Shelley's *Prometheus Unbound:* The Text and the Drafts

Shelley's *Prometheus Unbound:*
The Text and the Drafts

TOWARD A MODERN DEFINITIVE EDITION

Edited by Lawrence John Zillman

New Haven and London, Yale University Press

1968

Copyright © 1968 by Yale University.
Designed by John O. C. McCrillis,
set in Baskerville type,
and printed in the United States of America by
Vail-Ballou Press, Inc., Binghamton, N.Y.
Distributed in Canada by McGill University Press.

Library of Congress catalog card number: 68-13932

Thank you again, Lorene

Preface

The aim of the present edition of Shelley's *Prometheus Unbound* is twofold: to supply a more nearly definitive text of the poem than has been available, and to show the growth of that text as revealed in the extant manuscripts.

Reassessment of conditions pertaining to the derivation of the first edition (1820) and of Mary Shelley's two editions (1839, 1840) has thrown new light on the role of the modern editor of the poem. This has led to a more consistent and, it is hoped, a more meaningful presentation of Shelley's text, both in verbal accuracy and in consistency of punctuation and capitalization, an area that in the past has been grossly neglected. All debatable readings have been defended in the textual notes.

With respect to the manuscripts, the Shelley-Rolls gift to the Bodleian Library made available all of the remaining known Shelley items relevant to the drama, including a body of drafts about double the previous known amount. Since the minutiae of the E manuscript (the "fair copy") are readily accessible in the present editor's variorum edition of the poem, and of the drafts (including a reassessment of that portion given in the variorum) in his recently published literal transcription, the focus here is on an extensive but relatively uncomplicated presentation of this evidence to show the growth of the poem in the poet's mind as he faced the truth that "words are weak / The glory they transfuse with fitting truth to speak." Textual notes deal with such details as are pertinent.

To those who have responded so willingly to my appeals for help, a word of thanks and absolution from liability: Frederick A. Pottle, Donald Emery, and Norman Charles Brennan, for checking all or parts of the manuscript; the University of Washington Graduate Research Fund, for financial assistance in travel; and the friendly and cooperative staffs of the Bodleian Library and the Huntington Library, for access to Shelley manuscripts in their collections and for permission to draw on their holdings.

Lawrence John Zillman

University of Washington

Contents

PART ONE

Introduction

Introduction

On November 10, 1820, shortly after Shelley, in Pisa, had received his first copy of *Prometheus Unbound,* he wrote Charles and James Ollier, his London publishers:

> Mr. [John] Gisborne has sent me a copy of the "Prometheus," which is certainly most beautifully printed. It is to be regretted that the errors of the press are so numerous, and in many respects so destructive of the sense of a species of poetry which, I fear, even with[out?] this disadvantage, very few will understand or like. I shall send you a list of *errata* in a day or two.[1]

So began a story of editorial uncertainty and inaccuracy that has persisted for a century and a half.

Textual Backgrounds of the First Edition (1820)

The initial difficulties arose innocently enough. By April 6, 1819, Shelley could write from Rome to Thomas Love Peacock in London that the poem was "finished" in what he at the time considered to be the completed drama in three acts (*Letters,* 2, 94). Normally this would mean that he had made the fair copy (the Bodleian E manuscript) from the rough drafts and was awaiting Mary Shelley's opportunity to transcribe it for the printer. Mary was doing so by September 6 (2, 116), and by December 15 was copying the "additions" made necessary by Shelley's decision to add the fourth act (2, 163).

At this point the customary procedure would have led to transmission of Mary's transcribed copy to the Olliers for publication, with preliminary proofreading to be done in the press and with the sheets then sent to the poet for final checking.

A series of letters to Ollier reflected the poet's concern in this

---

1. *Letters, 2,* 246 (all references to *Letters* are to the edition of Frederick L. Jones). Short titles of critical works, and Edition for gatherings of Shelley's poems, are employed throughout the text, with adequate clues for full identification in the Bibliography.

important matter. On December 23, almost as soon as the printer's copy had been sent, he wrote a letter (known to us only through a catalogue description) which "Chiefly refers to proofs of *Prometheus Unbound*" (2, 165), and on March 13, 1820, he urged that "the *revised* sheets might be sent by the Post to me [for final checking] at Leghorn" (2, 178). The latter letter had followed quickly on one of March 6, expressing anxiety that no word had been received as to the status of the manuscript, and admonishing the publisher that " 'Prometheus Unbound,' I must tell you, is my favourite poem; I charge you, therefore, specially to pet him and feed him with fine ink and good paper" (2, 174).

In Ollier's view, however, distance made it inexpedient for proofs to be sent to Shelley (2, 178n.), so the poet seized hopefully on the departure of his friends John and Maria Gisborne on May 2 to give him an advocate, and wrote (still from Pisa) to Charles Ollier on May 14, reluctantly accepting the situation, but trusting that care would be taken "respecting the correction of the press; especially in the lyrical parts, where a minute error would be of much consequence"; and he indicated that "Mr. Gisborne will revise it; he heard it recited, and will therefore more readily seize any error" (2, 196).

Having thus reconciled himself to a situation he clearly disliked, Shelley sought reassurance by writing to the Gisbornes on May 26, indicating the difficulties that had developed, accepting the Gisbornes' offer of assistance in correction of the proofs, entrusting them with "what I am so interested in having done well," and enclosing "two little papers of corrections & additions;—I do not think you will find any difficulty in interpolating them into their proper places."[2] But by July he learned that Peacock rather than Gisborne was to undertake the proofreading (2, 212).

On November 8, after he had received the volume, Shelley acknowledged Peacock's contribution: "Thank you for your kindness in correcting 'Prometheus,' which I am afraid gave you a great deal of trouble" (2, 244)—a restrained sentence with possible ironic overtones in view of the evident disappointment expressed to Ollier, as noted above, "that the errors of the press are so numer-

2. *Letters*, 2, 201. These were probably copies of changes in E. There is no evidence that the changes were not made as Shelley wished.

ous," and his determination to send a "list of *errata* in a day or two" (2, 246).

It was not, however, until two months later that Shelley finally sent the list to the Olliers, with the following: "I send you . . . the Errata of 'Prometheus,' which I ought to have sent long since—a formidable list, as you will see" (2, 257). Nor did he quickly forget the inaccuracies, for on June 8 he was again outspoken to Charles Ollier, to whom he wrote: "I shall send [*Adonais* to] you, either printed at Pisa, or transcribed in such a manner as it shall be difficult for the reviser to leave such errors as *assist* the obscurity of the 'Prometheus!' "[3]

One can only speculate on the details of a corrected edition had Shelley lived to see one through the press, but comparison with other of his works for which he was responsible would suggest that it would have been something less than a model by modern editorial standards. His own manuscript eccentricities, even in the relatively fair copy from which Mary made her transcription for the printer,[4] are indicative of a mind careless in such matters, and must

3. *Letters, 2, 297.* Locock interpreted this reference to transcriber and reviser as indicative of Shelley's own opinion of the cause of the errors (Edition, *1*, 595-96).

4. Relatively, that is, to the drafts, which frequently offer seemingly insurmountable obstacles to the transcriber, as Mary was to discover when she edited the *Posthumous Poems* of 1824: "Did anyone see the papers from which I drew that volume, the wonder would be how any eyes or patience were capable of extracting it from so confused a mass, interlined and broken into fragments, so that sense could only be deciphered and joined by guesses which might seem rather intuitive than founded on reasoning" (Note [1839 ed. (M)] on "Poems of 1822"). Shelley himself recognized the problem. When Trelawny spoke of *With a Guitar, to Jane* as "a frightful scrawl; words smeared out with his finger, and one upon the other, over and over in tiers, and all run together in most 'admired disorder'; it might have been taken for a sketch of a marsh overgrown with bulrushes, and the blots for wild ducks," Shelley's explanation was: "When my brain gets heated with thought, it soon boils, and throws off images and words faster than I can skim them off. In the morning, when cooled down, out of the rude sketch as you so justly call it, I shall attempt a drawing" (Trelawny, *Recollections*, pp. 49-50).

With the recent gift of manuscripts from the Shelley-Rolls family to the Bodleian Library there are now known drafts representing 142 of the 196 Preface lines (plus 17 unused Preface draft lines), and 750 of the 2610 lines of the poem (plus 87 unused text draft lines). The implications of this mate-

to a degree excuse Mary for possible errors; for if Shelley's copy is
acceptably clean in appearance and penmanship, it does not escape
the prevailing characteristics to be found not alone in the drafts,
but in the poet's unfevered writing as well. Some of these offered
even Mary a severe challenge.

There is, for example, the general matter of grammar, perhaps
best described by Frederick A. Pottle:

> Shelley appears to have been quite innocent of any instruc-
> tion in English grammar: he writes just as he talked and his
> conversational tradition (Eton), though good, was not at all
> points identical with the formal written standard. Conse-
> quently his poetry anywhere may make the verb agree in num-
> ber with the nearest noun rather than with the actual subject;
> like Byron he is capable of sentences that never conclude. His
> larger compositions show occasional patches that read like
> improvisations that he never went back to finish. But these
> sketchy or unfinished areas are generally peripheral; they sel-
> dom affect the main design ["The Case of Shelley," p. 605].

If, however, the grammatical problems are combined with other
of the difficulties accompanying the manuscript of the *Prometheus*,
the "main design" *is* affected to the degree that uncertainty in
many details shadows the clear outline of the larger pattern.

One of these details stems from certain specific problems in the
handwriting even at its best. It is frequently difficult or impossible
to distinguish small and capital letters such as *c, e, m, n, o,* and *s,*
or to determine whether a small or capital letter was written first
after Shelley altered one by overwriting with the other; the loop
on small *e* is often suppressed or missing, leading to confusion with
i in those frequent instances where the poet failed to dot the *i,* or
to place the dot correctly over it—a situation made more difficult
by his own confusion with respect to *ei* and *ie* (he clearly wrote

---

rial for the study of Shelley's craftsmanship create an excitement tempered
only by the knowledge that other notebooks and loose sheets must once have
existed which have now been lost, or which lie in the dark of collections in
unknown hands.

For a list of the extant holdings see Appendix B, and for a full literal transcription of the *Prometheus* passages see the present editor's *The Complete
Known Drafts of Shelley's Prometheus Unbound.*

thier at times, as well as *viel, weild,* and *wierd*); *æ* frequently looks like a poorly written *e*; and the final *re* (e.g. *where, there*) is occasionally and confusingly indistinguishable from *n*.

In all but a few instances, familiarity with Shelley's handwriting, supported by careful attention to context, makes reasonable conjecture possible in the foregoing area, but less certainty can be assured in the matter of punctuation. Here it appears that the poet purposely left the burden of such matters to Mary as copyist, to the printer, or to the proofreader. The punctuation, if present, is frequently careless, even where (as at III.iii.40-62) the sentence structure is complex and the sense difficult to determine; or it is altered, leaving an ambiguity to plague the transcriber; or it is eccentric. But perhaps the overriding habit in this regard is found at line ends or line breaks. Except for the question mark, which he used with some consistency, the poet was quite likely to omit any pointing, or to indulge his favorite substitute, the dash, which he used in place of normally expected punctuation.[5] Yet it should be noted that despite these sins of omission and commission very often the best clue to Shelley's intent is to be found in such hints as his imperfect pointing offers—hints Mary too frequently ignored, it would appear, in making her copy for the printer.

As with punctuation, Shelley's use of capitals was so inconsistent as to require considerable assistance from his editor. At times intent can be inferred from analysis of all uses with respect to a given word, but in other instances no pattern of usage can be established.[6] The poet, like so many of his generation, overcapitalized

5. There are in the fair copy, for example, 864 line ends or line breaks in Act I, of which 273 are instances of enjambement that call for no punctuation. Of the remaining 591 line ends or line breaks, normally calling for punctuation, 343 (of which 95 are sentence endings) have no punctuation supplied. Thus in more than half of the instances Shelley bypassed this responsibility. In the matter of dashes, there are 120 in Act I, of which 74 apparently were resorted to as easy substitutes for more exact pointing such as colons, semicolons, etc.

6. As Locock pointed out with respect to *O Gentle moon* (IV.495) and *Oh Gentle [m] Moon* (IV.499): "Those who are inclined to lay too much stress on the preservation of Shelley's orthography might take warning. . . . It can hardly be supposed that any distinction was intended [by the poet]" (Edition, *1*, 630).

to such an extent that Mary, Peacock, or the editor reduced the numbers notably, if not always uniformly. Selected examples of Shelley's usage will illustrate the problem: *Heaven* is almost always capitalized in E (without distinction as to whether the reference is to Jupiter's realm, to the firmament, to a state of ideal perfection, or general) with a ratio of 69:4, with the related *Paradise* capitalized without exception in its four uses, and *Eternity* with a 4:1 ratio; *Hell* as the antithesis of *Heaven* shows a ratio of 9:3 in favor of capitalization, with other references to the word 1:4; while *Earth* as the globe or ground, which one would not expect to be capitalized, has a 35:12 ratio in favor of the capital (although *World,* as its synonym, shows only 4:29). The practice with respect to *Earth* used figuratively or as a personification gives 16:6, scarcely as high a ratio as one would expect. *Ocean,* used as a personification four times, of which three are capitalized, continues with the capital in its non-personified uses, for an overall ratio of 19:2. *Love,* which one might expect Shelley to capitalize with great regularity, shows a surprisingly low ratio of 9:6 when used as an entity or personification, and only 7:53 in non-personified uses.

The resulting cumulative score for the above list is 173:120, and indicates the predilection of the poet, while the evidence for individual words shows clearly the inconsistencies that resulted from his failure to adhere to any pattern of discrimination with respect to distinctions in meaning or reference.

In matters of spelling, too, Shelley's inconsistencies appear. For example, he used *inchantment* (or related words) five times, with an equal number for *enchantment,* but with no evidence that the use of *i* or *e* was influenced by neighboring vowel sounds.[7] Shelley also employed, without evident distinction, *O, Oh* (or *oh*—and

7. Forman's theory that Shelley used *desart* as a noun and *desert* as an adjective (Edition, 2, 434-35) is not valid for the *Prometheus* manuscript, where the poet used the former spelling consistently, regardless of context. (See also Neville Rogers, "Shelley's Spelling," pp. 23-24.) The now archaic *sate* (preferred by Rogers) was obsolescent in the early nineteenth century and appears to have been pronounced optionally with the long or short *a.* The long *a* is suggested where Shelley, in other poems, employed *sate* as a rime (although there the possibility of approximate rime cannot be overlooked), but in the two occurrences in *Prometheus Unbound* (I.723 and II.i.134, both non-riming) modern usage seems preferable.

rarely with a following comma); *thro* and *through,* and *tho* and *though* (with the shorter forms at times probably a concession to space limitations); *etherial* and *ætherial.*

In habits related to the foregoing the poet used, with only forty-two exceptions, the ampersand for *and* in non-initial positions; he never solved the finer distinctions between *like* and *as;* he preferred *forever* to the more usual British *for ever;* he used *1st., 2d.,* etc., consistently in E, rather than writing out the words; he used *thro* and *thro',* and *tho* and *tho';* he commonly confused *its* and *it's;* and he was inconsistent in his use of quotation marks, and of contractions (e.g. *'d, 'st*) for metrical considerations. A further difficulty was initiated when, in underlining a word for stet or as a hold for choice, he frequently placed the underline so high (or a deletion so low) as to make his intent unclear.

COPING WITH THE DIFFICULTIES: EARLY EFFORTS

Although Mary Shelley was to experience all too soon the necessity of drawing from the drafts the contents of *Posthumous Poems* (1824), for *Prometheus Unbound* she had but to face a fair copy that, as we have seen, is "fair" in a comparative sense only. Yet there are 190 verbal changes alone between E and 1820 (see Appendix C), a number that cannot be laid against Mary's transcription exclusively, but that does invite speculation as to what might have been in the copy, no longer extant, which she made for the press.[8]

There could have been little difficulty on the score of clarity, for she normally wrote a legible hand,[9] but unless she checked fre-

---

8. Although Mary made every effort to get all manuscripts from Ollier after the poet's death, and though Peacock, early in 1823, supposedly sent all the publisher had (see Mary Shelley, *Letters, 1,* 206n.), her transcription of the *Prometheus* has never come to light.

9. But see above (p. 5) for Shelley's determination to have *Adonais* "transcribed in such a manner as it shall be difficult for the reviser to leave such errors as *assist* the obscurity of the 'Prometheus,'" and the letter of Mary to Maria Gisborne on December 28, 1819: "If by any chance you have not sent the Prometheus [to England] add the word *bowers* after *from their obscurest* [IV.375] & in the other [IV.392] change it to *it's mother fears awhile*" (Mary Shelley, *Letters, 1,* 92). Inasmuch as E offers only slight difficulty at these points it is probable that the Gisbornes had been led to inquire about unclear

quently with Shelley she might well have indulged many of the misreadings to which the poet's copy is subject. Some of these would be so minor as not to be called to the poet's attention; others would appear legible at first glance, and so copied, when more careful scrutiny might have shown a faulty reading; but in several important instances it must be assumed that Shelley himself was consulted before either a specific reading, a choice between optional readings, or a final change in a tentative passage was determined. It is likely, also, that Mary corrected faulty grammar and spelling when she encountered them, that she made gratuitous emendations of a minor kind, and that she was understandably subject to the unconscious transfers, slips of the pen, and other errors resulting from human frailty or fatigue during trying days.[10]

It must be assumed also that omission of eight undeleted stage directions in E rested with Shelley, possibly in response to Mary's suggestions. Shelley had frequently canceled stage directions while writing the fair copy—usually, as Martin J. Freeman noted, retaining the poetic elements, but making them "organic—a part of the poem itself" ("Text," p. 36). Whether those that remained undeleted were in Mary's copy is, of course, not known, but evidence that they were is found (1) in the fact that they were never deleted in E, suggesting that the changes were made late (had each been called into discussion as Mary copied, it is reasonable to believe

---

or inaccurately written lines in Mary's transcription. It should be noted also that in copying Byron's *Don Juan* Mary made alterations or committed errors of the kind under discussion here (see Truman Steffan, *Byron's Don Juan*, 4 vols. Austin, University of Texas Press, 1957, *1*, 176-78). In copies of other Shelley poems, however, found principally in Bodleian MSS Shelley adds. d.7, d.8, and d.9, and in the Harvard Notebooks, Mary's handwriting is uniformly legible. A comparison of these copies with the manuscripts from which they were drawn shows her to have been an acceptably careful transcriber who held closely but not slavishly to the pointing and capitalization of Shelley, but who made no effort towards definitive treatment of such matters. Here, again, it would appear that these details were left for determination by the press, subject to final correction in the proofs.

10. In September, when she was copying Acts I-III, Mary was seven months pregnant with Percy, who was born on November 12. The infant's demands on her time during the period when she was copying Act IV are suggested by the fact that there are no journal entries between November 10 and December 31, when she commented on how little she had read since her earlier entry.

that the decisions would have been reflected in deletions in E at the time); and (2) in an extra space in 1820 between III.iii.83-84. This comes at the point where the short direction, "kissing the ground" (at the right margin) would have been deleted in Mary's copy. The deletion was apparently missed by a compositor who followed the left margin for spacing. These considerations would suggest that the stage directions were in Mary's transcription, and that they were deleted there by Shelley without taking the time to locate and delete them in E.

A corollary to the latter assumption would be that the poet read the transcription with at least so much evidence of care,[11] but in view of his evident laxity in such matters it must be supposed that Mary's responsibility as transcriber would include especially careful attention to verbal matters and to punctuation before the printer's copy was sent to Ollier.

Were both Shelley and Mary negligent? It is, I believe, quite possible that they were, and for a reason suggested, but not developed, by Charles H. Taylor, Jr., when he reminded us that "in the early part of the nineteenth century punctuation and spelling were generally left to the discretion of the printer."[12] There is excellent

11. The alternative, that Shelley sent instructions for these deletions to the Gisbornes, is discounted by the fact that to do so would have necessitated a rechecking of E for determination of the selected items, at which time there is every reason to believe that the directions would have been deleted in E.

12. *Early Editions,* p. 47. See also Ronald B. McKerrow's *An Introduction to Bibliography* (Oxford, Clarendon Press, 1928), pp. 246-51; Fredson Bowers' *Textual and Literary Criticism* (Cambridge University Press, 1959), Chap. IV, and esp. pp. 136-40 with notes; and Shelley's *The Esdaile Notebook,* ed. Kenneth Neill Cameron (New York, Knopf, 1964), pp. 332-33. Pertinent comments by Shelley to Ollier with respect to other writings are: February, 1817: "I send you the revise [of *A Proposal for Putting the Reform to the Vote*], which may be put to press when corrected" (*Letters, 1,* 532); December 3, 1817: "That Mc·Millan [probably Ollier's printer] is an obstinate old dog as troublesome as he is impudent. . . . Let him print the errata [of *Laon and Cythna*], & say at the top if he likes, that it was all the Author's fault, & that he is as immaculate as the Lamb of God" (*1,* 571); September 6, 1819: "In the *Rosalind & Helen* [the proofs of which, as well as of *Julian and Maddalo,* had been corrected by Peacock (2, 4, 29, 31, 108)] I see there are some few errors, which are so much the worse because they are errors in the sense [compare the same criticism of Peacock's proofreading of the *Prometheus,* above].—If there should be any *danger* of a 2d Edition I will correct them" (*2,* 117); April 30, 1820:

evidence to support the view that both E and the transcription were made on this premise, for such practice would make unnecessary two tedious and, in Shelley's case, uncongenial steps: the slow and careful pointing of the fair copy, and the detailed collation of the transcript with the fair copy. If he could trust Mary to transcribe E with reasonable accuracy, even at the risk of minor verbal changes[13] and a minimum of assistance with the punctuation, there would be no need for the time-consuming and irritating work involved in sending perfect copy to England. This would not imply that the poet was unconcerned about this aspect of his work (the opposite, as we have seen, was the case), or that he ignored Mary's copy: even if he read it with acceptable care there is no reason to suppose that he would have in mind the many tentative changes, the optional choices, or the alterations susceptible of misreading, to be found in E. All such matters could be given their final attention and correction when, after press style had been applied to the manuscript, the result set in type, and the preliminary proofreading done, the author could more easily check against verbal errors and the finer shades of meaning he intended, and attain satisfaction in the corrected proofs.

It should not be forgotten that Shelley expected proofs to be sent to him in Italy, and was, if the foregoing assumptions are valid, understandably alarmed because this was not done. Nor could he have been otherwise than concerned when, for reasons unknown, John Gisborne passed the responsibility for corrections on to Peacock, who had not "heard it recited," who was probably more likely than Gisborne would have been to initiate changes, and who

---

"I send a list of errata [for reprinting of *The Cenci*]; the incorrectness of, the forms of typography, etc., which are considerably numerous, you will be so obliging as to attend to yourself" (2, 188); February 16, 1821: "I have written it [*Epipsychidion*] so as to give very little trouble, I hope, to the printer, or to the person who revises. I would be much obliged if you could take this office on yourself" (2, 263). Compare Keats's "I will take care the Printer shall not trip up my Heels" (to John Taylor, February 27, 1818. See also his letters to Taylor of April 24, 1818 and June 11?, 1820).

13. They proved far more serious than he could have anticipated, although, as we shall see, probably not all could be charged against Mary's transcription.

was, according to Gisborne's report to Shelley, "surrounded with statements and accounts."[14]

If one keeps in mind Mary Shelley's comment in her note on *Prometheus Unbound*—"It requires a mind as subtle and penetrating as his own to understand the mystic meanings scattered throughout the poem"—the inability of Shelley to have an opportunity for final oversight of the published work is the more significant, the errors of 1820 more understandable, and the greater care Shelley might have taken with E (or both Shelley and Mary with the transcription, had they known the course events would take) not difficult to imagine.[15]

In summary, then, the early efforts to cope with the difficulties of the fair copy led only to disappointment for the poet—disappointment that could have stemmed from several sources: (1) possible faulty interpretation or transcription of the frequently imperfect E by Mary; (2) failure of Shelley himself to check the transcription with sufficient care; (3) the unfortunate turn of events that prevented the poet's final checking of the proofs; (4) the errors of the press, despite the poet's urgent admonition to Ollier; (5) Peacock's unsatisfactory role (probably for lack of time) as final proofreader—the most important and vulnerable link between the writing and publication of the poem, which Shelley himself had hoped to supply; and (6) the possible gratuitous emendations of Peacock.

Despite its weaknesses, the first edition offered a text of *Prometheus Unbound* that became, with the few corrections found in Mary Shelley's edition of 1839, the basis for the work of later edi-

14. Shelley, *Letters*, 2, 244. Peacock, recently employed as examiner by the India House, was clearly burdened with work. Gisborne's description would be applicable to the period of the proofreading. See also n. 12, above, under September 6, 1819.

15. It is easy to say, with hindsight as prompter, that Shelley and Mary should have worked more closely to assure an impeccable printer's copy, or that Mary, with Shelley at hand, should have come closer in detail to the intent of E. But the first is to overlook the realities of the situation outlined above: Shelley expected to correct the errors that might remain in the proofs; and the second is not likely to be a point of view shared by those who have attempted, with an expenditure of time and energy not available to Mary, to ferret out the answers to the problems of the "fair" copy.

tors throughout the nineteenth century. Press style undoubtedly determined general considerations of format, as well as such effort as was made toward standardization of spelling, reduction of the number of capitals (if Mary followed the poet in this respect), lyric indention based on rime scheme, a predilection for colons (frequently where Shelley's overused dash would have been superior), placement and abbreviation of non-centered names of characters, etc.

This edition led shortly to the first effort to establish a more accurate text. Shelley's own errata—"a formidable list, as you will see"—was sent to Ollier on January 20, 1821, with apology for the delay. But any hope that a corrected edition of the poem would be forthcoming within a reasonable time was finally lost when, after the poet's death in the following year and the publication of *Posthumous Poems* in 1824, Sir Timothy Shelley forbade Mary, on penalty of revocation of allowance, to publish, while he lived, any more of the poet's works. He relaxed this proscription only many years later, for the 1839 edition. Probably it was this dictum that prevented Mary's cooperation with A. and W. Galignani in a projected Paris edition of the poems of Shelley in 1826. In any event, nothing came of the proposal until, in 1829, the Galignanis undertook a new project, to comprise the works of Coleridge, Shelley, and Keats in one volume.

Unlike the piracies of William Benbow (1826) and John Ascham (1834)—both of whose *Prometheus* texts were set from 1820 as copy (as was that of Galignani)—the Galignanis sought and obtained, through an English friend, Cyrus Redding, assistance from Mary Shelley.[16] She drew a pencil sketch of the poet from which an unsatisfactory engraving was made, and she contributed errata or additions for at least *Adonais, Hellas,* and *Prometheus Unbound.* With respect to the latter it could well be that she saw in the Galignani publication an opportunity to do what she had been prevented from doing directly—improve some of the weaknesses of 1820. But, as Taylor has shown, although the changes for *Adonais* and *Hellas* were incorporated in the Galignani printing, only two verbal alterations were made in *Prometheus Unbound*—that at I.733 correcting *born* to *borne,* and that at II.iv.100, correcting

16. For a full discussion see Taylor's *Early Editions,* pp. 19-22, 28 n.

reigns to *rains*.[17] These were corrections, as Taylor noted, "which any attentive reader might have made." He offered a plausible explanation of this failure to apply the errata to the drama:

> In the Galignanis' edition the *Prometheus* is printed early, as the third piece in the text. The shorter poems are included among the "Miscellaneous Poems" in the last division of the text, and are thus separated from the drama by several long poems. What seems most probable to me is that the *Prometheus* was already set (or quite possibly the sheets for it had been printed) when the list of corrections reached Paris, but that the list arrived in time for changes to be made in the shorter poems, either on the printer's copy or in the formes [*Early Editions*, p. 22].

But the Galignanis did not follow 1820 slavishly. Their own characteristics of press style can be seen in consistent changes of *thro* and *tho* to *through* and *though*; in the use of *'d* for the unpronounced *-ed* syllable; in the simpler spellings: *desert, crystal, gulf, ay,* etc.; in the use of *a* rather than *an* before *hindrance, hundred,* and *universal*; in ninety-one minor punctuation changes (none of which clarified difficult passages); in eight minor capitalization changes; and in five uses of italics.

Galignani changes that probably stemmed from editorial emendation or errors of the press rather than normal press style are to be found in the faulty sense that resulted when "Hark! Spirits speak" (II.i.171) was rendered as "Hark! Spirits, speak" (as similarly at II.v.47); in the erroneous *illumined* for *illumed* (I.637), *which enchantment* for *which the enchantment* (II.ii.71), and *those that* for *those who* (III.iii.126); and in the correction, already noted, of *born* to *borne* (I.733) and *reigns* to *rains* (II.iv.100).

The Galignani modifications are thus seen to be typical of any moderately careful editorial concern unsupported by evidence other than the printed edition of the poem—a pattern, prevalent throughout the nineteenth century, that offered much interesting speculation and, frequently, considerable imaginative insight, but no textual authority except as it profited from Mary Shelley's use

17. *Early Editions*, p. 22. Taylor said "only one." He missed the I.733 change.

of the errata list and Mathilde Blind's review (discussed below) of
W. M. Rossetti's first edition. Our interest in the Galignani would,
as a result, be minimal were it not for the fact of its marked influence on Mary Shelley's editions of the poem, to which attention
should now be turned.

The first of Mary's two editions (M) appeared in four volumes
early in 1839. Within a year a second, reset, one-volume quarto
(M²) appeared with corrections and additions to the earlier printing.[18] For the first time since 1820 it was now possible to bring to
the *Prometheus* the textual corrections desired by Shelley, and in
her note to the poem Mary stated: "I may mention, for the infor-
mation of the more critical reader, that the verbal alterations in
this edition of Prometheus are made from a list of errata, written
by Shelley himself." It should be noted, (1) that the attention was
to "verbal alterations" rather than to those in punctuation, despite
the fact that the latter were to be a continuing difficulty throughout the editorial history of the poem; and (2) that the careful attention to a perfected text suggested by Mary's statement is deceptive.
She says nothing of having returned to the fair copy for collation;
and there is, in fact, no evidence that she attempted this onerous
task in the midst of a major undertaking and in the face of illness
while the work was in progress. She was apparently willing to rest
in the contribution (and its importance, though limited, cannot
be overstressed) of the errata list.

The genesis of the text for M is significant here. Taylor has
shown that instead of sending her first editions to the publisher as
printer's copy, Mary substituted the unauthorized editions of
Ascham and Galignani, correcting the proofs, not always carefully,
from her first editions or other sources. For *Prometheus Unbound*
she used the Galignani for copy, possibly, as Taylor suggested,

> deliberately, believing that it would be a better text for the
> poems concerned. She would surely have recalled that a decade
> earlier she had forwarded items of errata for the *Prometheus*

18. The resetting led to changes from M, not all of which, it must be supposed, can be ascribed to Mary's wishes: there were two minor spelling
changes, four minor alterations in capitalization, forty-six minor punctuation
changes, one major verbal change (*streams* for *steams* at II.ii.53), and two
typographical errors.

and a suppressed stanza of *Hellas* to Redding for the Galignanis' use, and would naturally have assumed that they had been incorporated in their text. When the proofs were returned to her, she would of course have discovered that the Galiganis had not corrected the *Prometheus,* so that she was obliged to do so herself, but it is quite possible that at the time when she decided to send the Paris edition to the printer, she believed the corrections were present.[19]

With this knowledge, it is possible to speculate with greater accuracy on the nature of the errata list from which Mary worked. C. D. Locock, it would seem, expected more than was justified when he asked:

> May we suppose that Mrs. Shelley never made use of [the "formidable list" of errata] at all? that what she did use was a *preliminary* list,—the list which Shelley "hoped to despatch in a day or two" (November 10, 1820)—not the "formidable list" . . . which may in the course of nine[teen] years have been mislaid? Failing this hypothesis, we can only assume that Shelley's "formidable list" was not nearly so formidable as it might have been [Edition, *1, 596*].

One might answer Locock by pointing out that in January, 1821, Shelley apologized for not having sent the list referred to in the letter of November 10 (there is no evidence of a distinction between a "preliminary" list and the final list); but even more directly one might suggest that to a disappointed poet twenty-nine major items (see below) might well appear "formidable." There is no evidence that Shelley undertook a collation of E at this time,

19. *Early Editions,* p. 42. For a full and convincing discussion see pp. 34-46 of Taylor's study. For those who might be critical of Mary's general procedure, Taylor commented: "It should be said in Mary Shelley's defense, however, that her major editorial effort was applied to the *Posthumous Poems,* which she deciphered and prepared with commendable accuracy considering the state of Shelley's manuscripts. It is not surprising that fifteen years later, jealous of her first editions and suffering from ill health, she chose a short cut in the preparation of copy for the *Poetical Works* and was then unable to correct the proof to meet even her own ideals of textual accuracy, not to mention those of the trained editors who followed her" (p. 45).

and hence it can be assumed that he ignored many details. He was occupied with other matters, and even a minute reading of 1820 with resulting detailed errata was hardly to be expected. From the evidence it is clear that he made a list of major errors only, which was sent first to Ollier, then later, by way of Mary, to Galignani and finally found its way into a printed text.

Probably the nearest approach to a reconstruction of the errata list can be sought by asking what alterations in M do not appear in either 1820 or Galignani (or if in Galignani, by coincidence), but do correspond to E. Such a list, shown in the accompanying table, comprises twenty-nine items, all but two of which are found in E, and only two of which are found (probably coincidentally) in Galignani.[20]

Discussion of Mary's text of the *Prometheus* inevitably leads to what may appear to be undue stress on the errata list, yet it is here that her principal contribution to textual accuracy of the poem is to be found. It is clear that the result might not have been completely satisfactory to the wishes of the poet as revealed in E. On this copy Shelley appears to have worked even after the poem was published, and it must be assumed, from the evident care with which he revised his work, that the errata and emendations in E represented his own final word on his dissatisfaction with the first

20. If the relationship between Mary's first edition (M) and that of Galignani (G) with respect to 1820 is analyzed more fully, the following tabulation results:

Items	G differs from 1820 and is followed by M	M differs from both G and 1820
Minor punctuation changes	91	59
Major punctuation changes	2	4
Minor verbal changes	3	0
Major verbal changes	5	31
Minor spelling changes	18	4
Minor capitalization changes	3	5
Minor italic changes	5	0

M followed the major G punctuation change to *Spirits,* (II.i.171 and II.v.47), and differed from both G and 1820 in *vanquished?* (I.312), *tyrant's* (I.388), and the unpointed *another's* (I.572), the latter a typographical error. For the major verbal differences adopted by M see textual notes on I.637, 733; II.ii.71; II.iv.100; III.iii.126. See Appendix C for a full tabulation of verbal changes involving E, 1820, and M.

THE PROBABLE LIST OF ERRATA FOR 1839[1]

Line		1839	1820
Preface	57	the vigorous awakening of spring (E)[2]	awakening spring
Dramatis Personae		The Spirit of the Moon (E: omitted)	omitted
I.	106	Though silence is as hell to us (E)	a hell
	408	clamour. Fear delay! (E: clamour, fear delay)[3]	clamour: fear delay:
	619	The ravin it has gorged (E)	The ruin
	687	We make there our liquid lair (E)	We make these
	733	It has borne me here as fleet (E)[4]	It has born
II. ii.	38	Like many a lake-surrounded flute (E)	a lake-surrounding
	50	And wakes the destined: soft emotion (E)[3]	destined soft emotion
	93	. . . the chained Titan's woful doom (E)	woful dooms
iv.	100	. . . but who rains down (E)[4]	who reigns down
v.	54	Child of Light! thy limbs are burning (E)	thy lips are burning
III. i.	5	The soul of man, like unextinguished fire (E)	like an unextinguished
	13	. . . though under my wrath's night (E)	my wrath's might
	20	. . . till the destined hour arrives (E)	the distant hour
	69	What then art thou (E)	What art thou
ii.	39	That sits i' the morning star (E)	That sits on
iii.	55	. . . and rapt Poesy (E)	and wrapt Poesy
	70	. . . this the mystic shell (E)	this is the
	102	Shall suck unwithering hues (E)	unwitting hues
iv.	121	The flight from which they find repose (E)	The light
IV.	225	Scattered in strings . . . (E)	in string
	274	Vast beams like spokes . . . (E)	like spoke
	282	. . . on crystalline columns poized (E)	columns poured
	355	. . . caves cloven by the thunder-ball (E)	by thunder-ball
	432	A half unfrozen dew-globe (E)	half infrozen
	483	As a lover or cameleon (E?)	or a cameleon
	559	Of dread endurance . . . (E)	Of dead endurance
	575	Neither to change, nor faulter . . . (E)	nor flatter

1. At IV.210, M has *curbed* for *curved*, an obvious typographical error. Possible, but unlikely, entries in the errata (see Textual Notes) might be: II.i.SD: *A lonely Vale* (E-1820: *A lovely Vale*); II.iii.50: *I see shapes* (E: *seest those shapes*; 1820: *I see thin shapes*); IV.554: *This the day* (E-1820: *This is the day*).

2. (E) indicates that M and E are in agreement.

3. I consider that, despite Mary's statement limiting the errata to "verbal alterations," this highly significant punctuation change might well have been included.

4. Although Galignani initiated this change, it is sufficiently important to have been included in the errata list.

edition. If so, it must be concluded that Mary did not make full use of the materials available to her with respect to this poem, and that she rested much too heavily on Galignani for copy. Yet credit must not be withheld for the work she did. Possibly William Michael Rossetti's comment in the Preface to his 1870 edition is most pertinent:

> Mrs. Shelley brought deep affection and unmeasured enthusiasm to the task of editing her husband's work. But ill health and the pain of reminiscence curtailed her editorial labours: besides which, to judge from the result, you would say that Mrs. Shelley was not one of the persons to whom the gift of consistent accuracy has been imparted; for even this too is a gift in its way, not wholly to be improvised for the occasion [Edition, *1*, xii].

Coping with the Difficulties: Later Efforts

Thirty years were to pass before any writer turned to Shelley's manuscript for evidence of the poet's intent that might go beyond the limits of the errata list. The writer was Mathilde Blind in a review of Rossetti's edition of 1870. Rossetti gave no evidence, in his Preface or notes, that he was aware of the existence of E,[21] and while his editorial aims were acceptably modest, his practice with respect to *Prometheus Unbound* was scarcely restrained, whether in matters of punctuation or in verbal conjectures and emendations, although the latter were in many instances indicative of imaginative insight even when they were not supported by later evidence in Shelley's hand. It was in refutation of some of these conjectures and emendations that Miss Blind called the manuscript into evidence in eleven instances where Rossetti had made changes from 1820 unsupported by M. In addition, she volunteered two readings and two misreadings from E. It would appear, however, that Miss Blind's access to the manuscript was limited, for in her own text of Acts I and IV of the drama for her selection of Shelley's poems (1872) she incorporated only the new readings

21. Nor did any editor before 1893 except George Woodberry, despite knowledge of the manuscript from Miss Blind's review. (In 1892 Woodberry referred to it as "the incomplete MS" used by Blind [Edition, 2, 426].) For full variant readings of all principal editions after M see the *Variorum*.

from her review, and otherwise, except for the few expected minor changes in punctuation and capitalization, reproduced the Rossetti text.

Gradually, however, through the errata list and Miss Blind's efforts, the first steps were being taken toward a corrected reading of the poem, and with the passage of another twenty-three years opportunity was finally given for the unrestricted study of Shelley's own fair copy. In 1893 Lady Shelley presented to the Bodleian Library, among other Shelleyana, the E manuscript; and shortly thereafter the German scholar, Julius Zupitza, turned his attention to its careful study, with the work completed by Joseph Schick following Zupitza's death.

Zupitza-Schick did not attempt an edition of the poem, but chose rather to make, in a series of articles, a comparison based on the popular Harry Buxton Forman edition of 1876. Forman had followed Mary Shelley in correcting obvious errors in the 1820 edition, and he profited from Miss Blind's article; but without access to E he could offer no fresh textual insight based on manuscrips sources, and so continued or initiated a number of errors. The result of the Zupitza-Schick effort was the first nearly full indication (it was not complete in details) of the nature of the manuscript and its contents; and while one may disagree with some of the readings and point out omissions and errors, all who work with textual matters in Shelley's poem must acknowledge a debt for the care and skill with which this pioneering work was done. In such matters involving chirographical difficulties approximation to the truth can come only through rethreading of the maze by many minds, with each later transcriber resting heavily on the work of those who have gone before.

So it was that Charles D. Locock, in his *Examination* (1903), acknowledged that he had compared his work with that of Zupitza-Schick; but his aim was much less inclusive than theirs, and although he admitted the importance of punctuation, he rested in an invitation to scholars to write to him on this matter. As might be expected, however, the fact of Locock's publication in English gave such readings as he discussed considerable weight, especially when they appeared in the edition of Thomas Hutchinson in the following year, and in Locock's own edition in 1911.

Hutchinson's edition (1904) was well received and through its inclusion in the Oxford Standard Authors series quickly became the most influential after Forman, superseding that work in later years. Yet it was an edition that in certain details left much to be desired. Although Hutchinson wrote in his note on *Prometheus Unbound*: "Our text is that of 1820, modified by ed. 1839, and by the Bodleian fair copy" (p. 200), he actually adhered closely to the text of Forman, and continued readings of the latter that were unsupported by either M or E. He also failed to give careful attention to the matters of punctuation that were so needful of study. Further, he made no mention of the Zupitza-Schick study, and gave no evidence of having worked directly with E; but he did introduce for the first time some of the readings of E that had been recorded in Locock's *Examination* and his work thus assumed an important position in the textual history of the poem at the turn of the century.

Richard Ackermann, in a separate edition of the poem published in Germany in 1908, drew on Zupitza-Schick, although he made no independent investigation of the manuscript, with the result that he gave more of the E readings than had any editor to that date. These were frequently used indiscriminately, however, and with inadequate attention to punctuation difficulties since no solution of these had been attempted by Zupitza-Schick. There is no evidence that Ackermann's edition was an influence on later editors, probably in part because of its foreign publication, but principally because of the growing popularity of Hutchinson and, in 1911, the major contribution of Locock's edition, for which Locock used the materials gathered earlier for the *Examination*.

Locock was thus the first editor to bring the results of a personal study of E to a text of *Prometheus Unbound*; but he was unnecessarily influenced by the manuscript in his inconsistent use of capitals and in the frequency with which he employed dashes, and by 1820-M for matters of general punctuation.[22] As to verbal vari-

---

22. Locock, without knowledge of the derivation of the M text, would naturally assume that where it agreed with 1820 it would represent Mary's final word on punctuation; but it is surprising that he made little or no effort to establish more consistency than he did. My indebtedness to his insights with respect to verbal matters, however, will be readily apparent in my textual notes.

ants, Locock found in the manuscript 136 that differed from both the 1820 and Mary Shelley editions, with forty-nine of these sufficiently superior to be introduced into his text.[23]

The handsome ten-volume Julian Edition of the complete works, edited by Roger Ingpen and Walter E. Peck (Volume II, containing the *Prometheus,* appeared in 1927) failed to give the definitive treatment of the poem that was expected. Although the editors offered a nice balance with respect to 1820, the changes made by Mary Shelley, and some of the readings of E as given by Locock, there was no evidence of independent examination of E, and their text was no more exact or final than were several others that preceded it. The principal contribution of the Julian Edition was the inclusion for the first time of an abstract of some sixty lines of early drafts from the manuscripts then in the possession of Sir John C. E. Shelley-Rolls.

The next significant attempt to cope with the difficulties of the manuscript occurred when Martin Joseph Freeman addressed himself to the problem in "A Text of Shelley's *Prometheus Unbound,*" a dissertation submitted for the doctoral degree at the University of Chicago in 1934. As part of his thesis Freeman, working from photostats, transcribed afresh the available manuscript materials and made his final text the basis of the poem as published in *The Reader's Shelley* (1942), edited in collaboration with Carl Grabo. But it was a text that held even closer to E than did that of Locock in matters of eccentric punctuation, capitalization, etc., and demonstrated that in such details there is a point beyond which fidelity to the manuscript should not go;[24] while with respect to verbal

23. Martin Freeman found "more than 150" ("Text," p. 9). The discrepancy was probably the result of difference in reading, or possibly of Freeman's inclusion in his count of slight differences such as *checked, check'd,* which Locock, who did not list his readings in full, might have treated as metrical rather than verbal changes. My own count is 165 (see Appendix C), with 59 incorporated in the present text.

24. It must be remembered that Shelley was clearly not attempting a printer's copy. He was hopelessly inconsistent in punctuation and capitalization, and to carry these inconsistencies into a text that is not in itself a transcription of the manuscript is to misinterpret editorial responsibility.

It is only fair to add, however, that if it has been necessary at times to stress the shortcomings of my predecessors (even as I await my turn in the dock), I would be remiss did I not also acknowledge with gratitude the efforts of

changes Freeman differed from Locock in fifteen readings, of which four were without manuscript authority, even in Freeman's transcription; seven were choices in debatable readings frequently unsupported by careful reading of E; one resulted in a tetrameter questionably defended; and three, again questionably defended, had been noted and rejected by Locock.

COPING WITH THE DIFFICULTIES: THE PRESENT EDITION

Against the foregoing background of efforts to arrive at greater textual accuracy for Shelley's poem the present edition has been undertaken. Three considerations have been of principal importance: (1) Since, as has been shown, 1820 was faulty in large part because too many details, especially in punctuation, were left for a proofreading that was unexpectedly taken out of Shelley's hands and delegated to Peacock, the authority of that edition, and the necessity or desirability of adhering closely to it are notably diminished. (2) Establishment by Charles H. Taylor, Jr., of the derivation of Mary Shelley's 1839 text from the Galignanis' edition (itself a close adherent to 1820), together with a detailed collation to determine the extent of her contribution, shows that her efforts did not involve a careful reappraisal of the manuscript or a detailed reworking of either 1820 or Galignani. The principal superiority of her text over that of the first edition thus rested in the influence of the errata list on a limited number of verbal corrections. As a result, her text, like that of 1820, must be treated with important reservations. (3) Unaware of these circumstances, later nineteenth-century editors for the most part either assumed, understandably, that Mary had confirmed 1820 when her text did not differ from it, or they indulged conjectures without authority in manuscript sources; while twentieth-century editors, working with varying degrees of attention to E after it was given to the Bodleian

---

Zupitza-Schick, Locock, and Freeman, who worked from E; their work has frequently confirmed my own tentative readings or forced me into further consideration of disputed passages. And let it be recorded here that if, as a result of continuing study of Shelley's handwriting and intent, I have suggested corrected readings for others, I have in the present work treated my own earlier readings in the *Variorum* with similar critical scrutiny. One quickly learns, with Mary Shelley, that "What at one time escapes the searching eye, dimmed by its own earnestness, becomes clear at a future period" ("Postscript" added in M² to the "Editor's Preface" of M).

Library, although on more certain ground, tended to lean heavily on Shelley's copy, regardless of its obvious shortcomings and inconsistencies.

It seems clear in the light of present knowledge that today's editor of the *Prometheus* must accept broader responsibility than have his predecessors in this role. In effect, what he must build on is a manuscript prepared under an early-nineteenth-century custom that left a surprising amount of important detail to the transcriber or the printer. To the extent that these have, for whatever reason, failed to provide a definitive text he must, with due respect for their work and the work of those who followed them—and within the limits imposed by a fair copy that frequently belies its epithet —substitute his best judgment for theirs with respect to the many facets of a subtle and challenging poem.

He must first, through a long period of association with E and the drafts, cope with the difficulties of Shelley's chirography, until he can determine with some confidence what the poet actually wrote. With this he must combine an attempt to gain, through what a colleague has called "knowledge by acquaintance," a sense of the working of Shelley's mind as the hesitant or bold drafts evolved into the fair copy—specifically, of the poet's probable intent in passages that defy easy certainty because they too frequently offer only minimal syntactic guidance. Only in this way can he hope to approximate the role of surrogate that Shelley thought was his in John Gisborne, who had "heard it recited, and will therefore more readily seize any error" (*Letters, 2, 196*).

Thus equipped, he must turn to the changes that entered the text between the writing of the fair copy and the printing of the first edition. He must determine the degree to which these alterations were authorized by Shelley, or contributed by Mary, Peacock, or the printer. Intuition will frequently be called to the aid of scholarship at this point, and the findings must be correspondingly tentative unless substantiated by the evidence of errata deduced from Mary's edition.

The editor next faces the area of difficulty most seriously neglected by Shelley and, it would appear, by Mary as well: punctuation, capitalization, and related matters. He must work carefully from such evidence as the manuscript offers, but avoid the mannerisms to which the poet was subject; determine the degree to which press style influenced 1820 and, through it, later editions; and, putting himself in the position of the original editor or compositor, in effect receive the E copy from Shelley's hands and proceed to the problems of mechanics delegated to him by the poet.

For if, as Shelley wrote to John Gisborne on January 26, 1822, "Prometheus was never intended for more than 5 or 6 persons" (*Letters, 2,* 388), the fact remains that many have found, and will continue to find, a rich experience in reading the poem, although they may agree, with Mary Shelley in her note, that "It requires a mind as subtle and penetrating as his [the poet's] own to understand the mystic meanings scattered throughout the poem. They elude the ordinary reader by their abstraction and delicacy of distinction"—to which she added, probably with less chance of agreement, "but they are not vague." Minds that are somewhat less subtle and penetrating than Shelley's may well feel that part of the elusiveness to which Mary referred—even an occasional vagueness which she denied—must be charged against the proffered text itself; and if the chosen five or six can ignore the dross that checks its flight, the many others may welcome, even at this late date, such assistance towards understanding the meaning, whether mystic or not, as accuracy and clarity of text can provide.

Editorial Principles in the Present Edition

The Text

Format. For the text, indentions, spacing, etc., follow the apparent intent of E since press style undoubtedly determined such matters in 1820-M. Manuscript readings and textual notes have, for ease of reference, been placed as close to the text as is practicable. Full variant readings, from which detailed reconstruction of E, 1820, and M can be made, have been relegated to an appendix since most are of minor significance. All important items have been discussed in textual notes.

Poeticisms. The conventional poetic use of the paradigm of *thou* and the now archaic second person singular in *-st* or *-est* have been retained since they are basic to the tone of the poem.[25] However,

---

25. Exceptions should be noted in four instances where Shelley violated the paradigm of *thou* for what clearly appear to be considerations of euphony, and where a change would seriously alter the rhythm or the tone of the lines:

greater consistency than in E-M has been sought by limiting the *'st* contractions to those lines where metrical integrity or euphony is threatened by a natural uncontracted reading. The pronounced final *-ed* (consistently unmarked but assumed in E-M) has been marked, in conformity with modern usage.

Consistency. Uniformity of modern usage in capitalization, spelling and punctuation has been sought.

Punctuation. In this most neglected and, in many ways, most sensitive area, the goal has been a restrained treatment for which an acceptable consistency can be claimed, and through which Shelley's apparent meaning can be most clearly and effectively communicated to the reader.[26]

Capitalization. Standard modern practice has been observed in this frequently confused area. *Heaven* (with the capital) has been reserved for reference to Jupiter's realm, *Hell* for its antithesis; with other capitalized words (*Earth, Ocean, Love,* etc.) restricted to personification or indication of character.

Spelling. British usage has been retained, and modern spellings have been substituted for those that were current in Shelley's day but are now obsolete or obsolescent.

Quotation Marks. The preferred British use of the single mark has replaced the prevailing inconstistencey of E-M.

---

my innumerable for *mine innumerable* (I.181); *As you speak* for *As thou speakest* (II.i.141); *shall chant* for *shalt chant* (III.iii.27); and *And you pretend* for *And thou pretendest* (IV.507). For a fifth ambiguous occurrence see textual notes on I.136-37.

26. Mark Twain, in an anonymous article (*Atlantic Monthly, 45,* 1880, 849-60, with the Twain identification by Charles Neider in *Harper's Magazine, 222,* June 1952, pp. 52-53), was not, but might well have been thinking of Shelley when he wrote: "Some people were not born to punctuate; these cannot learn the art. They can learn only a rude fashion of it; they cannot attain to its niceties, for these must be *felt;* they cannot be reasoned out. Cast-iron rules will not answer, here, any way; what is one man's comma is another man's colon. One man can't punctuate another man's manuscript any more than one person can make the gestures for another man's speech." In Shelley's case one is compelled to try, at least, to meet the subtleties of the poet's expression with his best efforts; and while hope for unanimous agreement with the present pointing may be as utopian as the poem's theme, it will be rewarding if the syntactical path has been made easier to follow than has formerly been the case. (For a general discussion of this matter see Neville Rogers, "The Punctuation of Shelley's Syntax.")

Stage Direction Enclosures. Enclosing brackets have supplied the omission of such punctuation in E, and replaced the inconsistencies of 1820-M, for stage directions within the running text.

Reading Choices. Where optional choices in E (or between E, 1820 and M) are present, final choices have been defended in the textual notes.

The Manuscripts

The manuscript use is designed to indicate the main features of the growth of the poem in the poet's mind, and to do so in a simplified format that will avoid the confusions of a literal transcription. Yet, since it is possible here to suggest something of the immediacy of Shelley's style—something of the "flavor" of his composition—without loss of clarity, this has been done by transcribing evidence of the poet's habits of punctuation, capitalization, use of the ampersand, etc., while avoiding such matters as are largely irrelevant to the present purpose but are accessible to the scholar in the present editor's variorum edition of the poem or literal transcription of the complete drafts: Shelley's line count, the paging of notebook entries, and minutiae of composition such as pen or pencil use, differences in ink, indention variations, inconsistent capitalization and use (or omission) of single and double quotation marks or stage direction enclosures, false starts (unless a different word is suggested), anticipations of a following repeated word, partial deletions where full deletions were clearly intended, eccentric spelling or obvious slips in spelling or writing, most fragmented jottings, and placement of manuscript changes. The last have been brought into the line here and indicated for clarity simply as [*word*] *changed word,* and may have resulted from overwriting, insertion above, below, or at either side of the line, alteration of a few letters, etc.

In the drafts, characters are seldom assigned to speeches: at times simple check marks are used for separation; at other times there is no demarcation. It has not seemed essential to indicate here the exceptions to this general practice unless a change of character for a given speech has been made.

PART TWO

Shelley's *Prometheus Unbound:*
The Text and the Drafts

Key to Abbreviations and Code Markings

SD	Stage (or Scene) Direction (used also for speech ascriptions)
E	Bodleian MSS Shelley E.1, E.2, and E.3
1820	The first edition of the poem
M	Mary Shelley's first edition (1839)
M²	Mary Shelley's second edition [1839] 1840
[ ]	As part of a manuscript reading: deletion by the poet
⟨ ⟩	As part of a manuscript reading: editorial comment or conjecture
→	As part of a manuscript reading: transition from one stage of a draft to another
*	As part of a manuscript reading: illegible letters or word
(1) (2) (3)	Designations of two or more drafts of given lines
E-1820 1820-M E-M	The reading is the same in both or all of the inclusive items

NOTE: In the textual notes all manuscript readings are from E unless specifically identified as being from the drafts.

E has *Prometheus Unbound* / *a Lyrical Drama* / *D.P.* and a partial list of dramatis personae (see Appendix A). 1820 carried only a half title at the point of the drama, but had the following title page set with varied type sizes: PROMETHEUS UNBOUND / A LYRICAL DRAMA / IN FOUR ACTS / WITH OTHER POEMS / BY / PERCY BYSSHE SHELLEY / AUDISNE HÆC, AMPHIARAE, SUB TERRAM ABDITE? / LONDON / C AND J OLLIER VERE STREET BOND STREET / 1820 M carried a preliminary page with title, subtitle, acts, and epigraph. M^2, reset in double columns, placed the material of the preliminary page in M as a heading for the first page of the text.

PROMETHEUS UNBOUND

A Lyrical Drama

IN FOUR ACTS

Audisne hæc, Amphiarae, sub terram abdite?

Drafts for Preface lines 1-47, plus a short unused passage, are in Bodleian MS Shelley adds. e.11; and for lines 75-178 in Huntington MS 2177. The fair copy is in Bodleian MSS Shelley E.1 and E.3.

1-6 There are two drafts of these lines.

1-6 (1): *[The story of] The Greek tragic writers were accustomed to choose a subject well known to their auditors & often treated by their [Contemporaries & rivals.]*—

1-2 (2): *The Greek tragic writers [in their treatment of] [when they chose,] in selecting as [a] their subject any portion of the history or mythology of their nation,*

4-5 (2): *felt themselves obliged*

7-8 Draft: *Such a plan would have been no more than the resignation of those claims to [emulation] preference*

10 Draft: *was [told] exhibited on the Greek theatre*

15-16 Draft: *to the empire of Heaven by [the] his marriage*

17 Draft: *on this view*   E: *[on] according to*

18-19 Draft: *& Hercules by the permission of Jupiter delivered Prometheus from the vulture & the ⟨option: his⟩ chains.* → received, but *by Hercules* lacking.

24-25 Draft: *the [consideration] thought of the [unfavourable] high comparison I [challenged] should so challenge*

26-27 Draft: *averse from a [conclusion so unw⟨arranted⟩] a catastrophe so feeble*

28 Draft (after *of mankind*): *Nor can I imagine how such a [story] scene could ever have [been exhibited without] excited any thing but disappointment.* Above the last word is *on the st* with *st* part of an obscured word. I doubt *stage* but possibly it is *steps* with a malformed *p*; or they may be irrelevant words already present when Shelley reached the page.

29-31 Draft: *the fable so powerful in the sufferings [of Prometheus] & the endurance of Prometheus [is annih⟨ilated⟩] would be annihilated*

30 E: *The endurance* A slight refinement of expression resulted from omission of *the* in 1820-M.

32-35 Draft: *quaking before his perfidious & successful adversary. Prometheus is I think a more poetical*   E: *perfidious & successful* with the transposition in 1820 either accidental or made for emphasis.

PREFACE.

The Greek tragic writers, in selecting as their subject any portion of their national history or mythology, employed in their treatment of it a certain arbitrary discretion. They by no means conceived themselves bound to adhere to the common interpretation, or to imitate in story as in title their rivals and predecessors. Such a system would have amounted to a resignation of those claims to preference over their competitors which incited the composition. The Agamemnonian story was exhibited on the Athenian theatre with as many variations as dramas.

I have presumed to employ a similar licence. The *Prometheus Unbound* of Æschylus supposed the reconciliation of Jupiter with his victim as the price of the disclosure of the danger threatened to his empire by the consummation of his marriage with Thetis. Thetis, according to this view of the subject, was given in marriage to Peleus, and Prometheus, by the permission of Jupiter, delivered from his captivity by Hercules. Had I framed my story on this model, I should have done no more than have attempted to restore the lost drama of Æschylus; an ambition which, if my preference to this mode of treating the subject had incited me to cherish, the recollection of the high comparison such an attempt would challenge might well abate. But, in truth, I was averse from a catastrophe so feeble as that of reconciling the Champion with the Oppressor of mankind. The moral interest of the fable, which is so powerfully sustained by the sufferings and endurance of Prometheus, would be annihilated if we could conceive of him as unsaying his high language and quailing before his successful and perfidious adversary. The only imaginary being resembling in any degree Prometheus, is Satan; and Prometheus is, in my judgement, a more poetical character than Satan, because, in addition to courage,

35

39-40 Draft: *ambition & revenge & injustice which*

41 Draft and E: *perpetually interfere*   1820-M: *perpetually* omitted, perhaps as too strong a word in this context.

42 Draft: *The character of* lacking.

43-44 Draft: *leads us to [excuse] weigh his faults [in return for his] with his wrongs [because the] & to excuse*

46 Draft: *read that magnificent*

48-73 There are no known drafts for these lines.

51 E: *[among] [in] upon*

54 E: *which [has] are [stretched out] extended in ever winding labyrinths [am⟨ong⟩] upon*

56 E: *[air] sky*

57 E: *of* (probably accidentally omitted in 1820) was restored in M probably from the errata since Galignani followed the 1820 reading.

61 E: *[There will be found] The imagery which I have*

71 E: The faulty *it is from the study* was corrected to the present reading in 1820.

74 Draft: *One word in candour on the manner in which* The draft also contains the following unused passage relevant here (the first part of the sentence is torn away): *from the impulses of that universal nature [which is] the book [of] from which poetry is a transcript → from which all poetry is beautiful inasmuch as it is a transcript*

and majesty, and firm and patient opposition to omnipotent force, he is susceptible of being described as
exempt from the taints of ambition, envy, revenge,
and a desire for personal aggrandisement, which, in
the hero of *Paradise Lost,* interfere with the interest.
The character of Satan engenders in the mind a per-
nicious casuistry which leads us to weigh his faults
with his wrongs, and to excuse the former because the
latter exceed all measure. In the minds of those who
consider that magnificent fiction with a religious feeling, it engenders something worse. But Prometheus
is, as it were, the type of the highest perfection of
moral and intellectual nature, impelled by the purest
and the truest motives to the best and noblest ends.

This poem was chiefly written upon the mountainous
ruins of the Baths of Caracalla, among the flowery
glades, and thickets of odoriferous blossoming trees,
which are extended in ever-winding labyrinths upon its
immense platforms and dizzy arches suspended in the
air. The bright blue sky of Rome, and the effect of
the vigorous awakening of spring in that divinest climate,
and the new life with which it drenches the spirits
even to intoxication, were the inspiration of this
drama.

The imagery which I have employed will be found,
in many instances, to have been drawn from the opera-
tions of the human mind, or from those external actions
by which they are expressed. This is unusual in
modern poetry, although Dante and Shakespeare are
full of instances of the same kind: Dante indeed
more than any other poet, and with greater success.
But the Greek poets, as writers to whom no resource
of awakening the sympathy of their contemporaries
was unknown, were in the habitual use of this power;
and it is the study of their works (since a higher
merit would probably be denied me) to which I am
willing that my readers should impute this singularity.

One word is due in candour to the degree in which the

75-78 Draft: *writing may have modified* with *my . . . mine.* lacking.

78-81 Draft: *any one [person] [writer] contemporary with such writers as [L. B. & Words. & Coleridge] stand in the ranks of literature of the present day can conscientiously assure themselves or others that their language*

83 Draft: *the [writings] productions of these*
85-86 Draft: *due less to the peculiarity*
87 Draft: *intellectual [education] condition*
88 Draft: *they were produced.*
89 Draft and E: *have the form*   1820 initiated the received change, which avoids the unfortunate repetition of *have*
90 Draft: *those whom they are supposed to imitate; [and it is not because]* → received.
94-118 The draft has the following unused passage, relevant here: *[In] how many second rate writers of the age of Queen Elizabeth [do we find a style &] possess a stlye & a form which is in every way admirable, who had they lived in the age of George the 2ᵈ might probably have deserved to figure among the heroes of the Dunciad. | Still men*
94-96 Draft: *I am undeniably persuaded [that a] the peculiar style [has not been in En⟨gland⟩] of intense & comprehensive [thought in poetry] imagery which distinguishes [England] modern writers, has not been*
97 Draft: *any particular one*
98-99 Draft: *mass of [genius] capabilities is probably at every period the same, [Ours in England is proved by the same vigorous & fervid spirit of language having prevailed in Germany.] the circumstances*
98 E: *[in] [is] remains*
101 Draft: *in extent & population*
102-09 Draft: *but that each under [similar] institutions similar to those of Athens, would produce philosophers & poets equal to those which have never (if we may except Shakespeare) been surpassed. So much experience warrants; & theory may promise & imagine more   We owe [probably to the Reformation] the great writers of the [age of] Elizabethan age to the fervid awakening of the public mind which [overthrew the hierarchy of Religion] shook the most oppressive form of the Christian Religion to the dust,*
102 E: *is [every] no reason*
103 E: *institutions [equally] not more [ex⟨cellent⟩] perfect*
109-10 E: *We owe [Pa⟨radise Lost⟩] Milton*
110 Draft: *the development & progress* with numerals to indicate the transposition.
111-13 Draft: *the sacred . . . religion.* lacking.
111 Draft: *spirit. [Chaucer was contemporary with Wickliff] The great*

study of contemporary writings may have tinged my composition, for such has been a topic of censure with regard to poems far more popular, and, indeed, more de-
servedly popular, than mine. It is impossible that any
one who inhabits the same age with such writers as those
who stand in the foremost ranks of our own, can conscientiously assure himself that his language and tone
of thought may not have been modified by the study of
the productions of those extraordinary intellects. It
is true that, not the spirit of their genius, but the forms
in which it has manifested itself, are due less to the pe-
culiarities of their own minds than to the peculiarity of
the moral and intellectual condition of the minds among
which they have been produced. Thus a number of
writers possess the form, whilst they want the spirit of
those whom, it is alleged, they imitate; because the
former is the endowment of the age in which they live,
and the latter must be the uncommunicated lightning
of their own mind.

The peculiar style of intense and comprehensive
imagery which distinguishes the modern literature of
England has not been, as a general power, the product of the imitation of any particular writer. The
mass of capabilities remains at every period materially
the same; the circumstances which awaken it to action
perpetually change. If England were divided into
forty republics, each equal in population and extent
to Athens, there is no reason to suppose but that,
under institutions not more perfect than those of
Athens, each would produce philosophers and poets
equal to those who (if we except Shakespeare) have
never been surpassed. We owe the great writers of
the golden age of our literature to that fervid awakening of the public mind which shook to dust the oldest
and most oppressive form of the Christian religion. We
owe Milton to the progress and development of the
same spirit: the sacred Milton was, let it ever be remembered, a republican, and a bold inquirer into

113 E: [*faiths*] *morals & religion*

114-115 Draft: *age are,* [*let us believe*] *we have reason to suppose the fore-runners of some*   E: *the companions or forerunners*

116-19 Draft: *The cloud . . . restored.*   lacking.

116 Draft and E: *condition, & in the*   The present reading follows 1820, which corrected the faulty structure.

120-24 There are two drafts of these lines.

120-24 (1): *Originality does not consist* [*in words & names, or stories*] *or combinations of metre & language different from those which have gone before, it does not consist only in avoiding a resemblance*   →   (2) received with variants as noted below.

121-22 (2): *representation;* [*its abstractions*] *poetical abstractions*

122-24 (2): *not because the portions of them have no previous*   E: *not because* [*they had no previous*] *the* [*parts*] *portions*

124 E: *of man or* [*of*] *in nature,*

125-26 Draft: *the whole has* [*a sen⟨sible⟩*] *an intelligible analogy*

125 E: *whole* [*which those parts*] *produced by their combination*

127-28 Draft and E: *and with . . . them.*   lacking.   This was almost certainly a Shelley addition. After *thought* the draft has: *it abstracts from all that has been imagined, or is the* [*visible*] *object of sensation what* ⟨option: *that which*⟩ *is most beautiful,*

128-29 Draft: [*Poets*] *One real Poet is to another a piece of Nature, which he studies & imitates*

128 E: [*the*] *One*

130-37 Draft: *He might . . . ineffectual.*   lacking.

133 E: *as* [*that he would*] [*to*] *exclude*

134 E: *in the* [*prod⟨uctions⟩*] *writings*

135 E: *presumption in* [*all*] *any*

136 E: *in him* [*could he accomplish such*] *would be*

137-40 Draft: *A* [*man*] *poet is the joint product of such internal powers as modify the natures of others, & of external* [*ones*] *influences which excite*

140-41 Draft: *he . . . both.*   lacking.

140 E: *as* [*modify the*] *excite*   and   *he is not one* [*of*]*, but*

141-143 Draft: *modified by* [*every word*] *all the objects of nature & of art, by every word, &* [*tone*] *sentence which he ever admitted*

142 E: [*but*] *by every*

145 Draft: *many outward forms*

146-49 Draft: *Poets . . . escape.*   lacking.

146-47 E: [*Men, are*] *Poets, not otherwise than philosophers or* [*artis⟨ts⟩*] *painters sculptors or musicians,*   1820 initiated the received changes, which resulted in a more direct and effective sentence structure.

150-84 There are two drafts of these lines.

150-53 (1): *It is with us, as with our ancestors* [*in*] *of the* [*Elizabethan*] *age of Shakespeare, we have writers, some more or less powerful, but all modelled on* [*one spirit.*] *the spirit of one   Who w⁴ call Virgil an imitator of Homer? the*

morals and religion. The great writers of our own
age are, we have reason to suppose, the companions
and forerunners of some unimagined change in our   115
social condition, or the opinions which cement it. The
cloud of mind is discharging its collected lightning,
and the equilibrium between institutions and opinions
is now restoring, or is about to be restored.

As to imitation, poetry is a mimetic art. It creates,   120
but it creates by combination and representation.
Poetical abstractions are beautiful and new, not
because the portions of which they are composed had
no previous existence in the mind of man or in nature,
but because the whole produced by their combination   125
has some intelligible and beautiful analogy with those
sources of emotion and thought, and with the contemporary condition of them. One great poet is a master-
piece of nature which another not only ought to study
but must study. He might as wisely and as easily   130
determine that his mind should no longer be the
mirror of all that is lovely in the visible universe,
as exclude from his contemplation the beautiful which
exists in the writings of a great contemporary. The
pretense of doing it would be a presumption in any   135
but the greatest; the effect, even in him, would be
strained, unnatural, and ineffectual. A poet is the
combined product of such internal powers as modify
the nature of others, and of such external influences
as excite and sustain these powers; he is not one, but   140
both. Every man's mind is, in this respect, modified
by all the objects of nature and art; by every word
and every suggestion which he ever admitted to act
upon his consciousness; it is the mirror upon which
all forms are reflected, and in which they compose   145
one form. Poets, not otherwise than philosophers,
painters, sculptors, and musicians, are in one sense
the creators, and in another the creations, of their
age. From this subjection the loftiest do not escape.
There is a similarity between Homer and Hesiod, be-   150

[ideal] conceptions had been new modelled within his mind, they had been born again—

150 E: *similarity, [among sufficient distinctions,] between*

151-52 (2): *between Virgil & Horace,* lacking.

153-57 (2): *between Dryden . . . imitated.* lacking, but with: *Fletcher, [between Swift] all great writers of [the same age.] a contemporary epoch*

154 E: *each has a [specific] generic*

155-56 E: *similarity [is] be*

158-84 (1): *[There is one mistake] [I have heard one mistake expressed concerning my writing   It has been alledged that my writings are [destined] consecrated by me to the working of a gre⟨at reform?⟩] They are the productions indeed of a person who verily believes himself to possess something like a reasoned system [on the great ques⟨tion⟩] & what spirit [is devoid of such a faith] is so torpid as to have formed to itself no decision on the great question of [morality] the conduct of men towards each other in human life*

158-59 (2): *[I am twitted ⟨?⟩ with] Let me take this opportunity of acknowledging*

158 E: *[Concede to me] Let this opportunity*   and   *acknowledging [what] that*

159-60 (2): *characteristically calls*

161-64 (2): *to write his book he does not explain. My comfort is, that I shall be damned in good company [Plato, Lord Bacon, Milton. ⟨sic⟩ Rousseau]*

162 E: *explain.—[But] For*

166-68 (2): *inforcement of that reform, or that I consider them in any degree a reasoned system on [the forms] theory of human life*

166 E: *of [that]*

169-70 (2): *Nothing can equally well be expressed in prose [ought to be expressed in verse.] but is tedious*

169 E: *equally well be*   The present reading was initiated in 1820 and gives a stronger construction.

171-73 (2): *They are attempts to familiarize the imagination of poetical readers with [the] beautiful*

171-72 E: *[rather] simply*

172 E: *familiarize the [imagination of po⟨etical⟩] highly*

174-78 (2): *excellence. [Of course if I designed I] Until [a heart] the mind can love & admire & trust & hope, & endure to what end would you propose principles of moral conduct? [When] They are seeds thrown upon the highway of life, & the hungry [passenger tramples them on to dust.]*

176 E: *endure, [that] reasoned*

180-84 E is almost illegible at this point, but appears to have developed as follows (Mary would almost certainly have called on Shelley for clarification and final choices for the 1820 reading): *that is, produce a systematical development of [the principles which should regulate human life] what appear to me to be the genuine [elements of] sources of our human society, let not the advocates of [despotism] injustice & superstition [assure] flatter themselves that I*

tween Æschylus and Euripides, between Virgil and
Horace, between Dante and Petrarch, between
Shakespeare and Fletcher, between Dryden and Pope;
each has a generic resemblance under which their
specific distinctions are arranged. If this similarity   155
be the result of imitation, I am willing to confess
that I have imitated.

Let this opportunity be conceded to me of acknowledging that I have, what a Scotch philosopher characteristically terms, 'a passion for reforming the   160
world.' What passion incited him to write and publish
his book, he omits to explain. For my part, I had
rather be damned with Plato and Lord Bacon, than
go to Heaven with Paley and Malthus. But it is a
mistake to suppose that I dedicate my poetical compo-   165
sitions solely to the direct enforcement of reform, or
that I consider them in any degree as containing a
reasoned system on the theory of human life. Didac-
tic poetry is my abhorrence; nothing can be equally
well expressed in prose that is not tedious and supere-   170
rogatory in verse. My purpose has hitherto been sim-
ply to familiarize the highly refined imagination of the
more select classes of poetical readers with beautiful
idealisms of moral excellence, aware that until the
mind can love, and admire, and trust, and hope, and   175
endure, reasoned principles of moral conduct are seeds
cast upon the highway of life which the unconscious
passenger tramples into dust, although they would
bear the harvest of his happiness. Should I live to
accomplish what I purpose, that is, produce a system-   180
atical history of what appear to me to be the genuine
elements of human society, let not the advocates of
injustice and superstition flatter themselves that I
should take Æschylus rather than Plato as my model.

---

should take [Euclid] rather than [Aeschylus] → *Aeschylus rather than [Eu-*
clid] Plato as my model.—

186-88 E: *apology* [*to a*] *candid mind and* [*those who are*] *uncandid* [*may speak as they will*] *injure* [*not*] *me* [*but*] *their own hearts & minds, by* [*calumny*] *misrepresentation.* → *received.*

189-90 E: [*has*] *may possess or instruct* is clear in E; *and instruct* of 1820 was probably an overlooked slip by Mary, uncorrected in M, since E is a more appropriate reading in this context.

191-93 E: *to exert them;* [*if he cannot amuse*] *if his* [*efforts*] *attempt be ineffectual let the punishment of an unaccomplished* [*attempt*] *purpose have been sufficient, let none*

193 E: [*no one*] *none*

194 E: *his* [*hopes*] *efforts.—*[*it is already trembling upon*] *The*

195 E: *betray* [*the spot*] *his grave*

There are three passages in Bodleian MS Shelley adds. e.11 (pp. 47, 52) that may be relevant to the Preface (the first possibly pertinent to the final paragraph above): (1) *As it does not look to any practical change in politics* ⟨option: *human nature*⟩ *but merely points out what w^d be the effect of the most favourable which it enters into the mind to conceive* (2) *In the human world,* [*love is*] *one of the commonest expressions of love is social intercourse, &* [*the*] *in describing the deepest effects of abstract love the author could not avoid the danger of exciting some ideas* [*of*] *connected with* [*it*] *this mode of expression. In this he has exposed himself to the danger of awakening ludicrous or unauthorized images; but in the obedience to an impulse* (3) *I am not conscious of having deviated from the* ⟨*custom*⟩ *of antique mythology —The Spirits indeed* [*may belong*] [*or Genii*] *belong under various names to every system of supernatural agency, it is a generic name including Genii, Lamiæ, elementary powers* [*the*] *Angels fairies, ghosts, demons*

The having spoken of myself with unaffected free- 185
dom will need little apology with the candid, and let
the uncandid consider that they injure me less than
their own hearts and minds by misrepresentation.
Whatever talents a person may possess to amuse or
instruct others, be they ever so inconsiderable, he is 190
yet bound to exert them: if his attempt be ineffectual,
let the punishment of an unaccomplished purpose
have been sufficient; let none trouble themselves to
heap the dust of oblivion upon his efforts; the pile
they raise will betray his grave, which might otherwise 195
have been unknown.

E: *Demogorgon, Ocean, Apollo* lacking.   E-1820: *The Spirit of the Moon* lacking and first introduced in M, probably from the errata list.

DRAMATIS PERSONÆ

Prometheus
Demogorgon
Jupiter
The Earth
Ocean
Apollo
Mercury
Hercules
Asia ⎤
Panthea ⎬ Oceanides
Ione ⎦
The Phantasm of Jupiter
The Spirit of the Earth
The Spirit of the Moon
Spirits of the Hours
Echoes
Fauns
Furies
Spirits

Drafts for Act I, found in Bodleian MS Shelley adds. e.12, are meager, and represent only fifteen of the 833 lines in the act. Unless otherwise noted, therefore, all manuscript readings are from E, where they are found in Bodleian MSS E.1 and E.3.

1-216 There are no known drafts of these lines.

12-13 The present punctuation is more indicative of Shelley's intent (E has *hours | And moments,*) than is that of 1820-M, which is: *Three thousand years of sleep unsheltered hours, | And moments aye divided* etc.

14 Although Freeman defended *seem* of E inasmuch as "the moments are still continuing" ("Text," p. 42), the 1820-M reading *seemed* is preferable since it is the accumulation of hours, etc., in the past that has built Prometheus' present empire.

15 *Scorn & despair—[more glorious than thy throne] these are mine empire.* It is quite possible (as F. A. Pottle suggested to me) that Shelley "dropped his r's" and pronounced *empire* as ɛm pɑi ə, thus giving a pentameter rather than the apparent tetrameter. (Cf. J. S. Kenyon, *American Pronunciation,* 10th ed. (Ann Arbor, Whare, 1958), sect. 353; and n. on IV.294, below.)

16-17 *More glorious far than [thine unenvied throne | Of gold & blood, are these] O Mighty God!* → received.

21 *[Ba⟨re⟩] Black*

26 *[Sky—] Heaven—* The personification is properly capitalized.

PROMETHEUS UNBOUND

ACT I

Scene: A Ravine of icy Rocks in the Indian Caucasus. Prometheus
is discovered bound to the Precipice. Panthea *and* Ione *are seated
at his Feet. Time, Night. During the Scene, Morning slowly breaks.*

Prometheus

Monarch of Gods and Dæmons, and all Spirits
But One, who throng those bright and rolling worlds
Which thou and I alone of living things
Behold with sleepless eyes!—regard this earth
Made multitudinous with thy slaves, whom thou   5
Requitest for knee-worship, prayer, and praise,
And toil, and hecatombs of broken hearts,
With fear, and self-contempt, and barren hope;
Whilst me, who am thy foe, eyeless in hate,
Hast thou made reign and triumph, to thy scorn,   10
O'er mine own misery and thy vain revenge.
Three thousand years of sleep-unsheltered hours
And moments—aye divided by keen pangs
Till they seemed years—torture and solitude,
Scorn and despair—these are mine empire: 15
More glorious far than that which thou surveyest
From thine unenvied throne, O Mighty God!
Almighty, had I deigned to share the shame
Of thine ill tyranny, and hung not here
Nailed to this wall of eagle-baffling mountain,   20
Black, wintry, dead, unmeasured; without herb,
Insect, or beast, or shape or sound of life—
Ah me, alas, pain, pain ever, forever!

No change, no pause, no hope!—yet I endure.
I ask the Earth, have not the mountains felt?   25
I ask yon Heaven—the all-beholding Sun—
Has it not seen? the Sea, in storm or calm—

28 [*An*] [*Its*] *Heaven's* and   *below*[?]—

35 E has *its own* but *his own* of 1820 draws the proper contrast since the
beak in itself would have no poison.

37 *The* [*shapeless*] *ghastly* and   *dream*[*s*], Following l. 37 is: [*Where
thou descend'st each night with open eyes | In torture, for a tyrant seldom
sleeps, | Thou never;*] → received.

42 [*spirits*] *genii*

44 *And yet* ⟨option: *And even*⟩

48 [*The*] *Their*   Although careful analysis establishes this order of change,
the overwriting apparently misled Mary to give *The* for 1820-M.

53 [*alas*] *ah*

54 It is surprising that, if *the wide* was an error in 1820, the errata list did
not carry a correction; but *thro wide* of E is superior since it localizes the reference (Jupiter's realm), and the unqualified closing spondee carries a stronger
feeling of space.

59 [*Then*] *Once*

64 [*& thou*] *Thou* [*pure*] *serenest*

Heaven's ever-changing shadow, spread below—
Have its deaf waves not heard my agony?
Ah me, alas, pain, pain ever, forever!   30

The crawling glaciers pierce me with the spears
Of their moon-freezing crystals; the bright chains
Eat with their burning cold into my bones;
Heaven's wingèd hound, polluting from thy lips
His beak in poison not his own, tears up   35
My heart; and shapeless sights come wandering by,
The ghastly people of the realm of dream,
Mocking me; and the Earthquake-fiends are charged
To wrench the rivets from my quivering wounds
When the rocks split and close again behind;   40
While, from their loud abysses, howling throng
The genii of the storm, urging the rage
Of whirlwind, and afflict me with keen hail.
And yet to me welcome is Day and Night,
Whether one breaks the hoar frost of the morn,   45
Or starry, dim, and slow, the other climbs
The leaden-coloured east; for then they lead
Their wingless, crawling hours, one among whom—
As some dark priest hales the reluctant victim—
Shall drag thee, cruel King, to kiss the blood   50
From these pale feet, which then might trample thee
If they disdained not such a prostrate slave.
Disdain? Ah no! I pity thee. What Ruin
Will hunt thee undefended through wide Heaven!
How will thy soul, cloven to its depth with terror,   55
Gape like a hell within! I speak in grief,
Not exultation, for I hate no more
As then, ere misery made me wise. The curse
Once breathed on thee I would recall. Ye Mountains,
Whose many-voicèd Echoes, through the mist   60
Of cataracts, flung the thunder of that spell!
Ye icy Springs, stagnant with wrinkling frost,
Which vibrated to hear me, and then crept
Shuddering through India! Thou serenest Air,

80 [*thro*] *'mid*   1820-M corrected the current but old-fashioned *had ran*
of E.

85 Below *Been cloven* is *And silence* probably irrelevant here, but possibly
a jotting later adopted for line 106.

88 [*fi⟨ery⟩*] *flaming*

Through which the Sun walks burning without beams!   65
And ye swift Whirlwinds, who on poisèd wings
Hung mute and moveless o'er yon hushed abyss,
As thunder, louder than your own, made rock
The orbèd world! If then my words had power—
Though I am changed so that aught evil wish   70
Is dead within; although no memory be
Of what is hate—let them not lose it now!
What was that curse? for ye all heard me speak.

First Voice: from the Mountains

Thrice three hundred thousand years
   O'er the Earthquake's couch we stood;   75
Oft, as men convulsed with fears,
   We trembled in our multitude.

Second Voice: from the Springs

Thunderbolts had parched our water,
   We had been stained with bitter blood,
And had run mute, 'mid shrieks of slaughter,   80
   Through a city and a solitude.

Third Voice: from the Air

I had clothed, since Earth uprose,
   Its wastes in colours not their own;
And oft had my serene repose
   Been cloven by many a rending groan.   85

Fourth Voice: from the Whirlwinds

We had soared beneath these mountains
   Unresting ages; nor had thunder,
Nor yon volcano's flaming fountains,
   Nor any power above or under
   Ever made us mute with wonder.   90

First Voice

But never bowed our snowy crest
As at the voice of thine unrest.

98 *And* [*died—as the mad*] → received.

99 Mary possibly interpreted *Earth* (E-M) as a reference to the character.

103-04 It has usually been assumed that Shelley was indulging either a sole-
cism or a convention in this rime combination (see *Variorum*, p. 354). It is now
clear that to about 1830 the pronunciation *-in* for *-ing* was almost universal
and that *ruin-pursuing* was an exact rime for Shelley. (See "Preface to the
New Edition" in F. A. Pottle, *Shelley and Browning* [Hamden, Conn., Archon
Books, 1965].)

105 [*Make*] *Made*

106 *as* is slightly blotted in E, and was susceptible of misreading as *a* by
Mary for 1820. The restoration of *as* in M was probably from the errata list
(Galignani: 1820). Below line 106 is the SD: *they pass with a terrible sound*
This is the first of several stage directions, undeleted in E but unused, whose
failure to appear in 1820 was almost certainly Shelley's decision. In this instance there is no compensation (as there usually is) in repeated elements of
the SD in the text lines.

107 *The Earth* ⟨option: *A Voice*⟩ / *The tongueless* [*clefts within the mountains then*] → received with [*hollows*] *caverns*

108 *Cried Misery*[*!*], [*&*] *then, the* [*startled*] *hollow*

110 *howled* [*it*] [*back* ⟨?⟩] *to* [*all*] *the lashing winds*

113-14 *Which I gave forth.* [*O Mother dare thy sons* / *Scorn him without
whom, by* [*under*] *the might of Jove*] → received.

117 [*wind?—*] *wind!—Know* [*they*] *ye*

118 [*su*⟨fferings⟩] *agony*

119 [*thine*] [*their*] [*mans* ⟨?⟩] *your*

120 [*Ye*] *O* and *snow*[*ing*]-*fed streams   streams* might be read as *stream*,
but what follows the *m* is more curved (like Shelley's *s*) than straight (like his
usual comma).

121 *Now* [*dimly*] *seen* [*thro' tempests*] *athwart*

Second Voice

Never such a sound before
To the Indian waves we bore.
A pilot asleep on the howling sea   95
Leaped up from the deck in agony,
And heard, and cried, 'Ah, woe is me!'
And died as mad as the wild waves be.

Third Voice

By such dread words from earth to Heaven
My still realm was never riven: 100
When its wound was closed, there stood
Darkness o'er the day like blood.

Fourth Voice

And we shrank back; for dreams of ruin
To frozen caves our flight pursuing
Made us keep silence—thus—and thus—   105
Though silence is as hell to us.

The Earth

The tongueless caverns of the craggy hills
Cried 'Misery!' then; the hollow heaven replied,
'Misery!' and the ocean's purple waves,
Climbing the land, howled to the lashing winds,   110
And the pale nations heard it—'Misery!'

Prometheus

I hear a sound of voices—not the voice
Which I gave forth. Mother, thy sons and thou
Scorn him without whose all-enduring will
Beneath the fierce omnipotence of Jove   115
Both they and thou had vanished like thin mist
Unrolled on the morning wind. Know ye not me,
The Titan? he who made his agony
The barrier to your else all-conquering foe?
O rock-embosomed lawns and snow-fed streams   120
Now seen athwart frore vapours, deep below,
Through whose o'ershadowing woods I wandered once

136-37 The ambiguity of *love* (is it that *I love* or that *thou love*⟨st⟩?) stems from Shelley's inconsistent use of the paradigm of *thou* (see Intro., n. 25, above). I believe that *thou* is the subject of *love,* but that emendation to *lovest* (as also at II.i.141 and IV.507) would be to support consistency with pedantry and sacrifice the euphony which I believe dictated Shelley's use in these instances. See the *Variorum,* pp. 139-40, for the extended debate on the present passage, especially the parallel with *To a Skylark,* l. 80.

140 *Heaven's [fierce] fell*

With Asia, drinking life from her loved eyes—
Why scorns the spirit which informs ye, now
To commune with me? me alone, who checked—   125
As one who checks a fiend-drawn charioteer—
The falsehood and the force of him who reigns
Supreme, and with the groans of pining slaves
Fills your dim glens and liquid wildernesses?
Why answer ye not, still? Brethren!

                    The Earth

                              They dare not.   130

                    Prometheus

Who dares? for I would hear that curse again. . . .
Ha, what an awful whisper rises up!
'Tis scarce like sound: it tingles through the frame
As lightning tingles, hovering ere it strike.
Speak, Spirit! from thine inorganic voice   135
I only know that thou art moving near
And love. How cursed I him?

                    The Earth

                              How canst thou hear
Who knowest not the language of the dead?

                    Prometheus

Thou art a living spirit—speak as they.

                    The Earth

I dare not speak like life, lest Heaven's fell King   140
Should hear, and link me to some wheel of pain
More torturing than the one whereon I roll.
Subtle thou art and good; and though the Gods
Hear not this voice, yet thou art more than God,
Being wise and kind: earnestly hearken now.   145

                    Prometheus

Obscurely through my brain, like shadows dim,
Sweep awful thoughts, rapid and thick. I feel

151-52 *Only to those who die . . .* ⟨sic⟩ *I am the Earth* → received.
151 [*who*] *what*

157-58 *like a* [*cloud / Of glory arise—*] → *like a beam / From sunrise,*
[*burst*] *leap*— If E represented a late change to avoid the Wordsworthian
echo, and was neglected by Mary in copying (or was added after the transcription), one would expect the point to be of major concern for the errata.
Since M followed 1820 (the present reading) it must be concluded, with Locock, that "Shelley preferred the older, and perhaps more appropriate meta-
phor" (*Examination*, p. 29).

161 *And our* [*invisible*] *almighty* [*invisible*] is deleted in pencil, suggesting
that the word was held for a time as an option.

165 *moonlike* (probably a tentative option for *sphered*) was perhaps rejected when Shelley noted the *like-light* echo.

166 [*shaken*] *lifted with* *lifted by* of 1820-M is more exact, as possibly
Mary, Shelley, or Peacock realized.

167 [*lifted*] *rifted* The change was probably made when *lifted* was substituted in line 166.

169-76 *Lightning & Inundation vexed the plains* / [*Pestilence fell*] *on man
& beast & worm* / *And Famine, & black blight on herb & tree,* / [*Blue thistles
bloomed in cities, foodless toads* / [*Without*] *Within voluptuous chambers
panting crawled,* / *And* [*wind*] *air-fed efts* [*lizards*]; *for my withered breast
was dry*] → received with changes as noted below.

172-173 The punctuation of E-M (*and worm,* [E: *worm*] / *And Famine;*)
left an ambiguity, since Plague and Famine both fell on man.

172 [*For*] *When* The change dictates the comma above after *crawled* as
against the semicolon of the revised E (and M) or the colon of 1820.

173 [*blue*] *black*

174 [*The corn fields & the vineyards & the meadows*] → received.

Faint, like one mingled in entwining love;
Yet 'tis not pleasure.

The Earth

No, thou canst not hear:
Thou art immortal, and this tongue is known   150
Only to those who die.

Prometheus

And what art thou,
O melancholy Voice?

The Earth

I am the Earth,
Thy mother; she within whose stony veins,
To the last fibre of the loftiest tree
Whose thin leaves trembled in the frozen air,   155
Joy ran, as blood within a living frame,
When thou didst from her bosom, like a cloud
Of glory, arise—a spirit of keen joy!
And at thy voice her pining sons uplifted
Their prostrate brows from the polluting dust,   160
And our almighty Tyrant with fierce dread
Grew pale, until his thunder chained thee here.
Then—see those million worlds which burn and roll
Around us: their inhabitants beheld
My spherèd light wane in wide heaven; the sea   165
Was lifted by strange tempest, and new fire
From earthquake-rifted mountains of bright snow
Shook its portentous hair beneath Heaven's frown;
Lightning and inundation vexed the plains;
Blue thistles bloomed in cities; foodless toads   170
Within voluptuous chambers panting crawled,
When plague had fallen on man and beast and worm—
And famine—and black blight on herb and tree;
And in the corn, and vines, and meadow grass
Teemed ineradicable poisonous weeds   175
Draining their growth—for my wan breast was dry
With grief—and the thin air, my breath, was stained

179 [*for*] *aye,*

181 Shelley's customary usage would call for *mine* before the vowel, but with the *n*'s of *innumerable* the line is more euphonious with *my* (as in E-M).

195 This line is followed by [*Which thou henceforth art doomed to inter-weave*]

202 [*lo⟨vely⟩*] *beauteous*

204 [*peopled*] *shaken*   The final choice of *peopled* for 1820 would appear to have been Shelley's since there is no evidence of a correction in the errata list. *peopled* restored the less commonplace and contextually more appropriate word.

208-09 [*on his throne | Of*] *throned | On*   Despite the rhetorically stronger final reading of E one must assume that it was not used because the resulting tetrameter of line 208 was detected.

With the contagion of a mother's hate
Breathed on her child's destroyer.—Aye, I heard
Thy curse, the which, if thou rememberest not,   180
Yet my innumerable seas and streams,
Mountains, and caves, and winds, and yon wide air,
And the inarticulate people of the dead,
Preserve, a treasured spell. We meditate
In secret joy and hope those dreadful words,   185
But dare not speak them.

Prometheus

Venerable mother!
All else who live and suffer take from thee
Some comfort: flowers, and fruits, and happy sounds,
And love, though fleeting. These may not be mine;
But mine own words, I pray, deny me not.   190

The Earth

They shall be told. Ere Babylon was dust,
The Magus Zoroaster, my dead child,
Met his own image walking in the garden.
That apparition, sole of men, he saw.
For know, there are two worlds of life and death: 195
One that which thou beholdest; but the other
Is underneath the grave, where do inhabit
The shadows of all forms that think and live,
Till death unite them, and they part no more;
Dreams and the light imaginings of men,   200
And all that faith creates, or love desires—
Terrible, strange, sublime and beauteous shapes.
There thou art, and dost hang, a writhing shade
'Mid whirlwind-peopled mountains; all the Gods
Are there, and all the powers of nameless worlds—   205
Vast, sceptred phantoms; heroes, men, and beasts;
And Demogorgon, a tremendous Gloom—
And he, the supreme Tyrant, on his throne
Of burning gold. Son, one of these shall utter
The curse which all remember. Call at will   210

212 *Hades, [Osiris] or [Saturn] Typhon or what [later] mightier Gods*

216 *supreme [shall] may*
217-18 The draft of *As . . . palace.* differs only in *winds* for *wind*
218 (last half)-752 There are no known drafts of these lines.

221 This line is followed by a canceled SD, compensated for in lines 231-39:
[*The sound beneath as of earthquake & the driving of whirlwinds—The Ravine is split, & the Phantasm of Jupiter [appears] rises, surrounded by heavy clouds which dart forth lightning*]
222 SD: [*Panthea] Ione*
223 The weaker *o'er* of 1820-M probably resulted from transfer from line 222 in copying or printing, or it could have been a gratuitous attempt to give parallel construction. Apparently it was not noted for the errata list.
225 [*uprise] arise*

235 [*proud] [pale] pale*

237-238 *Its* ⟨option: *His*⟩ and *he* ⟨option: *it*⟩ In view of *Like one who* in l. 239, *he* in ll. 256-57, and the undeleted *His* and *he* here, it is likely that (despite *it* of l. 227 where the context is different) *Its* and *it* were merely tentative options.

Thine own ghost, or the ghost of Jupiter,
Hades, or Typhon, or what mightier Gods
From all-prolific Evil since thy ruin
Have sprung, and trampled on my prostrate sons.
Ask, and they must reply: so the revenge   215
Of the Supreme may sweep through vacant shades
As rainy wind through the abandoned gate
Of a fallen palace.

Prometheus

    Mother, let not aught
Of that which may be evil pass again
My lips, or those of aught resembling me.   220
Phantasm of Jupiter, arise, appear!

Ione

My wings are folded o'er mine ears;
My wings are crossed over mine eyes;
Yet through their silver shade appears,
And through their lulling plumes arise   225
   A shape, a throng of sounds:
    May it be no ill to thee
   O thou of many wounds!
Near whom, for our sweet sister's sake,
Ever thus we watch and wake.   230

Panthea

The sound is of whirlwind underground,
Earthquake, and fire, and mountains cloven;
The shape is awful, like the sound,
Clothed in dark purple, star-inwoven.
   A sceptre of pale gold,   235
    To stay steps proud o'er the slow cloud,
   His veinèd hand doth hold.
Cruel he looks, but calm and strong,
Like one who does, not suffers wrong.

Phantasm of Jupiter

Why have the secret powers of this strange world   240

247 *He* (initiated in 1820) corrected the grammatical error (*be* / *Him*) of E.

252-53 [*Listen, and though ye weep, rejoicing know* | *That our strong curse cannot be unfilfilled*] → received with [*must be fulfilled*] *ye dare not speak cannot* was initiated in 1820 and was not likely to have been done without Shelley's approval, even though it is weaker than the original. The Phantasm speaks in an unaccustomed audible voice (ll. 242-45) which, it must be assumed, *could* be echoed, and cannot only because they dare not. Possibly the fact that *dare not* had shortly before been used three times (ll. 130, 140, 186) led to the change.

256 SD: [*Ione*] *Panthea*
256 [*Look*] *See*

257 [*O sister*] *O shelter*

258 [*cruel,*] [*calm*] *proud* with [*cruel*] underlined for option. This line was originally followed by l. 261.

Driven me, a frail and empty phantom, hither
On direst storms? What unaccustomed sounds
Are hovering on my lips, unlike the voice
With which our pallid race hold ghastly talk
In darkness? And, proud Sufferer, who art thou?   245

Prometheus

Tremendous Image! as thou art must be
He whom thou shadowest forth. I am his foe,
The Titan. Speak the words which I would hear,
Although no thought inform thine empty voice.

The Earth

Listen! and though your echoes must be mute,   250
Grey mountains, and old woods, and haunted springs,
Prophetic caves, and isle-surrounding streams,
Rejoice to hear what yet ye cannot speak.

Phantasm

A spirit seizes me, and speaks within:
It tears me as fire tears a thunder-cloud!   255

Panthea

See how he lifts his mighty looks! the heaven
Darkens above.

Ione

He speaks! O shelter me!

Prometheus

I see the curse on gestures proud and cold,
And looks of firm defiance, and calm hate,
And such despair as mocks itself with smiles,   260
Written as on a scroll . . . yet speak—O speak!

Phantasm

Fiend, I defy thee! with a calm, fixed mind,
    All that thou canst inflict I bid thee do.
Foul Tyrant both of Gods and humankind,
    One only being shalt thou not subdue.   265

275 [*power*] *tower*

277 *Its* is clear in E, and the context strongly supports it. Again Mary or the printer could have lapsed momentarily and permitted the more obvious *In darkness* to slip in for 1820, without change in M. (Cf. n. on III.i.13.)

282 [*Lord*] [*King*] *God & Lord—*

294 *this universe* is clear in E, but 1820 offers the less restrictive reading, followed here.

301 Below this line is an unused but undeleted SD: *the Phantom vanishes* for which there is no compensation in the text lines. (See n. on I.106.)

Rain then thy plagues upon me here,
Ghastly disease and frenzying fear;
And let alternate frost and fire
Eat into me, and be thine ire
Lightning, and cutting hail, and legioned forms   270
Of furies, driving by upon the wounding storms.

Aye, do thy worst. Thou art omnipotent.
   O'er all things but thyself I gave thee power,
And mine own will. Be thy swift mischiefs sent
     To blast mankind, from yon æthereal tower.   275
      Let thy malignant spirit move
      Its darkness over those I love:
      On me and mine I imprecate
      The utmost torture of thy hate,
And thus devote to sleepless agony   280
This undeclining head while thou must reign on high.

But thou who art the God and Lord—O thou
   Who fillest with thy soul this world of woe;
To whom all things of earth and Heaven do bow
     In fear and worship—all-prevailing foe!   285
      I curse thee! let a sufferer's curse
      Clasp thee, his torturer, like remorse,
      Till thine Infinity shall be
      A robe of envenomed agony;
And thine Omnipotence a crown of pain   290
To cling like burning gold round thy dissolving brain.

Heap on thy soul, by virtue of this curse,
   Ill deeds; then be thou damned, beholding good
Both infinite as is the universe,
     And thou, and thy self-torturing solitude.   295
      An awful image of calm power
      Though now thou sittest, let the hour
      Come, when thou must appear to be
      That which thou art internally;
And after many a false and fruitless crime   300
Scorn track thy lagging fall through boundless space and time.

302-05 Locock felt that these lines (written flush in E) should be indented by rime (Edition, *1*, 601). I consider them rather as transitional rimed pentameters suggesting the blank verse form commonly assigned to these characters.

305 This line is followed by the uncompensated SD: [*he bends his head as in pain*]   The deletion must be accepted but seems unfortunate in view of the following speech of The Earth.

312-13 Although one would expect these lines to form a single divided hexameter to balance l. 311 (cf. also IV.56), Shelley's line count indicates that he read them as two lines, and they have been so read in all editions.
312 First Echo: *Fallen & vanquished?*   →   received.

316 [*yon*] *the*

319 [*unsandalled*] *golden-sandalled*

325 [*Heaven-walking*] *world-wandering*   On the facing page is a smudged SD: *Enter Mer⟨cury⟩*

Prometheus

Were these my words, O Parent?

The Earth

They were thine.

Prometheus

It doth repent me: words are quick and vain;
Grief for awhile is blind, and so was mine.
I wish no living thing to suffer pain.   305

The Earth

Misery, O misery to me,
That Jove at length should vanquish thee.
Wail, howl aloud, Land and Sea,
The Earth's rent heart shall answer ye.
Howl, spirits of the living and the dead,   310
Your refuge, your defence lies fallen and vanquishèd.

First Echo

Lies fallen and vanquishèd?

Second Echo

Fallen and vanquishèd!

Ione

Fear not—'tis but some passing spasm;
The Titan is unvanquished still.   315
But see where—through the azure chasm
Of yon forked and snowy hill,
Trampling the slant winds on high
With golden-sandalled feet that glow
Under plumes of purple dye   320
Like rose-ensanguined ivory—
    A shape comes now,
Stretching on high from his right hand
    A serpent-cinctured wand.

Panthea

'Tis Jove's world-wandering herald, Mercury.   325

328 Only Rossetti (followed by Woodberry) attempted to correct the faulty punctuation here, by giving *represses,—* I have preferred to initiate the interrogative mood at this point, as being more in keeping with the context.

331 *Joves [tempest-walking] hounds* No substitute is present for the deleted phrase, which was probably cut before *[Heaven-walking]* of l. 325 was changed, and whose reinstatement was assumed when the echo in l. 325 was removed. It is not likely that the reinstatement would have been made without Shelley's approval.

332 E has *gluts on* but 1820 offers the more exact preposition, followed here.

337 *[Yes: but the] Titan looks firm, [though] not proud.* → received. This line is followed by a canceled SD (for which compensation is found in the following lines): *[Enter Mercury followed by the Furies whom he represses with his wand.]*

338 *[smell] scent* The change of *in* (E) to *into* (1820-M) offers a more exact meaning despite an unobtrusive (because divided) hexameter.

339-42 *smells like [fresh corpses] | To a death-bird after battle! Herald of Gods | Darest thou delay? take cheer, [a richer prey] | [Children of Hell] If the Son of Maia soon* ⟨Shelley then substituted an SD: *He pauses* for *Children of Hell*⟩ → received.

341 With the reading emphasis properly on the initial dactylic *Darest thou* the uncontracted form gives strength to the line without loss of metrical integrity. The question mark after *Herald* in E could easily have been misread as an exclamation mark by Mary for 1820-M.

345-46 Shelley appears to have first written: *And gnash, beside the streams of fire & wail | Your foodless teeth! . .* ⟨sic⟩ Omission of the expected comma after *wail* would not be unusual, and this is basically the reading of 1820, which justified Mathilde Blind's identification of the allusion as the infernal rivers Cocytus and Phlegethon ("Shelley," p. 80). (She erroneously read a comma after *wail* to support her case—there is ink spatter but no comma.) M, however, showed a comma after *fire* and examination of E shows that Shelley apparently added, not a comma but two slanting dots at that point (possibly to balance *teeth! . .* below). Was Mary following the errata list in her change, which would make *wail* a verb rather than a substantive, negate the allusion suggested by Blind, and leave at best an extremely awkward construction (i.e. "gnash your teeth and wail ⟨through⟩ your teeth")? I believe that there is no authority for this assumption, but that M simply followed Galignani's gratuitous comma after *fire*, and that if *fire . .* was indeed an intended alteration by Shelley he overruled the change. In view of the many parallels from *Paradise Lost* in the *Prometheus* (see *Variorum*) the reminiscence of Milton's "Cocytus, nam'd of lamentation loud | Heard on the ruful stream; fierce Phlegeton | Whose waves of torrent fire inflame with rage," and "Gorgons and Hydra's, and Chimera's dire" (*Paradise Lost* II.579-81, 628) seems to offer positive evidence of Shelley's original (and perhaps reestablished) intent.

Ione

And who are those with hydra tresses
And iron wings that climb the wind—
Whom the frowning God represses—
Like vapours steaming up behind,
Clanging loud, an endless crowd?   330

Panthea

These are Jove's tempest-walking hounds,
Whom he gluts with groans and blood
When, charioted on sulphurous cloud,
    He bursts Heaven's bounds.

Ione

Are they now led from the thin dead,   335
On new pangs to be fed?

Panthea

The Titan looks as ever, firm, not proud.

First Fury

Ha! I scent life!

Second Fury

Let me but look into his eyes!

Third Fury

The hope of torturing him smells like a heap
Of corpses to a death-bird after battle!   340

First Fury

Darest thou delay, O Herald? take cheer, Hounds
Of Hell—what if the Son of Maia soon
Should make us food and sport? Who can please long
The Omnipotent?

Mercury

            Back to your towers of iron,
And gnash, beside the streams of fire and wail,   345
Your foodless teeth! . . . Geryon, arise! and Gorgon,

349 [*hate*] *love* The uncertainty as to which word to use here is commented on by Shelley in a note: *The contrast would have been* ⟨*more com-*
plete⟩ *if the sentiment had been transposed: but wherefore sacrifice the philo-*
sophical truth, that love however monstrous in its expression is still less worthy
of horror than hatred ⟨. . .⟩ I now agree with Locock (Edition, *1*, 602) that
the third word from the end is *horror* and that *still* has the sense of "never-
theless." (Zupitza read *honor* but Shelley consistently used the spelling *honour*.)

353 [*one*] *thee*

357 *do more* in E was an obvious oversight corrected for 1820.

365-66 *And long must teach—thy* [*mighty*] *Torturer arms* / [*Even now,*]
with [*new &*] *unimagined pains* → received.

369 The change from *and savage* in E to *or savage* in 1820-M was a possible
transfer from the line opening, but the fact that no correction was made in M
suggests an intentional change for the sharpened meaning.

375 *& bid* [*them gird*] *it clasp*

Chimæra; and thou Sphinx, subtlest of fiends,
Who ministered to Thebes Heaven's poisoned wine—
Unnatural love and more unnatural hate:
These shall perform your task.

First Fury

                       O mercy! mercy!   350
We die with our desire—drive us not back!

Mercury

Crouch then in silence.
                 Awful Sufferer!
To thee unwilling, most unwillingly
I come, by the great Father's will driven down
To execute a doom of new revenge.   355
Alas! I pity thee, and hate myself
That I can do no more. Aye from thy sight
Returning, for a season, Heaven seems Hell,
So thy worn form pursues me night and day,
Smiling reproach. Wise art thou, firm and good,   360
But vainly wouldst stand forth alone in strife
Against the Omnipotent, as yon clear lamps
That measure and divide the weary years
From which there is no refuge, long have taught
And long must teach. Even now thy torturer arms   365
With the strange might of unimagined pains
The powers who scheme slow agonies in Hell,
And my commission is to lead them here,
Or what more subtle, foul, or savage fiends
People the abyss, and leave them to their task.   370
Be it not so! . . . There is a secret known
To thee, and to none else of living things,
Which may transfer the sceptre of wide Heaven,
The fear of which perplexes the Supreme.
Clothe it in words, and bid it clasp his throne   375
In intercession; bend thy soul in prayer,
And like a suppliant in some gorgeous fane
Let the will kneel within thy haughty heart;

382 *He has;* [&] [*I placed it in his choice to be* | *The crown, or trampled refuse of the world* ⟨options: *To be the Sun of gladness to all life* or *To be the sun of joy to the dark world*⟩ | *With but one law itself a glorious boon—* | *I gave*]—& *in return he chains me here*

385 *cling*[*s*]

386 Careful examination of the manuscript shows that *trampled* was changed to *trodden* Since the word looks more like *trodden* at first glance (and no correction of 1820's *trampled* was made in M), it must be assumed that Shelley was consulted and made the final choice.

398 [*The*] *Like*

408 The change from *clamour, fear delay* (E) to *clamour: fear delay:* (1820) to *clamour. Fear delay!* (M) suggests a continuing effort to remove the ambiguity of the reference, and (since Galignani followed 1820) was, I believe, a reflection of the errata list. There would be no reason to suggest that the Hellhounds (Furies) fear delay, but every reason (in view of l. 409) to warn Mercury that he should do so since he has caused the delay through restraint of the Furies (l. 352).

409 [*scowls*] *lowers*

412 [*When sayest thou*] [*Thou knowest not when the destined change arrives* ⟨option: (l. 414)⟩] → received.

For benefits and meek submission tame
The fiercest and the mightiest.

Prometheus

Evil minds   380
Change good to their own nature. I gave all
He has, and in return he chains me here
Years, ages, night and day—whether the sun
Split my parched skin, or in the moony night
The crystal-wingèd snow cling round my hair—   385
Whilst my belovèd race is trampled down
By his thought-executing ministers.
Such is the Tyrant's recompense. 'Tis just:
He who is evil can receive no good;
And for a world bestowed, or a friend lost,   390
He can feel hate, fear, shame—not gratitude:
He but requites me for his own misdeed.
Kindness to such is keen reproach, which breaks
With bitter stings the light sleep of Revenge.
Submission, thou dost know, I cannot try: 395
For what submission but that fatal word,
The death-seal of mankind's captivity—
Like the Sicilian's hair-suspended sword
Which trembles o'er his crown—would he accept,
Or could I yield? Which yet I will not yield.   400
Let others flatter Crime where it sits throned
In brief omnipotence; secure are they,
For Justice, when triumphant, will weep down
Pity, not punishment, on her own wrongs,
Too much avenged by those who err. I wait,   405
Enduring thus, the retributive hour
Which since we spake is even nearer now.
But hark! the Hell-hounds clamour. Fear delay!
Behold! Heaven lowers under thy Father's frown.

Mercury

O that we might be spared: I to inflict   410
And thou to suffer! Once more answer me:
Thou knowest not the period of Jove's power?

413 [*they*] *it*

416 [*Then*] *Yet*

418 [*years*] *age on* [*years*] *age*

423 *unreprieved.* (with the period of E as against the question mark of 1820-
M) offers a more positive close to this statement by Mercury, which comes between two questions.

424 *them—* (as in E). Shelley's intent in E was clearly for a pointing stronger
than the comma of 1820-M in order that the inevitable passing of the years
might be emphasized. Although they did not know E, both Rossetti and Forman apparently sensed this. Rossetti gave *them. The*   Forman, who followed 1820-M in his first edition, gave *them:* in his second.

425 With the diminished accent on *might'st* the contraction of E-M en-
hances the euphony of the line.

430 The unpunctuated *serene* of E emphasizes the intended contrast more
effectively than does the comma punctuation of 1820-M.

432 *Call up the fiends.* is followed by a compensated SD: [*thunder & lightning*] (see n. on I.106).

Prometheus

I know but this, that it must come.

Mercury

Alas!
Thou canst not count thy years to come of pain?

Prometheus

They last while Jove must reign; nor more nor less   415
Do I desire or fear.

Mercury

Yet pause, and plunge
Into eternity, where recorded time,
Even all that we imagine, age on age,
Seems but a point, and the reluctant mind
Flags wearily in its unending flight,   420
Till it sink, dizzy, blind, lost, shelterless.
Perchance it has not numbered the slow years
Which thou must spend in torture, unreprieved.

Prometheus

Perchance no thought can count them—yet they pass.

Mercury

If thou might'st dwell among the Gods the while,   425
Lapped in voluptuous joy?

Prometheus

I would not quit
This bleak ravine, these unrepentant pains.

Mercury

Alas! I wonder at, yet pity thee.

Prometheus

Pity the self-despising slaves of Heaven,
Not me, within whose mind sits peace serene   430
As light in the sun, throned. . . . How vain is talk!
Call up the fiends.

436 *[How] Most*

Ione

   O sister, look! White fire
Has cloven to the roots yon huge snow-loaded cedar:
How fearfully God's thunder howls behind!

Mercury

I must obey his words and thine—alas!   435
Most heavily remorse hangs at my heart!

Panthea

See where the child of Heaven with wingèd feet
Runs down the slanted sunlight of the dawn.

Ione

Dear sister, close thy plumes over thine eyes
Lest thou behold and die: they come—they come   440
Blackening the birth of day with countless wings,
And hollow underneath, like death.

First Fury

              Prometheus!

Second Fury

Immortal Titan!

Third Fury

Champion of Heaven's slaves!

Prometheus

He whom some dreadful voice invokes is here:
Prometheus, the chained Titan. Horrible forms,   445
What and who are ye? Never yet there came
Phantasms so foul through monster-teeming Hell
From the all-miscreative brain of Jove.
Whilst I behold such execrable shapes,
Methinks I grow like what I contemplate,   450
And laugh and stare in loathsome sympathy.

First Fury

We are the ministers of pain, and fear,

459 [*the*] *these*

464 [*de*⟨light⟩] *exult*

471 [*shape*] *form*
472 The transposition from *are we* of E to *we are* of 1820-M was probably a
natural mistake in transcribing or printing.

475 [*Y*⟨ou⟩] *Thou*   and   [*you*] *thee*

And disappointment, and mistrust, and hate,
And clinging crime; and as lean dogs pursue
Through wood and lake some struck and sobbing fawn,   455
We track all things that weep, and bleed, and live,
When the great King betrays them to our will.

Prometheus

O many fearful natures in one name,
I know ye; and these lakes and echoes know
The darkness and the clangour of your wings.   460
But why more hideous than your loathèd selves
Gather ye up in legions from the deep?

Second Fury

We knew not that: Sisters, rejoice, rejoice!

Prometheus

Can aught exult in its deformity?

Second Fury

The beauty of delight makes lovers glad,   465
Gazing on one another: so are we.
As from the rose which the pale priestess kneels
To gather for her festal crown of flowers
The aerial crimson falls, flushing her cheek—
So from our victim's destined agony   470
The shade which is our form invests us round;
Else are we shapeless as our mother Night.

Prometheus

I laugh your power, and his who sent you here,
To lowest scorn. Pour forth the cup of pain.

First Fury

Thou thinkest we will rend thee bone from bone,   475
And nerve from nerve, working like fire within?

Prometheus

Pain is my element, as hate is thine;
Ye rend me now: I care not.

479 [*your*] *thy*

483 E: *Thou thinkest* Unlike l. 475, the uncontracted *thinkest* would threaten the metrical integrity of the line here.

487, 491 The punctuation (E gives *men—* and an unpointed *agony* while 1820-M gives *men:* and *agony.*) has been altered here because Prometheus' answer indicates that this speech is a double question.

490 [*without*] *within* [*your*] *thy*

Second Fury

                    Dost imagine
We will but laugh into thy lidless eyes?

Prometheus

I weigh not what ye do, but what ye suffer,   480
Being evil. Cruel was the Power which called
You, or aught else so wretched, into light.

Third Fury

Thou think'st we will live through thee, one by one,
Like animal life; and though we can obscure not
The soul which burns within, that we will dwell   485
Beside it, like a vain loud multitude
Vexing the self-content of wisest men?—
That we will be dread thought beneath thy brain,
And foul desire round thine astonished heart,
And blood within thy labyrinthine veins   490
Crawling like agony?

Prometheus

                    Why, ye are thus now;
Yet am I king over myself, and rule
The torturing and conflicting throngs within,
As Jove rules you when Hell grows mutinous.

Chorus of Furies

From the ends of the earth, from the ends of the earth,   495
Where the night has its grave and the morning its birth,
              Come, come, come!
O ye who shake hills with the scream of your mirth
When cities sink howling in ruin, and ye
Who with wingless footsteps trample the sea,   500
And close upon Shipwreck and Famine's track
Sit chattering with joy on the foodless wreck:
              Come, come, come!
    Leave the bed, low, cold, and red,
    Strewed beneath a nation dead;   505
    Leave the hatred, as in ashes

511 [*enchanted*] *inchanted*   The return to *enchanted* for 1820-M standard-
ized the usage, and there could be little choice for euphony since both *in* and
en are echoed within the line.

520 Below this line is the compensated SD: [*Enter rushing by groups of horrible forms; they speak as they* [*rush by*] *pass in chorus*]

522 [*Alas the*] [*The*] *These solid mountains* [*tremble*] *quiver*   The latter
change was probably made because of the *tremble-tremulous* echo, but the
result was a fresher word.
   523 [*look not I pray*] *their shadows make*

525 There is a certain risk that the furies in this new group may be confused with those speaking between ll. 443-520. Shelley probably assumed that
ll. 521-24 would clarify the matter.
   527 Galignani modernized the spelling *gulphs* (E-1820) to *gulfs* and was followed by M.

531 Since the furies have come from a world as yet unchanged, logic could
have dictated the alteration of *was* in E to the present tense of 1820-M.

Fire is left for future burning:
It will burst in bloodier flashes
When ye stir it, soon returning;
Leave the self-contempt implanted 510
In young spirits, sense-enchanted,
Misery's yet unkindled fuel;
Leave Hell's secrets half unchanted
To the maniac dreamer: cruel
More than ye can be with hate, 515
    Is he with fear.
        Come, come, come!
We are steaming up from Hell's wide gate,
And we burthen the blasts of the atmosphere,
But vainly we toil till ye come here. 520

Ione

Sister, I hear the thunder of new wings.

Panthea

These solid mountains quiver with the sound
Even as the tremulous air: their shadows make
The space within my plumes more black than night.

First Fury

Your call was as a wingèd car 525
Driven on whirlwinds fast and far;
It rapt us from red gulfs of war;

Second Fury

From wide cities, famine-wasted;

Third Fury

Groans half heard, and blood untasted;

Fourth Fury

Kingly conclaves stern and cold, 530
Where blood with gold is bought and sold;

Fifth Fury

From the furnace, white and hot,
In which—

538 Following this line is an unused and uncompensated SD: [*Another*] *a Fury rushing from the crowd*

539 Following *veil!* is an undeleted, unused, but compensated (ll. 550-59) SD: *The Furies, having mingled in a strange dance, divide, & in the background is seen a plain covered with burning cities*

542 The anapestic movement accepts easily the uncontracted *wakenedst* of E (1820-M: *waken'dst*).

552 This line is followed by a compensated SD: [*a shadow passes over the scene & a piercing shriek is heard*]

553 *Hark* at this point was probably (and excusably) misread by Mary as *Mark* for 1820 and overlooked for the errata list. In the context *Hark* is the superior reading.

A Fury

Speak not: whisper not!
I know all that ye would tell,
But to speak might break the spell   535
Which must bend the Invincible,
The stern of thought;
He yet defies the deepest power of Hell.

A Fury

Tear the veil!

Another Fury

It is torn!

Chorus

The pale stars of the morn
Shine on a misery dire to be borne.   540
Dost thou faint, mighty Titan? We laugh thee to scorn.
Dost thou boast the clear knowledge thou wakenedst for man?
Then was kindled within him a thirst which outran
Those perishing waters; a thirst of fierce fever,
Hope, love, doubt, desire—which consume him forever. 545
One came forth of gentle worth,
Smiling on the sanguine earth;
His words outlived him, like swift poison
Withering up truth, peace, and pity.
Look! where round the wide horizon   550
Many a million-peopled city
Vomits smoke in the bright air.
Hark that outcry of despair!
'Tis his mild and gentle ghost
Wailing for the faith he kindled.   555
Look again! the flames almost
To a glow-worm's lamp have dwindled:
The survivors round the embers
Gather in dread.
Joy, joy, joy!   560
Past ages crowd on thee, but each one remembers,

564 [*Hah, agony drops*] *Drops*
565 [*Fast from*] *his* [*qui*⟨vering⟩]   →   received.

577 SD: *All the Furies depart but one*   The present reading follows 1820-M, which offers a refinement of expression.

578 SD: [*Panthea*] *Ione*

580 [*deep*] *sea* with *deep* reinstated by underline.
581 [*sea*] [*waves*] with *sea* reinstated by underline, probably when the change was made in l. 580.

583 [*once*] *twice*

And the future is dark, and the present is spread
Like a pillow of thorns for thy slumberless head.

Semichorus I

Drops of bloody agony flow
From his white and quivering brow.   565
Grant a little respite now—
See! a disenchanted nation
Springs like day from desolation;
To Truth its state is dedicate,
And Freedom leads it forth, her mate;   570
A legioned band of linkèd brothers
Whom Love calls children—

Semichorus II

          'Tis another's—
See how kindred murder kin!
'Tis the vintage-time for Death and Sin:
Blood, like new wine, bubbles within,   575
Till Despair smothers
The struggling world, which slaves and tyrants win.
       [*All the* Furies *vanish, except one.*]

Ione

Hark, sister! what a low yet dreadful groan
Quite unsuppressed is tearing up the heart
Of the good Titan, as storms tear the deep,   580
And beasts hear the sea moan in inland caves.
Darest thou observe how the fiends torture him?

Panthea

Alas! I looked forth twice, but will no more.

Ione

What didst thou see?

Panthea

       A woeful sight: a youth
With patient looks nailed to a crucifix.   585

586 [*above*] *around*

589 *Tho* of E is clearly superior to *And* of 1820-M. If Shelley was aware of
the change it is surprisingly uncorrected in M, unless he considered the matter
of minor importance.

594-95 *Behold,* [*behold how those who do endure* / [*Stripes*] *Wounds for*
mankind] → received with *and chains,* [*& des*⟨pair⟩] *but heap*
596 This line is followed by an unused but undeleted SD: *a* [*shadow*] *dark-*
ness floats slowly across the scene   (See n. on I.106.)

598 [*that*] *those*

600 [*O fix*] *Fix fix*

602 [*thy*] *those*

Ione

What next?

Panthea

The heaven around, the earth below
Was peopled with thick shapes of human death,
All horrible, and wrought by human hands;
Though some appeared the work of human hearts,
For men were slowly killed by frowns and smiles.   590
And other sights too foul to speak and live
Were wandering by. Let us not tempt worse fear
By looking forth: those groans are grief enough.

Fury

Behold an emblem: those who do endure
Deep wrongs for man, and scorn, and chains, but heap   595
Thousandfold torment on themselves and him.

Prometheus

Remit the anguish of that lighted stare;
Close those wan lips; let that thorn-wounded brow
Stream not with blood—it mingles with thy tears!
Fix, fix those tortured orbs in peace and death,   600
So thy sick throes shake not that crucifix,
So those pale fingers play not with thy gore.
O horrible! Thy name I will not speak:
It hath become a curse. I see, I see
The wise, the mild, the lofty, and the just,   605
Whom thy slaves hate for being like to thee:
Some hunted by foul lies from their heart's home,
An early-chosen, late-lamented home,
As hooded ounces cling to the driven hind;
Some linked to corpses in unwholesome cells;   610
Some—hear I not the multitude laugh loud?—
Impaled in lingering fire: and mighty realms
Float by my feet, like sea-uprooted isles,
Whose sons are kneaded down in common blood
By the red light of their own burning homes.   615

619 *ravin[e]*   The word is clear in E, and correction of *ruin* (1820) in M
was probably from the errata list (Galignani: 1820).

628 *And [so] all*

634 *I speak no[t!] more!*   and   *ah woe [is me]*   E has *Exit* as the SD but
Vanishes. of 1820-M makes for consistency with l. 577.

635 I now believe that what appears to be a question mark after *forever*
was a pen slip at the top of an exclamation mark. Shelley would naturally
echo here the earlier cries of ll. 23 and 30.

637 *illumined* was introduced by Galignani (*illumed* in E-1820) and missed
for correction in M.

Fury

Blood thou canst see, and fire; and canst hear groans:
Worse things, unheard, unseen, remain behind.

Prometheus

Worse?

Fury

                In each human heart terror survives
The ravin it has gorged; the loftiest fear
All that they would disdain to think were true: 620
Hypocrisy and custom make their minds
The fanes of many a worship, now outworn.
They dare not devise good for man's estate,
And yet they know not that they do not dare.
The good want power, but to weep barren tears;   625
The powerful goodness want: worse need for them;
The wise want love, and those who love want wisdom;
And all best things are thus confused to ill.
Many are strong and rich, and would be just,
But live among their suffering fellow men   630
As if none felt: they know not what they do.

Prometheus

Thy words are like a cloud of wingèd snakes;
And yet I pity those they torture not.

Fury

Thou pitiest them? I speak no more!
                        [*Vanishes.*]

Prometheus

                        Ah woe!
Ah woe! Alas! pain, pain ever, forever!   635
I close my tearless eyes, but see more clear
Thy works within my woe-illumèd mind,
Thou subtle Tyrant! . . . Peace is in the grave.
The grave hides all things beautiful and good:
I am a God and cannot find it there;   640

642 *This is defeat not victory!* [*to*] →   received.

646 The dropping of *more* in 1820-M could have resulted from an error in transcription or printing, but its apparent omission from the errata list is surprising in view of its strength in the line.

650 *And nations* of E was probably changed to *The nations* for 1820-M when the originally unpunctuated *emblazonry* was pointed. (Omission of punctuation would have led naturally to *And*)

657 [*I*] *To*

659 [*lairs*] *homes*

661 *they behold* of 1820-M, a change probably approved by Shelley, was a reading superior in euphony to *and they see* of E.

662 [*Within*] *Beyond*

Nor would I seek it. For, though dread revenge,
This is defeat, fierce King, not victory!
The sights with which thou torturest gird my soul
With new endurance, till the hour arrives
When they shall be no types of things which are.   645

Panthea

Alas! what sawest thou more?

Prometheus

                    There are two woes:
To speak and to behold; thou spare me one.
Names are there, Nature's sacred watchwords: they
Were borne aloft in bright emblazonry.
The nations thronged around, and cried aloud,   650
As with one voice, 'Truth, Liberty, and Love!'
Suddenly fierce confusion fell from Heaven
Among them: there was strife, deceit, and fear;
Tyrants rushed in, and did divide the spoil.
This was the shadow of the truth I saw.   655

The Earth

I felt thy torture, son, with such mixed joy
As pain and virtue give. To cheer thy state
I bid ascend those subtle and fair spirits
Whose homes are the dim caves of human thought,
And who inhabit, as birds wing the wind,   660
Its world-surrounding ether; they behold
Beyond that twilight realm, as in a glass,
The future: may they speak comfort to thee!

Panthea

Look, sister, where a troop of spirits gather
Like flocks of clouds in spring's delightful weather,   665
Thronging in the blue air!

Ione

                    And see! more come,
Like fountain-vapours when the winds are dumb,

687 *these* of 1820 was probably an error in transcription (*there* is subject to misreading) restored to *there* in M from the errata list (Galignani: 1820).

693 Shelley's *radiant like* in E was the result of his customary confusion between *like* and *as*.

695-96 The intent (indicated by *cast*— of E and confirmed by *cast.* of 1820-M) seems to be: I fled amid the darkness cast upward by the sound of battle. As I did so, cries of "Freedom! Hope! Death! Victory!" rose from the dust of outworn creeds, etc., but these gave way to the single sound of universal love.

That climb up the ravine in scattered lines.
And hark! is it the music of the pines?
Is it the lake? is it the waterfall? 670

Panthea

'Tis something sadder, sweeter far than all.

Chorus of Spirits

From unremembered ages we
Gentle guides and guardians be
Of Heaven-oppressed mortality;
And we breathe, and sicken not, 675
The atmosphere of human thought:
Be it dim, and dank, and grey,
Like a storm-extinguished day
Travelled o'er by dying gleams;
Be it bright as all between 680
Cloudless skies and windless streams,
Silent, liquid, and serene.
As the birds within the wind,
As the fish within the wave,
As the thoughts of man's own mind 685
Float through all above the grave,
We make there our liquid lair,
Voyaging cloudlike and unpent
Through the boundless element:
Thence we bear the prophecy 690
Which begins and ends in thee!

Ione

More yet come, one by one: the air around them
Looks radiant as the air around a star.

First Spirit

On a battle-trumpet's blast
I fled hither, fast, fast, fast, 695
'Mid the darkness upward cast.
From the dust of creeds outworn,
From the tyrant's banner torn,

707 Below this line is the following deleted passage: [2^d *Spirit* | *I leaped on the wings of the Earth-star damp* | *As it rose on the steam of a slaughtered camp*— | *The sleeping newt heard not our tramp* | *As swift* [*and silent we did pass*] *as the wing of fire may pass* | [*Among*] *We threaded the points of long thick grass* | *Which hide the green pools of the morass*| *But shook a water-serpents couch* | *In a cleft skull, of many such* | *The widest; at the meteors touch* | *The snake did seem to see in dream* | *Thrones & dungeons overthrown* | [*A*] *Visions how unlike his own* . . . . ⟨sic⟩ | *'Twas the hope the prophecy* | *Which begins & ends in thee*]

708 SD: [3^d] 2^d to adjust when the above speech was canceled.

711 [*t*⟨he⟩] *a*

712 Mary apparently missed a comma, placed high, after *Between*

714 I believe that Shelley's dash (*half*—) in E (1820-M: *half:*) invites a full stop.

723 SD: [4th] 3^d See n. on I.708. For *sate* of E-M see Intro., n. 7, above.

Gathering round me, onward borne,
There was mingled many a cry—   700
'Freedom! Hope! Death! Victory!'
Till they faded through the sky;
And one sound above, around,
One sound beneath, around, above,
Was moving: 'twas the soul of love;   705
'Twas the hope, the prophecy,
Which begins and ends in thee.

Second Spirit

A rainbow's arch stood on the sea,
Which rocked beneath, immoveably;
And the triumphant storm did flee,   710
Like a conqueror swift and proud,
Between, with many a captive cloud,
A shapeless, dark, and rapid crowd,
Each by lightning riven in half.
I heard the thunder hoarsely laugh.   715
Mighty fleets were strewn like chaff
And spread beneath a hell of death
O'er the white waters. I alit
On a great ship, lightning-split,
And speeded hither on the sigh   720
Of one who gave an enemy
His plank—then plunged aside to die.

Third Spirit

I sat beside a sage's bed,
And the lamp was burning red
Near the book where he had fed,   725
When a Dream with plumes of flame
To his pillow hovering came,
And I knew it was the same
Which had kindled long ago
Pity, eloquence, and woe;   730
And the world awhile below
Wore the shade its lustre made.

733 1820: *born* Galignani: *borne* which was probably also in the errata list.

745 *bees i[n]* Although Shelley's intent is clear, this is the only contraction of *in* in 39 uses in Act I (see also II.v.35 and III.ii.39) and with no more justification than would be true of several others. *in* of 1820-M gives the more natural and euphonious reading (but see n. on III.ii.39).

752 E: *Beholdst* Shelley's intent, followed by 1820-M, is clear, and appropriate to the initial iamb. Cf. n. on I.341.

753-54 There is a draft of these lines which reads simply: *Twin nurslings of the all sustaining air | Whom one nest sheltered*

753 E: [*twin*] *two* This line is followed by: [*Sink through the lapses of the yielding air?—*]

755-64 There are no known drafts of these lines.

758 Shelley started to cancel *words* before he decided on the change in l. 759.

759 [*words.*] *voice.*

761 *deepning* of E suggests an intended *deep'ning* but there is no apostrophe. The uncontracted form of 1820-M offers a more forceful reading.

762 [*sad*] *soft*

It has borne me here as fleet
As Desire's lightning feet:
I must ride it back ere morrow,   735
Or the sage will wake in sorrow.

Fourth Spirit

On a poet's lips I slept
Dreaming like a love-adept
In the sound his breathing kept;
Nor seeks nor finds he mortal blisses,   740
But feeds on the aerial kisses
Of shapes that haunt thought's wildernesses.
He will watch from dawn to gloom
The lake-reflected sun illume
The yellow bees in the ivy-bloom,   745
Nor heed nor see what things they be;
But from these create he can
Forms more real than living man,
Nurslings of immortality!
One of these awakened me,   750
And I sped to succour thee.

Ione

Behold'st thou not two shapes from the east and west
Come, as two doves to one belovèd nest,
Twin nurslings of the all-sustaining air,
On swift still wings glide down the atmosphere?   755
And hark! their sweet, sad voices! 'tis despair
Mingled with love, and then dissolved in sound.

Panthea

Canst thou speak, sister? all my words are drowned.

Ione

Their beauty gives me voice. See how they float
On their sustaining wings of skiey grain,   760
Orange and azure deepening into gold:
Their soft smiles light the air like a star's fire.

763 First SD: [5*th* Spirit] Chorus of Spirits

765-67 Draft: [*O Love thou God & King*] *descend* [*with*] *on* ⟨option: *from*⟩ *world embracing* [*pinion* ⟨?⟩] *wings,* / *Scattering the liquid joy of life* [*& these dream people slumbers*] *from thine immortal tresses* / [*Let* ⟨option: *Where*⟩ *thy footsteps pave the world with light*]   There is no indication as to which character was to speak this invocation, but the change of mode in E is more in keeping with the intent of the passage, as are the verbal changes.

766 E: [*Scattered*] *Scattering*   Draft: [*hair*] *tresses*

768-71 There are no known drafts of these lines.

770 I believe that the E punctuation (an unpointed *Night* and *oer*—) indicates Shelley's intent here, as against *night. I wandered oer,* of 1820-M.

771 Consistency (*Turnedst*) must yield to euphony in this instance, as E-M recognized.

772-73 Draft: [*Ah desolation is a*] *delicate thing*— / *It walks* → *For it walks* [*sister*] *mine* occurs in a preliminary jotting, with *sister* recovered for E.

774 Draft: *But* [*seeks with*] *treads with lulling* ⟨option: *unfelt*⟩ *footstep*[*s*], *& fans with silent wings*   *silent footstep* of 1820-M was probably the result of transfer from the same line either by Mary or the printer, but surprisingly uncorrected in M.   Mathilde Blind, excusably, read E as *killing* ("Shelley," p. 80), which was not corrected by Zupitza-Schick. Locock, prompted by a "nocturnal conjecture, later verified" (Edition, *1,* 606), gave *lulling* which is certainly correct.

775 Draft: *The* [*tender hearts &*] *soft hopes*

776 Draft: [*As the*] [*And lulled into*] → *received with plume*   E: ['*Till,*] *Who*

777 Draft: [*And the dream inspiring motion,*] → *And the music-stirring* [*trampling*] *of* [*the*] *its soft* → *received.*

779 Draft: *And wake &* [*dream* [*sleep*] *no more*] → *And wake* [*& live the dream*] [*to live the dreamless sleepless death of life,*] → *And wake & die, like early flowers when the winds that waked them, fleet.*   E: *their shadow* Although poorly written, the word is *their* (and must refer to *visions*). Perhaps Shelley or Mary noted that the parallel between *Pain* and *Ruin* (l. 780) dictated *the* (i.e. Though the shadow of Love be not alone pain but even ruin, etc.). [*him*] *he* ⟨*his?*⟩   If the change was to *his* (there is no dot for the *i*) the preference must be for *he* of 1820-M (i.e. *he* [Prometheus], like others of *the best and gentlest* (l. 775), has found the pain of desolation because he has dreamed *visions of aerial joy* (l. 778) that have not been fulfilled).

780-833 There are no known drafts of these lines.

780 SD: [5*th*] *Chorus*

Chorus of Spirits

Hast thou beheld the form of Love?

Fifth Spirit

As over wide dominions
I sped, like some swift cloud that wings the wide air's
    wildernesses,
That planet-crested shape swept by on lightning-braided
    pinions,   765
    Scattering the liquid joy of life from his ambrosial
    tresses:
His footsteps paved the world with light, but as I passed
    'twas fading,
    And hollow Ruin yawned behind. Great sages bound in
    madness,
And headless patriots and pale youths who perished,
    unupbraiding,
    Gleamed in the night I wandered o'er; till thou, O
    King of Sadness,   770
Turned by thy smile the worst I saw to recollected
    gladness.

Sixth Spirit

Ah, sister! Desolation is a delicate thing:
It walks not on the earth, it floats not on the air,
But treads with lulling footstep, and fans with silent wing
The tender hopes which in their hearts the best and
    gentlest bear,   775
Who, soothed to false repose by the fanning plumes above,
And the music-stirring motion of its soft and busy feet,
Dream visions of aerial joy, and call the monster Love,
And wake, and find the shadow pain, as he whom now we greet.

Chorus

Though Ruin now Love's shadow be,   780
Following him destroyingly
    On Death's white and wingèd steed,
Which the fleetest cannot flee—

791 1820-M: *the snow-storms   the* (not in E) might have been an unconscious addition by Mary or the printer, not noted for the errata list. E gives
the stronger reading, one more consistent with the prevailing rhythm of the
passage. Lines 791-95 form an extended parenthesis that needs to be set off
more definitely than in E (*breathe . . . blow—*) or 1820-M (*breathe, . . . blow:*).

800 An unused but undeleted SD: *They vanish* is compensated for in the
next line.
801 First SD: [*Panthea*] *Ione*

804 *Languish* [*though*] *yet the* [*echoes are not*] *mute* → received.

> Trampling down both flower and weed,
> Man and beast, and foul and fair,   785
> Like a tempest through the air—
> Thou shalt quell this horseman grim,
> Woundless though in heart or limb.

Prometheus

Spirits! how know ye this shall be?

Chorus

> In the atmosphere we breathe—   790
> As buds grow red when snow-storms flee
> From spring gathering up beneath,
> Whose mild winds shake the elder brake,
> And the wandering herdsmen know
> That the white-thorn soon will blow—   795
> Wisdom, Justice, Love, and Peace,
> When they struggle to increase,
> Are to us as soft winds be
> To shepherd-boys: the prophecy
> Which begins and ends in thee.   800

Ione

Where are the spirits fled?

Panthea

> Only a sense
> Remains of them, like the omnipotence
> Of music when the inspired voice and lute
> Languish, ere yet the responses are mute
> Which through the deep and labyrinthine soul,   805
> Like echoes through long caverns, wind and roll.

Prometheus

How fair these air-borne shapes! and yet I feel
Most vain all hope but love; and thou art far,
Asia! who, when my being overflowed,
Wert like a golden chalice to bright wine   810
Which else had sunk into the thirsty dust.

824 This line is followed by (still assigned to Prometheus): [*But the eastern star is pale*]

825 *In truth* [*most deeply*]—*but the Eastern star* [*is pale*] → received with *looks wan*   The substitution of *wan* for *pale* in E was probably dictated by a desire to avoid a rime with *vale* in the next line (cf. II.i.17, 107 for *white* and *pale* in the same context).   *wan* is clear in E, and the change to *white* in 1820-M was possibly made to give a word more in keeping with the promise of the new day. Shelley's punctuation (*truth—* and *exile—* [line 827]) gives a misleading sense of parenthesis. 1820-M gave a semicolon in both positions although a dash in the second is more in keeping with the intent.

827 *The sense of her sad exile—*[*tho her presence | Makes fruits & flowers & sunwarm winds, & sounds smooth oer*] → received.

All things are still. Alas! how heavily
This quiet morning weighs upon my heart.
Though I should dream, I could even sleep with grief
If slumber were denied not. I would fain   815
Be what it is my destiny to be,
The saviour and the strength of suffering man,
Or sink into the original gulf of things. . . .
There is no agony and no solace left;
Earth can console, Heaven can torment no more.   820

Panthea

Hast thou forgotten one who watches thee
The cold dark night, and never sleeps but when
The shadow of thy spirit falls on her?

Prometheus

I said all hope was vain but love: thou lovest.

Panthea

Deeply in truth; but the eastern star looks white,   825
And Asia waits in that far Indian vale,
The scene of her sad exile—rugged once,
And desolate and frozen, like this ravine,
But now invested with fair flowers and herbs,
And haunted by sweet airs and sounds, which flow   830
Among the woods and waters, from the ether
Of her transforming presence, which would fade
If it were mingled not with thine. Farewell!

END OF THE FIRST ACT.

The drafts for Act II, representing 200 of the 687 lines (plus 42 unused lines), are found in Bodleian MS Shelley E.4, in Bodleian MSS Shelley adds. c.4, e.11 and e.12, and in Huntington MSS 2176 and 2177. Many of these passages are extremely difficult to transcribe, and the readings are correspondingly tentative. The fair copy is in Bodleian MSS Shelley E.2 and E.3.

SD In M, *lonely* for *lovely* of E-1820 was probably a printer's error uncorrected in M², but inclusion in the errata list is possible (if unlikely in view of Prometheus' lines at I.829-32) since it was a change from Galignani.

1-132 There are no known drafts of these lines, for which the following manuscript readings are from E.

10 [*of*] *or*

15 *long*[-]*desired*

25 It is probable that *sunrise* of E was changed to *sun-light* of 1820-M in view of *sunrise* in l. 14, but *sunlight* is also the more exact word in this context.

ACT II

Morning. A lovely Vale in the Indian Caucasus. Asia *alone.*

Asia

From all the blasts of heaven thou hast descended:
Yes, like a spirit, like a thought which makes
Unwonted tears throng to the horny eyes,
And beatings haunt the desolated heart
Which should have learnt repose, thou hast descended   5
Cradled in tempests; thou dost wake, O Spring!
O child of many winds! As suddenly
Thou comest as the memory of a dream
Which now is sad because it hath been sweet;
Like genius, or like joy which riseth up   10
As from the earth, clothing with golden clouds
The desert of our life. . . .
This is the season, this the day, the hour;
At sunrise thou shouldst come, sweet sister mine,
Too long desired, too long delaying, come!   15
How like death-worms the wingless moments crawl!
The point of one white star is quivering still
Deep in the orange light of widening morn
Beyond the purple mountains; through a chasm
Of wind-divided mist the darker lake   20
Reflects it—now it wanes—it gleams again
As the waves fade, and as the burning threads
Of woven cloud unravel in pale air:
'Tis lost! and through yon peaks of cloudlike snow
The roseate sunlight quivers—hear I not   25
The Æolian music of her sea-green plumes
Winnowing the crimson dawn?
                              [Panthea *enters.*]
                    I feel, I see
Those eyes which burn through smiles that fade in tears,
Like stars half quenched in mists of silver dew.
Belovèd and most beautiful, who wearest   30
The shadow of that soul by which I live,

38-39 *Satiate with sweet flowers.* [*I slept peacefully* / *Before thine exile &*
his grievous woe]   →   received.

41-42 *Unhappy love,* [*and ere by use & pity*] / *Both love & woe* [*had grown*
[*mine own*] *my hearts own mates* .. ⟨sic⟩ *I slept*]   →   received.

43 [*have*] *had*

44 [*Within*] *Under*

55 [*woe*] *pain*

How late thou art! the spherèd sun had climbed
The sea, my heart was sick with hope, before
The printless air felt thy belated plumes.

                    Panthea
Pardon, great sister! but my wings were faint   35
With the delight of a remembered dream,
As are the noontide plumes of summer winds
Satiate with sweet flowers. I was wont to sleep
Peacefully, and awake refreshed and calm,
Before the sacred Titan's fall and thine   40
Unhappy love had made, through use and pity,
Both love and woe familiar to my heart
As they had grown to thine. Erewhile I slept
Under the glaucous caverns of old Ocean,
Within dim bowers of green and purple moss,   45
Our young Ione's soft and milky arms
Locked then, as now, behind my dark, moist hair,
While my shut eyes and cheek were pressed within
The folded depth of her life-breathing bosom:
But not as now, since I am made the wind   50
Which fails beneath the music that I bear
Of thy most wordless converse; since dissolved
Into the sense with which love talks, my rest
Was troubled and yet sweet, my waking hours
Too full of care and pain.

                    Asia
                              Lift up thine eyes   55
And let me read thy dream.

                    Panthea
                              As I have said,
With our sea-sister at his feet I slept.
The mountain mists, condensing at our voice
Under the moon, had spread their snowy flakes,
From the keen ice shielding our linkèd sleep.   60
Then two dreams came. One I remember not.
But in the other, his pale, wound-worn limbs
Fell from Prometheus, and the azure night

66 Possibly the echo between *dizzy* and *dim* of E led to the superior *giddy* of 1820-M.

83 [*Then*] *And* [*as*] *like*
84 [*Which hang*] *Gathering again in drops* [*on the*] *upon*
85 [*So*] *And*

88 *ere they died* of 1820-M is clearly superior in this context to *as they died* of E.
89 [*lost music . . . ⟨sic⟩ but I heard*] → [*weak*] *far melody* Locock discovered the correct reading *far* which is on *weak* and could easily have been missed by Mary—whose error, surprisingly, was apparently overlooked by Shelley and omitted from the errata list. I agree with Locock (Edition, *1*, 607) that Shelley changed to *far* probably because of II.ii.33, where *weak melody* occurs again. This line was followed by: [*Among the many sounds, one word, thy name*] → received.

98 *I know not* [*even—so sweet that it is sweet*] *yet it is* *ing → received.
99 *it is* [*some*] *sport* [*of thine*] → received.
100 [*some*] [*an*] with [*some*] underlined for stet, probably after the change in l. 99.

Grew radiant with the glory of that form
Which lives unchanged within, and his voice fell   65
Like music which makes giddy the dim brain
Faint with intoxication of keen joy:
'Sister of her whose footsteps pave the world
With loveliness—more fair than aught but her
Whose shadow thou art—lift thine eyes on me!'   70
I lifted them: the overpowering light
Of that immortal shape was shadowed o'er
By love, which, from his soft and flowing limbs,
And passion-parted lips, and keen, faint eyes,
Steamed forth like vaporous fire, an atmosphere   75
Which wrapped me in its all-dissolving power
As the warm ether of the morning sun
Wraps ere it drinks some cloud of wandering dew.
I saw not, heard not, moved not, only felt
His presence flow and mingle through my blood   80
Till it became his life, and his grew mine,
And I was thus absorbed—until it passed,
And like the vapours when the sun sinks down,
Gathering again in drops upon the pines,
And tremulous as they, in the deep night   85
My being was condensed; and as the rays
Of thought were slowly gathered, I could hear
His voice, whose accents lingered ere they died
Like footsteps of far melody. Thy name,
Among the many sounds, alone I heard   90
Of what might be articulate; though still
I listened through the night when sound was none.
Ione wakened then, and said to me:
'Canst thou divine what troubles me tonight?
I always knew what I desired before,   95
Nor ever found delight to wish in vain.
But now I cannot tell thee what I seek:
I know not—something sweet, since it is sweet
Even to desire. It is thy sport, false sister!
Thou hast discovered some enchantment old,   100
Whose spells have stolen my spirit as I slept
And mingled it with thine; for when just now

108 Asia: [*Lift up thine*] *Thou speakest,*

110 [*spirit*] *soul.* At this point is the following deleted passage (regarded by
Locock as the "germ" of the "Life of Life" lyric at II.v.48-71 [Edition, *1*, 631]):
[*Lift up thine eyes Panthea—they pierce—they burn!* | *Panthea* | *Alas I
am consumed—I melt away* | *The fire is in my heart—* | *Asia* | *Thine eyes
burn burn!—* | *Hide them within thine hair* | *Panthea* | *O quench thy
lips* | *I sink I perish* | *Asia* | *Shelter me now—they burn* | *It is his spirit
in their orbs . .* ⟨sic⟩ *my life* | *Is ebbing fast—I cannot speak—* | *Panthea* |
Rest, rest! | *Sleep death annihilation pain! aught else*] The next two leaves
in the manuscript were torn out, so there could have been more in this passage which was, perhaps, deleted because of its unfortunately melodramatic
tone.

112 [*what*] *that*

115 Although Shelley would normally avoid an echo such as *to two* (E has
in two), 1820 was probably changed for more exact expression.

119 [*within*] *beyond*

122 *moon* of E could easily have been misread as *morn* (1820-M) by Mary.
The errata list apparently overlooked the word, which was confirmed by
Mathilde Blind ("Shelley," p. 80).

123 I now agree with Freeman that the word is *thou* rather than *thine* of
1820-M. The word could easily have been misread by Mary, but careful examination of the manuscript suggests that an apparent dot over an *i* (for *thine*)
might be a defect in the paper. Logically, of course, *thou* follows from *He* of
l. 120, and from *depart not yet!* of this line.

126 Mary possibly read *oer* of E as *on* (Zupitza, too, was uncertain ["Zu . . .
Prometheus," *103*, 93]), but I find *oer* acceptably clear.

128 *it,* [*&*] *its*

We kissed, I felt within thy parted lips
The sweet air that sustained me; and the warmth
Of the life-blood for loss of which I faint   105
Quivered between our intertwining arms.'
I answered not, for the eastern star grew pale,
But fled to thee.

Asia

     Thou speakest, but thy words
Are as the air: I feel them not. . . . O lift
Thine eyes, that I may read his written soul!   110

Panthea

I lift them, though they droop beneath the load
Of that they would express: what canst thou see
But thine own fairest shadow imaged there?

Asia

Thine eyes are like the deep, blue, boundless heaven
Contracted to two circles underneath   115
Their long, fine lashes; dark, far, measureless;
Orb within orb, and line through line inwoven.

Panthea

Why lookest thou as if a spirit passed?

Asia

There is a change: beyond their inmost depth
I see a shade, a shape: 'tis he, arrayed   120
In the soft light of his own smiles, which spread
Like radiance from the cloud-surrounded moon.
Prometheus, it is thou! depart not yet!
Say not those smiles that we shall meet again
Within that bright pavilion which their beams   125
Shall build o'er the waste world? . . . The dream is told.
What shape is that between us! Its rude hair
Roughens the wind that lifts it; its regard
Is wild and quick; yet 'tis a thing of air,
For through its grey robe gleams the golden dew   130
Whose stars the noon has quenched not.

133-208 The drafts include most of these lines.

133-35 Draft: *I [had a dream] had dreams of spring | Last night methought
that flower infolding buds | Burst [forth] on yon*   E: [*Methou⟨ght⟩ it
was | A dream of spring*] → received.

134 For *sate* of E see Intro., n. 7, above.

136 Draft: *And then [arose] [swept] from yon white*

137 Draft: *swept down*

138 E: [*bloo⟨ms⟩*] *blossoms*

139-41 Draft: *And on each leaf, as on a hyacinth's bell | Was written ai ai*

140 E: [*speak*] *tell*

141 For this shift from *thou* to *you* see Intro., n. 25, above.

142-44 There are no known drafts of these lines.

143 *these* of E offers a more specific reference to Panthea's description; *the*
of 1820-M was either an oversight in transcription or an error of the press.

145-46 Draft: *of white & fleecy clouds | Were creeping*

145 [*thin⟨?⟩*] *dense*

147 Draft: The line is followed by: *Upon the giddy chasm, above*

148 Draft: *new bladed corn*

149 Draft: [*Oer⟨?⟩*] *piercing* Also, unused but possibly for this context:
*While from bowers & lawns | Ridges & fanes overshadowed by oak trees |
Asia—*

150-61 There are no known drafts of these lines.

151 E: Although the superior *moving* is reasonably clear, Mary probably
misread it as *morning* for 1820, with no correction in M.

153-55 In the key positions 1820-M gave only commas at *by* and *fire* The
need for more exact pointing has been frequently recognized.

Dream

Follow, follow!

Panthea

It is mine other dream.

Asia

It disappears.

Panthea

It passes now into my mind. Methought
As we sat here the flower-infolding buds
Burst on yon lightning-blasted almond tree;   135
When swift from the white Scythian wilderness
A wind swept forth, wrinkling the earth with frost.
I looked, and all the blossoms were blown down;
But on each leaf was stamped—as the blue bells
Of Hyacinth tell Apollo's written grief—   140
O follow, follow!

Asia

As you speak, your words
Fill, pause by pause, mine own forgotten sleep
With shapes. Methought among these lawns together
We wandered, underneath the young grey dawn,
And multitudes of dense white fleecy clouds   145
Were wandering in thick flocks along the mountains,
Shepherded by the slow, unwilling wind;
And the white dew on the new-bladed grass,
Just piercing the dark earth, hung silently.
And there was more which I remember not;   150
But on the shadows of the moving clouds
Athwart the purple mountain slope was written
Follow, O follow! as they vanished by;
And on each herb from which heaven's dew had fallen
The like was stamped as with a withering fire.   155
A wind arose among the pines; it shook
The clinging music from their boughs, and then
Low, sweet, faint sounds, like the farewell of ghosts,
Were heard: *O follow, follow, follow me!*

162 Draft: SD: *Voice*   E: [*Voice*] *Echo*

163 Draft: *The* [*rocks*] *crags this bright*
164 Draft: *As if* [*they lived*] *they were* / *Asia* / [*Ah no*] *list list,* [*I pray*] *it is some* [*spirit*] *being*

165 Draft: *what* [*clear*] *small clear sound—*

166 Draft: SD: *Voice*   E: SD: [*V⟨oice⟩*] *Echoes unseen*
167 Draft: [*Our words*] *We cannot stay*   E: [*As*] *We*

171 E: [*aerial*] *liquid*   Galignani introduced the sense-changing comma after *Spirits* (as also at II.v.47), which was uncorrected in M.
172 Draft: *tongues* [*now die*] *yet sound*   SD: *Eros* ⟨?⟩ *or Panthea*

173 (1): SD lacking.   (2) and (3): SD: *Voice*
173-77 There are three drafts of these lines, with (3) very close to the received.
174 (1): [*As the voice recedeth*]   (2): *Where the* [*forest*] *music leadeth*
175 (1): [*Under*] [*Thro caverns hollow*]   (3): [*Round*] *Thro the*
176 (1): [*Where the woods are* [*spreading*] *spreadeth*]   (3): following l. 176: [*Till the dark gloom like midnight grew*]   E: *the* might be misread as *this* but in view of the context I believe the intent is clear.

180 Draft: [*nightbird*] *wild bee*

And then I said, 'Panthea, look on me.'   160
But in the depth of those belovèd eyes
Still I saw, *follow, follow!*

Echo

Follow, follow!

Panthea

The crags, this clear spring morning, mock our voices,
As they were spirit-tongued.

Asia

It is some being
Around the crags. What fine clear sounds! O list!   165

Echoes *unseen*

Echoes we: listen!
We cannot stay:
As dew-stars glisten
Then fade away,
Child of Ocean!   170

Asia

Hark! Spirits speak! The liquid responses
Of their aerial tongues yet sound.

Panthea

I hear.

Echoes

O follow, follow,
As our voice recedeth
Through the caverns hollow   175
Where the forest spreadeth;
[*More distant.*]
O follow, follow,
Through the caverns hollow;
As the song floats, thou pursue,
Where the wild bee never flew,   180
Through the noontide darkness deep,
By the odour-breathing sleep

183 Draft: *Of [sweet] faint night-flowers, [by] & the waves*   E: *[sweet] faint*

184 E: *[Of] At*

185-86 Draft: *As the music wild & sweet / [Echoes [your] thine aerial] Answers to thy soft light feet*

185 E: *[the] our*

186 E: *[Mocked] Mocks*

188 Draft: SD: *[Asia] Panthea*   E restored the speech to Asia and changed the assignment of l. 189 accordingly.   Draft: *it [is] grows*

189 Draft: SD: *Asia* (See preceding note.)   Draft: *Hark the [strain floats] strains float*   E: *[It] the strain*

190 Draft: SD: *Voice*   E: SD: *Echo*   *Echoes* of 1820-M (despite the singular of the draft also) makes for consistency. By l. 166 the plural has been established, although the Echoes speak with a single voice (cf. l. 174). Draft: *In the [unknown] world unknown* → *[Beyond the world of [being] Nature]* → *[In the shade of shadows]* with the first attempt finally chosen for E.

196 (1): SD lacking.   (2): SD: *Voice more distant*   E: SD: *Echo* (See note on l. 190.)

196-201 There are two drafts of these lines.

200-03 (1): *[Hunt the babbling of the fountains / To their cradles in the mountains / [Deep beneath] Where on Demogorgons throne / A veiled darkness sits Alone]*

200 (2): *forests & the fountains*

201 (2): *[To their cradling mountains]* → received with *labyrinthine mountains*

202 (2): *By the [caverns & the chasms] gulphs & rents & chasms*

207 (2): *[take thine] hold ⟨?⟩ my hand in thine*   E: *thine hand in mine* Shelley apparently failed to notice the *thine-mine* echo (although he seems to have been aware of it in the draft).

Of faint night-flowers, and the waves
At the fountain-lighted caves,
While our music, wild and sweet,   185
Mocks thy gently-falling feet,
   Child of Ocean!

Asia

Shall we pursue the sound? It grows more faint
And distant.

Panthea

List! the strain floats nearer now.

Echoes

In the world unknown   190
Sleeps a voice unspoken;
By thy step alone
Can its rest be broken,
   Child of Ocean!

Asia

How the notes sink upon the ebbing wind!   195

Echoes

O follow, follow,
  Through the caverns hollow;
As the song floats thou pursue,
By the woodland noontide dew,
By the forests, lakes, and fountains,   200
Through the many-folded mountains,
To the rents, and gulfs, and chasms
Where the Earth reposed from spasms
On the day when he and thou
Parted, to commingle now,   205
   Child of Ocean!

Asia

Come, sweet Panthea, link thy hand in mine,
And follow, ere the voices fade away.

SD E: *A forest [surrounded by Mountains] intermingled*

SD E: *Semi-Chorus of Spirits—1*

1-62 There are drafts of most of these lines, plus an unused passage probably relevant to this scene which includes the following final state: *And from those woods forever run | From their chrystalline mines below | To feed old Indus onward flow | The streams that never see the sun | And thro earth's diamond vaulted caves | Then leap like meteor kindled showers | To light the pale & sunless flowers | Which overhang their glimmering waves | With the great Earths entwined beams | From their own sands & lucid streams | Their earthy birthplace shakes like thunder | And from deep caves to Indies bring | Loud as his own loud murmurings | A sound like earthquake stifled under | But here their [flow] breathes & moans | In soft & melancholy tones*

1-2 There are two drafts of these lines.

1-2 (1): fragmented but including: *[In that wood no tall trees | that were woods] | Of laurel, myrtle, pine & yew*

1 (2): *by* ⟨option: *the*⟩ *which*

2-3 (2): *Has past to* ⟨option: *by*⟩ *myrtle pine & yew | [And sabled dark tree] that ever grew*

5-23 There are two drafts of these lines.

5 (1): *[Neither] wind [nor sun] nor rain → Nor sun nor wind nor [star] moon nor rain*   (2): *Nor [wind] star nor sun nor wind*

6 (1): *[those] its interwoven [leaves] [shades] bowers*

7 (1) and (2) at first: *Save when some cloud of wandering dew*   Then (1): *some purling cloud of dew*   (2): *some trailing cloud of dew →* received. E: *when* (confirmed by both drafts) was evidently misread as *where* by Mary for 1820, without correction in M. The parallelism with l. 14 is strengthened with *when*

8 (1): *[Is] Slow driven on*   (2): *[Is driven on the earth creeping] Drifted along the wandering breeze* Note that *earth-creeping* was recovered for E.

9 (2): *[Among] Between*

10 (1): *[And] hangs [its drops] [one pearl] each a pearl in the white* (2): received with *i the white*   E: *[faint] pale*

12 (1): *[Or weighs] And [bends* ⟨space⟩ *as it passes by] →* received with *[fades] dies*   (2): *[bends]* without substitute.

13 (1): *[The] One* This line was followed by *[That on thy] [That by some mossy *]*

14 (1): *[Some] [one] some*

15 (1): *That walk & wander thro [drear night] the night*   (2): *climb & wander thro [the night] steep night*   E: *climb & wander   climbs* of 1820-M focused attention on the single star.

16 (1) and (2): *found that spot*   E: *[spot] cleft*

17 (1): *Beams [come] fall from [Heaven] high [that bower] those paths upon*   (2): received with *fall from heaven*   E: There is a faint pen-

SCENE II

A Forest, intermingled with Rocks and Caverns. Asia *and* Panthea
pass into it. Two young Fauns are sitting on a Rock, listening.

Semichorus I of Spirits

The path through which that lovely twain
Have passed, by cedar, pine, and yew,
And each dark tree that ever grew,
Is curtained out from heaven's wide blue;
Nor sun, nor moon, nor wind, nor rain,   5
Can pierce its interwoven bowers;
Nor aught, save when some cloud of dew,
Drifted along the earth-creeping breeze
Between the trunks of the hoar trees,
Hangs each a pearl in the pale flowers   10
Of the green laurel, blown anew,
And bends, and then fades silently,
One frail and fair anemone;
Or when some star of many a one
That climbs and wanders through steep night,   15
Has found the cleft through which alone
Beams fall from high those depths upon,
Ere it is borne away, away,
By the swift heavens that cannot stay:
It scatters drops of golden light,   20
Like lines of rain that ne'er unite;

---

ciled *bow* present as a possible option (*bower*) for *depths* (note *bower* in the
draft).

19 (1): *that will not* (option: *cannot*) *stay* Locock, "with some doubts"
(but I believe correctly) put a colon after *stay* because "a skeleton of the sentence, as previously punctuated, demonstrates a flaw in the syntax:—'Nothing
can pierce its interwoven bowers . . . save (1) where [now established as *when*]
some cloud of dew hangs a pearl . . . or (2) when some star has found a cleft
. . . *It* scatters drops.' Evidently this 'It' is wrong" (Edition, *1*, 609-10. Locock's
ellipses).

20 (1): *It scatters beams*   (2): [*beams*] *lines*   E: [*beams*] *drops*

21 (1): *Which stream in lines that*   (2): [*Which fall in lines that neer
unite*] → received with *rain which*

22 (1): *And [round there is] the gloom divine is still around*   (2): *For the gloom divine is still around*

23 (1): *underneath the [grassy] mossy*

24-25 Draft: *[And] there the voluptuous nightingale[s] / [Are] Is awake [in] through [all] thro the*

25-26 1820-M, with commas after *noon-day* and *fails* (E: unpointed), left an ambiguous structure and failed to subordinate the parenthetical ll. 27-29.

27 Draft: *And [in] thro the windless ivy [leaves] [fl⟨owers⟩] boughs—*

28 Draft: *[Lost] Sick as with deep love [away] / Drops [How the]* → received with *Sick as with*

30 Draft: *[on] from the [laurel] swinging blossom*

31 Draft: *[Watches] Watching to catch the dying ⟨option: languid⟩ [song] close*   E: *[strain] close*

32-33 Draft: *Of [the] its last strain, and [lifts] on high / The [Heaven-upclimbing] wings of the weak melody*

33 E: *[faint] weak*

34 Draft: *[Till new delights are]* → received with *streams*   E: *[strain] stream*   The word was probably (and excusably) misread as *strain* by Mary for 1820, and overlooked for the errata list since *strain* is also in M.

35 Draft: *[Beyond our] [To] That song [and it is almost mute]* → received with *That song*

36 Draft: *[And] When*   and   *still air*

38 1820: *lake-surrounding*   Restoration of *lake-surrounded* (the E reading) was probably from the errata list (Galignani: 1820).

40 Draft: *[Till like that aye renewed strain]* → received plus *[He dies away]*

41-63 The intended sense is probably as follows: The echoes draw all spirits. The echoes come first as a gentle sound, waking the destined spirits, who believe that they respond to an inner desire; but they are actually floated on a wind formed by the stream of sound—floated seemingly on their own way until, as the storm of sound becomes loud and strong, though still sweet, the destined spirits increase their speed (l. 60) likewise, and as the billows of sound gather (strengthen?) they bear the destined spirits like clouds to the fatal mountain. The unexpressed object (the destined spirits) of *bear* (l. 62) makes for a principal difficulty in this passage. (See also n. on ll. 59-61.)

41-42 Draft: *There [these] those enchanted [echoes dwell / Which draw]* → received.

44 Draft: *or ⟨option: and⟩ strange awe*   E: With *sweet* occurring above (l. 40) and twice below (ll. 56 and 58) it is unlikely that Shelley was responsible for the change of *deep* (in E) to yet another *sweet* (1820-M) within so short a span.   *deep* is the more meaningful word.

45 Draft: *All spirits [around by the way] on that trackless way*

46 Draft: *[as are the swift leaves [swept] / Which to ruin]* → *[As so light boats are driven to]* → received with *[the woodmen's] inland*

47 Draft: *[By] Down*

48-51 Draft: *[And first the sound is like the truths / Left melancholy]* →

And the gloom divine is all around,
And underneath is the mossy ground.

Semichorus II

There the voluptuous nightingales
Are awake through all the broad noonday.   25
When one with bliss or sadness fails—
And through the windless ivy-boughs,
Sick with sweet love, droops dying away
On its mate's music-panting bosom—
Another from the swinging blossom,   30
Watching to catch the languid close
Of the last strain, then lifts on high
The wings of the weak melody,
Till some new stream of feeling bear
The song, and all the woods are mute;   35
When there is heard through the dim air
The rush of wings, and rising there
Like many a lake-surrounded flute,
Sounds overflow the listener's brain
So sweet that joy is almost pain.   40

Semichorus I

There those enchanted eddies play
Of echoes, music-tongued, which draw,
By Demogorgon's mighty law,
With melting rapture or deep awe,
All spirits on that secret way,   45
As inland boats are driven to ocean
Down streams made strong with mountain-thaw;
And first there comes a gentle sound
To those in talk or slumber bound,

And first there [came] comes a [sound so low] faint low sound | Which like the twilight shade around | [Is] [Was] Is sad yet sweet, [when o'er it crept] Then fragments: [Pursues on beyond where we saw] | [Those radiant sisters I saw cast ⟨?⟩] | [Vanish as it past] At this point Shelley abandoned the fragments, picked up *Is sad yet sweet* above, and continued: *With soft emotion | [Thou] The [wanderers] follow those who saw* etc.

50 1820: Omission of punctuation after *destined* could have resulted from Mary's oversight (E has *destined—*), or from a faulty attempt to interpret the lines (by Mary, Peacock, or the printer). The correction in M was probably from the errata list (Galignani: 1820) and was first confirmed by Mathilde Blind ("Shelley," p. 80).   **52** E: [*steaming*] *breathing*

53 E: [*Then ⟨?⟩*] *There*   M²: *streams* was almost certainly a typographical error, but an interesting coincidence since Galignani had given *streams* which was corrected to *steams* in M.   **54** Draft: *Which* [*drives ⟨moves?⟩*] *sweeps*

55 Draft: *Believe* [*in the fleet*] *their own swift* [*feet*] *wings* [*&*] *feet*

56 Draft: [*Their own desires*] → received.

57 Draft: [*And as they pass*] *And so*   **58** *Until* [*most*] *still*

59-61 E: Despite the limited punctuation, I believe that the key strong-pause dash after *hurrying* (confirmed by the draft semicolon and the colon of M [probably from the errata list since Galignani followed the unpointed 1820]) clarifies Shelley's intent. It is the storm of sound that, formerly but a gentle awakener, now grows loud and strong and hurrying, tending to leave the destined spirits behind. (See also n. on ll. 41-63.)

59 Draft: [*carries*] *is driven*

60 Draft: *Sucked in,* ⟨space⟩ [*dominion*] with the latter word probably a tentative hold. The received reading is written above the space.

61-62 Draft:[*Along its billows*] [*When*] *Behind its gathering billows meet* / [*As winds amid the yielding air*] / [*Behind the * clouds they bear*] / [*Amid ⟨?⟩*] → received.   **62** For *bear* see n. on ll. 41-63.

63 E: An unused but compensated SD is present: *enter* [*two young female*] *Fauns* (See n. on I.106.)

64 The drafts for II.ii end with the following unused passage, probably for the Faun: *And who are they* / *Bathed in* [*sweet*] *deep luxury of each others looks* / *Which flows forth like the inmost light of being* / *Making the* [*day*] *noon obscure? unforeseeing* / *Of*

66 E: [*moist & mossy*] *least frequented*

69-82 On the inside back cover of E.2 is the following, in Clare Clairmont's handwriting: *Thin bursts arose from the depth of the water then one loudly drove on before the wind   The fen bubbles the pavilions of water spirits * ⟨y for yours?⟩ still* / *Clare*

71 M: The inferior *which enchantment* was introduced by Galignani and uncorrected in M.

76 E: *Which the noontide*   Considerations of meter probably dictated omission of *the* in 1820-M.

78 *shining homes* and *lucid homes* are present as options for *lucent domes* The final choice was clearly the superior one.

80-81 *They rein* [*its*] *their headlong speed, & glide* [*with it*] → received with *They ride on* [*it & them*] *it & reign*   I now agree with Freeman that the undeleted *it* is present. It is almost illegible and could easily have been missed by Mary, who probably related [*them*] (the deletion could also be missed easily) to *domes* (as did Freeman in his text) whereas the context clearly calls for *air* as the reference.   **82** [*Into*] *Under*

And wakes the destined: soft emotion   50
Attracts, impels them. Those who saw
Say from the breathing earth behind
There steams a plume-uplifting wind
Which drives them on their path, while they
Believe their own swift wings and feet   55
The sweet desires within obey;
And so they float upon their way,
Until, still sweet but loud and strong,
The storm of sound is driven along,
Sucked up and hurrying: as they fleet   60
Behind, its gathering billows meet
And to the fatal mountain bear
Like clouds amid the yielding air.

First Faun

Canst thou imagine where those spirits live
Which make such delicate music in the woods?   65
We haunt within the least frequented caves
And closest coverts, and we know these wilds,
Yet never meet them, though we hear them oft:
Where may they hide themselves?

Second Faun

        'Tis hard to tell:
I have heard those more skilled in spirits say,   70
The bubbles, which the enchantment of the sun
Sucks from the pale faint water-flowers that pave
The oozy bottom of clear lakes and pools,
Are the pavilions where such dwell and float
Under the green and golden atmosphere   75
Which noontide kindles through the woven leaves;
And when these burst, and the thin fiery air,
The which they breathed within those lucent domes,
Ascends to flow like meteors through the night,
They ride on it, and rein their headlong speed,   80
And bow their burning crests, and glide in fire
Under the waters of the earth again.

83 *If* [*these*] *such*

85 *or* [*in the violets heart*] → received.
87 *Or on* of 1820-M was probably the result of an uncorrected transfer from
l. 86. Mathilde Blind first noted the correct reading *Or in* ("Shelley," p. 80).
88 [*imagine*] *divine*
89 *stay* offers difficulty. Zupitza thought that it might be *stay* altered to *try*
("Zu . . . Prometheus," *103, 94*), and Locock thought that *se* (he conjectured
seek) had been altered to *try* (Edition *1*, 611). Careful study of the manuscript
leads me to conclude that the word is *stay*   I agree with Locock on *se* (I read
see) but think that Shelley changed the first *e* to *a*, put *y* over the second *e*,
and put the *t* in above *s*, letting the upstroke of *s* meet the shank of *t*. I now
believe that *try* was never intended.   [*the*] *noontide*
93 *doom* is clear in E, with *dooms* of 1820 possibly a printer's error. The
correct reading was restored in M probably from the errata list (Galignani:
1820).
96-97 The first version of these lines (see next note) at first followed l. 91 to
close the scene.
96 [*Which cheer our lonesome*] *twilights, & which charm* → received
when ll. 92-95 were added.

1-50 An unused draft passage, relevant to these lines, includes the following:
I hear ⟨option: *ye hear*⟩ / *The sudden whirlwind* [*of her dread uprise*] /
Gathering before her destined path [*most*] *like* / *The tempestuous tumult
of a thousand storms* / *Splintering the mountainous* [*palaces & towers*] [*temples*] *fanes, & rocky towers* / *Till their heaven cleaving wedges, & split domes
/* [*Stand*] [*Pierce*] *desolate &* [*shattered*] *jagged & toppling, pierce* / *The thin
realms of the uninhabited air* / *And earthquake cracking from the centre up
/ And splitting the great globe like brittle ice*
1-27 There are no known specific drafts of these lines.
1 [*'tis*] *to*
3 *chasm.* ⟨?⟩   The apparent period is, I believe, ink spatter.
4 Shelley himself probably changed the *breathed up* of E to the superior
hurled up of 1820-M to avoid the *breathing-breathed* repetition.

12 The awkwardness of an obsolescent *beest* in E was corrected in 1820-M.

14 [*must*] *should be*
15 [*Like all we love,*] [*As these perchance*] → received with [[*al*]*though*]
yet

First Faun

If such live thus, have others other lives,
Under pink blossoms or within the bells
Of meadow flowers, or folded violets deep,   85
Or on their dying odours, when they die,
Or in the sunlight of the spherèd dew?

Second Faun

Aye, many more, which we may well divine.
But should we stay to speak, noontide would come,
And thwart Silenus find his goats undrawn,   90
And grudge to sing those wise and lovely songs
Of fate, and chance, and God, and Chaos old,
And love, and the chained Titan's woeful doom,
And how he shall be loosed, and make the earth
One brotherhood: delightful strains which cheer   95
Our solitary twilights, and which charm
To silence the unenvying nightingales.

SCENE III

A Pinnacle of Rock among Mountains. Asia *and* Panthea.

Panthea

Hither the sound has borne us—to the realm
Of Demogorgon, and the mighty portal,
Like a volcano's meteor-breathing chasm,
Whence the oracular vapour is hurled up
Which lonely men drink wandering in their youth,   5
And call truth, virtue, love, genius, or joy;
That maddening wine of life, whose dregs they drain
To deep intoxication, and uplift,
Like Mænads who cry loud, Evoe! Evoe!
The voice which is contagion to the world.   10

Asia

Fit throne for such a power! Magnificent!
How glorious art thou, Earth! and if thou be
The shadow of some spirit lovelier still,
Though evil stain its work, and it should be
Like its creation, weak yet beautiful,   15

26 *illumed* of E might easily have been misread as *illumined* (1820-M) by Mary, and unnoted for the errata list. (Cf. I.637.)

28-98 The drafts include most of these lines.

28-42 The following unused draft leads into these lines: [*How horrible . . tis noonday,*] *but the stars* / *Are* [*shining*] *glittering* [*overhead*], *as if* [*deep*] *night* → *Are glittering keen*[*ly*], *as if the* [*dead*] *ghost* / *Had risen at noon from* [*her*] [*its*] *her untimely grave* / *Where she keeps watch* [*a spirit*] *oer peace & sleep & death* / [*With all the lamps*] *And lit these lamps within their sepulcher*

28-30 Draft: *keen heaven* [*pier⟨cing⟩*] *cleaving mountains* / *From pyramids of sunlike radiance, fling* / *The daylight, as the Ocean's*

29 E: [*pyramids*] *icy spires*

31 Draft: [*Is*] *From some* [*way⟨ward?⟩*] *windless reef is* [*scattered*] *hurled thro the clear air*

32 Draft: *Spangles the* [*stormless air*] [*atmo⟨sphere⟩*] *wind*

33-35 Draft: [*Girdling*] *Girdles this* [*mighty chasm . . ⟨sic⟩ then a howl*] *grave how with a roar* / *Of waterfalls, from* [*many*] *the* [*frost cloven chasms*] *thaw riven ravines* / *Is* [*filling the calm air*] *Satiates the listening air continuous,* [*wide*] *vast*

36-38 Draft: *hark* [*the s⟨now⟩*] *tis the driven snow* / *Which the* [*keen*] *clear north thrice sifted* [*and which fell*] *slow gathering there*

38 E: [*has*] *had*

39 Draft: [*as an*] [*on*] *in* [*heaven chosen*] *Heaven defying minds*

41 E: [*mountains*] *nations*

42 Draft: *And shake even to their roots—as ye do now* / [*Bare skinless bones of this outwearing world!* / *To your own awful voices*] *To your own voice*

43-53 There are no known drafts of these lines.

46 1820-M: *on some* avoids the echo of *on an* in E, and offers a more effective image.

48 Considerations of sound (*wind-which* in E) possibly dictated the change to *wind that* of 1820-M.

50 E at first: *Grows dizzy—I see shapes within the mist.* Shelley then made the reading extremely difficult by lightly deleting *I*, crowding *st those* above and between *see shapes* and improvising a question mark to give: *seest those shapes within the mist?* The lightly deleted *I*, the confusing *?* and the crowded *those* that might well be read *thin* would explain Mary's 1820 reading, surprisingly overlooked for the errata: *I see thin shapes within the mist.* As to the omission of *thin* in M, probably accidental, Locock suggested that Mary, "being aware from her 'formidable list' of errata that 'thin' was a misprint, consulted the MS and, failing to decipher it, decided to be content with what was easily legible" (Edition, *1*, 611-12). It is doubtful, as we have seen, that Mary made such use of the manuscript for her edition, and, in any event, one would expect an errata list to have contained the correct phrase without further deciphering. (One cannot, of course, overlook the unlikely possibility that the M reading was from the errata, but the following speech of Panthea

I could fall down and worship that and thee.
Even now my heart adoreth. Wonderful!
Look, sister, ere the vapour dim thy brain:
Beneath is a wide plain of billowy mist,
As a lake, paving in the morning sky,   20
With azure waves which burst in silver light,
Some Indian vale. Behold it, rolling on
Under the curdling winds, and islanding
The peak whereon we stand—midway, around
Encinctured by the dark and blooming forests,   25
Dim twilight lawns and stream-illumèd caves,
And wind-enchanted shapes of wandering mist;
And far on high the keen sky-cleaving mountains
From icy spires of sunlike radiance fling
The dawn, as lifted ocean's dazzling spray,   30
From some Atlantic islet scattered up,
Spangles the wind with lamp-like water-drops.
The vale is girdled with their walls; a howl
Of cataracts from their thaw-cloven ravines
Satiates the listening wind, continuous, vast,   35
Awful as silence. Hark! the rushing snow!
The sun-awakened avalanche! whose mass,
Thrice sifted by the storm, had gathered there
Flake after flake, in Heaven-defying minds
As thought by thought is piled, till some great truth   40
Is loosened, and the nations echo round,
Shaken to their roots, as do the mountains now.

Panthea

Look, how the gusty sea of mist is breaking
In crimson foam, even at our feet! it rises
As ocean at the enchantment of the moon   45
Round foodless men wrecked on some oozy isle.

Asia

The fragments of the cloud are scattered up;
The wind that lifts them disentwines my hair;
Its billows now sweep o'er mine eyes; my brain
Grows dizzy; seest those shapes within the mist?   50

seems a natural answer to the question of E.) As to what follows *mist* Zupitza read an *s* combined with a period changed to a question mark, and Locock held that the question mark itself might be an *s*, which I am sure it is not. (All preceding references to the mist [lines 19, 22, 27, 43, 44] are in the singular.) I believe that Shelley originally used a period and a *t* crossing which, as frequently, just touched the right side of the shank—in this instance it angled slightly upward. When the revision called for changed punctuation he added a small loop, easily missed by Mary, and a heavier, slightly elongated period to convert this angled crossing into a semblance of a question mark.

54 The drafts continue at this point.

56 Draft: *[shadow] shade*

58 Draft: *Of death [of] & of life*
59 Draft: *veil, within the bar*
60 Draft: *Of [the] things*
61 Draft: *Even to the [ch⟨air?⟩] footsteps ⟨option: step⟩ of the Eternal throne*   E: *Even to the [threshold of the] steps*

63 Draft: *Track the sound, which* → *[As] While the sound, [eddies] round* → *received.*

65 Draft: almost illegible, but possibly: *As [the bugle the sound]* or *As [the eagle the *]* → an acceptably clear *As a stag draws the hound*
66 Draft: *As [the] lightning [the] a vapour*

70 Draft: *a ⟨option: the⟩ stone*

72 Draft: *Thro the void of the Abyss* → *[Deep] thro the grey Abysm* → *received.*
74 Draft: *[There] Where*

78 Draft: *Nor the [darkness] is* → *received.*

Panthea

A countenance with beckoning smiles: there burns
An azure fire within its golden locks!
Another and another—hark! they speak!

Song of Spirits

To the deep, to the deep,
  Down, down!   55
Through the shade of sleep,
Through the cloudy strife
Of Death and of Life;
Through the veil and the bar
Of things which seem and are,   60
Even to the steps of the remotest throne,
  Down, down!

While the sound whirls around,
  Down, down!
As the fawn draws the hound,   65
As the lightning the vapour,
As a weak moth the taper;
Death, despair; love, sorrow;
Time both; to-day, to-morrow;
As steel obeys the spirit of the stone,   70
  Down, down!

Through the grey, void abysm,
  Down, down!
Where the air is no prism,
And the moon and stars are not,   75
And the cavern-crags wear not
The radiance of heaven,
Nor the gloom to earth given;
Where there is One pervading, One alone,
  Down, down!   80

81 The draft has an unused line, relevant here: [*There*] *Where these Depths are unveiled*

83 Draft: *Like* [*a dew mist*] [*grey death*] *the lightning asleep* This is followed by: [*Which the winds might embolden* / *To climb bright & golden* / [*Up*] *the pale vault of the dawn* / *Till the sun ride*[*s*] *thereon* / [*Up*]*on the brink, your limbs sink* / *Down, Down* / *A spell is muffled*]

84 Draft: *Like* [*a*] *that spark nursed in* [*embers*] [*ashes*] *embers*   E: *that spark* (as in the draft). Mary either erred with *the spark* (1820-M) or sought a parallel structure with *the last look* (l. 85). The reference to l. 85 is clarified by the E reading.

85 Draft: *Like the* [*word*] *last look*

86-88 Draft: fragmented, with only [*Like a * diamond*] *star* and [*Like*] *Over sepulchral wealth, a* present to suggest these lines. Shelley also tried: [*Like a clear lamp*]   and   [*Like a snake coiled in* [*slumber*] *dreams*]

88 E: [*buried*] *hidden but* [*for*] *from* The final choice of *treasured but for* would almost certainly have been made by Shelley on the basis of sense: the spell would not be hidden *from* Asia alone; it would be hidden (or *treasured*, the more suggestive word) *for* her alone, since she alone could implement it (see II.i.192).

90 Draft: *It seizes it bears* [*thee*] *ye* → [*It*] *has bound thee, it bears thee* → received.

92 Draft: *With thy*   E: [*thy*] [*the*] [*that*] *the*

94 Draft: [*For*] *Such*

95-98 Draft and E: These lines gave Shelley continuing difficulty. The draft at first followed l. 94 with: [*Though* ⟨sic⟩ *the graves rocky portal* / *The*] → [*The serpent spell coiled*] *for thee alone* → received l. 95, followed by: [*Thro the graves crag portal*] *The key of Death's portal* / *Will* [*send*] [*wake*] *loose the serpent coiled under his throne* / [*For*] *Through that alone*

96 E: [*With the key of life's portal*] → [*Will loose*] *Must* [*unchain, at*] → received.

97 E: *coiled* [*up*]

98 Draft: [*For*] *Through*   E: The following unused lines were possibly intended for this context: [*The living frame which sustains my soul* / *Is sinking beneath the fierce controul*] / *Down through the lampless deep of song* / *I am drawn & driven* ⟨space⟩ *along—*

There are no known drafts for Scene iv. All manuscript readings below are from E.

SD [*Demogorgon on his throne*] The deletion is compensated for in the opening line.

1 [*A veiled s*⟨hape⟩] *What*

2 [*darkness*] *Darkness* The uncapitalized *darkness* of 1820-M is more appropriate here since the darkness has not yet been identified as a "living spirit."

3 [*that*] [*the*] *the*

In the depth of the deep,
          Down, down!
Like veiled lightning asleep,
Like that spark nursed in embers,
The last look Love remembers,   85
Like a diamond which shines
On the dark wealth of mines,
A spell is treasured but for thee alone.
          Down, down!

We have bound thee, we guide thee   90
          Down, down!
With the bright form beside thee.
Resist not the weakness:
Such strength is in meekness
That the Eternal, the Immortal,   95
Must unloose through life's portal
The snake-like Doom coiled underneath his throne
          By that alone!

SCENE IV

The Cave of Demogorgon. Asia *and* Panthea.

Panthea

What veilèd form sits on that ebon throne?

Asia

The veil has fallen!

Panthea

          I see a mighty darkness
Filling the seat of power, and rays of gloom
Dart round, as light from the meridian sun,
Ungazed upon and shapeless: neither limb,   5
Nor form, nor outline; yet we feel it is
A living spirit.

Demogorgon

          Ask what thou wouldst know.

Asia

What canst thou tell?

8 The uncontracted *darest* of E (*dar'st* in 1820-M) gives the more natural and euphonious reading, without metrical violation.

10 [*sense*] *thought*   The change, as Freeman suggested ("Text," p. 169), probably came when Shelley used *sense* in l. 12.

14 Locock felt (I think questionably) that " 'in youth alone' means, not 'only in youth,' but 'in youth and when no others are present,' " and that Shelley "inadvertantly" made *fills* serve for both *which* and *when* (Edition, *1*, 612-13). For the extended debate on ll. 12-14 see *Variorum,* pp. 208-09. The sense is acceptably clear: When the winds of spring or the voice of love ⟨come⟩ . . . the sense fills the faint eyes, etc.

27 This line is followed by: [*Or looks which tell that while the lips are calm | And the eyes cold, the spirit weeps within | Tears like the sanguine sweat of agony;*]   (Cf. *Prince Athanase* 303-05 and *The Cenci* I.i.109-13.)

Demogorgon

All things thou darest demand.

Asia

Who made the living world?

Demogorgon

God.

Asia

Who made all
That it contains—thought, passion, reason, will,   10
Imagination?

Demogorgon

God: Almighty God.

Asia

Who made that sense which, when the winds of spring
In rarest visitation, or the voice
Of one belovèd heard in youth alone,
Fills the faint eyes with falling tears which dim   15
The radiant looks of unbewailing flowers,
And leaves this peopled earth a solitude
When it returns no more?

Demogorgon

Merciful God.

Asia

And who made terror, madness, crime, remorse,
Which from the links of the great chain of things   20
To every thought within the mind of man
Sway and drag heavily, and each one reels
Under the load towards the pit of death;
Abandoned hope, and love that turns to hate;
And self-contempt, bitterer to drink than blood;   25
Pain, whose unheeded and familiar speech
Is howling, and keen shrieks, day after day;
And Hell, or the sharp fear of Hell?

32 Earth is conceived of here as the mother of Saturn, hence properly capitalized in E-M.

35 An optional *world's* is present. The final choice could have been either
Shelley's or Mary's, with the question whether to echo *Earth* of l. 32.

39 [*spirit*] *birthrights* and [*wisdom &*] *knowledge birthrights* of E was
probably changed to *birthright* for 1820-M to make it properly generic.

Demogorgon

He reigns.

Asia

Utter his name—a world pining in pain
Asks but his name: curses shall drag him down.   30

Demogorgon

He reigns.

Asia

I feel, I know it; who?

Demogorgon

He reigns.

Asia

Who reigns? There was the Heaven and Earth at first,
And Light and Love; then Saturn, from whose throne
Time fell, an envious shadow; such the state
Of the earth's primal spirits beneath his sway,   35
As the calm joy of flowers and living leaves
Before the wind or sun has withered them,
And simi-vital worms; but he refused
The birthright of their being—knowledge, power,
The skill which wields the elements, the thought   40
Which pierces this dim universe like light,
Self-empire, and the majesty of love;
For thirst of which they fainted. Then Prometheus
Gave wisdom, which is strength, to Jupiter,
And with this law alone, 'Let man be free,'   45
Clothed him with the dominion of wide Heaven.
To know nor faith, nor love, nor law; to be
Omnipotent but friendless, is to reign—
And Jove now reigned; for on the race of man
First famine, and then toil, and then disease,   50
Strife, wounds, and ghastly death unseen before,
Fell; and the unseasonable seasons drove,
With alternating shafts of frost and fire,
Their shelterless, pale tribes to mountain caves;

66 *chase* is certainly the word, although poorly written and crowded. Possibly Mary, guided by the more conventional phrase, saw *prey* (1820-M). The failure to correct in M is surprising, however, since *beast of chase* is fresher and superior: fire, in its tamed state, is no longer a devouring beast of prey but lovely and playful, like a more gentle beast.

82 [*until it*] *till marble*
83 Compare note at IV.414.

And in their desert hearts fierce wants he sent,   55
And mad disquietudes, and shadows idle
Of unreal good, which levied mutual war,
So ruining the lair wherein they raged.
Prometheus saw, and waked the legioned hopes
Which sleep within folded Elysian flowers,   60
Nepenthe, Moly, Amaranth, fadeless blooms,
That they might hide with thin and rainbow wings
The shape of Death; and Love he sent to bind
The disunited tendrils of that vine
Which bears the wine of life, the human heart;   65
And he tamed fire, which like some beast of chase
Most terrible, but lovely, played beneath
The frown of man; and tortured to his will
Iron and gold, the slaves and signs of power,
And gems and poisons, and all subtlest forms   70
Hidden beneath the mountains and the waves.
He gave man speech, and speech created thought,
Which is the measure of the universe;
And Science struck the thrones of earth and Heaven,
Which shook but fell not; and the harmonious mind   75
Poured itself forth in all-prophetic song,
And music lifted up the listening spirit
Until it walked, exempt from mortal care,
Godlike, o'er the clear billows of sweet sound;
And human hands first mimicked and then mocked,   80
With moulded limbs more lovely than its own,
The human form, till marble grew divine,
And mothers, gazing, drank the love men see
Reflected in their race—behold, and perish.
He told the hidden power of herbs and springs,   85
And Disease drank and slept. Death grew like sleep.
He taught the implicated orbits woven
Of the wide-wandering stars, and how the sun
Changes his lair, and by what secret spell
The pale moon is transformed, when her broad eye   90
Gazes not on the interlunar sea.
He taught to rule, as life directs the limbs,
The tempest-wingèd chariots of the ocean,

100 *rains* is clear, and *reigns* of 1820 could have resulted from Mary's slip in copying (perhaps a thought transfer from ll. 31-32), or an error of the press. *rains* was first reinstated by Galignani, which might account for the correction in M, although the change could well have been included in the errata list.

106 [*for*] *while*

And the Celt know the Indian. Cities then
Were built, and through their snow-like columns flowed   95
The warm winds, and the azure ether shone,
And the blue sea and shadowy hills were seen.
Such, the alleviations of his state,
Prometheus gave to man, for which he hangs
Withering in destined pain: but who rains down   100
Evil, the immedicable plague, which, while
Man looks on his creation like a God
And sees that it is glorious, drives him on,
The wreck of his own will, the scorn of earth,
The outcast, the abandoned, the alone?   105
Not Jove: while yet his frown shook Heaven, aye, when
His adversary from adamantine chains
Cursed him, he trembled like a slave. Declare
Who is his master? Is he too a slave?

                    Demogorgon

All spirits are enslaved who serve things evil: 110
Thou knowest if Jupiter be such or no.

                    Asia

Whom calledst thou God?

                    Demogorgon

                              I spoke but as ye speak,
For Jove is the supreme of living things.

                    Asia

Who is the master of the slave?

                    Demogorgon

                              If the abysm
Could vomit forth its secrets—but a voice   115
Is wanting, the deep truth is imageless;
For what would it avail to bid thee gaze
On the revolving world? what to bid speak
Fate, Time, Occasion, Chance and Change? To these
All things are subject but eternal Love.   120

122 [*answer*] *response*

124-26 *One more demand* . . . ⟨sic⟩ *and be thine answer now* | *Nor doubtful nor obscure* ⟨option: *Nor dark nor dim*⟩ →   received.

128 [*shall*] *will*   Apparently Mary thought the reverse for 1820-M.

132 *their* [*speed*] *flight*

138-40 *clasped it; their bright hair* | *Streams* [*on the blast like meteors & they*] *all* →   *Streams like a comets* [*scattered hair*] *and all* | *Sweep onward*— It may be assumed that Shelley was responsible for the final 1820-M changes (followed here) which do not appear in E.

143 [*Waits with its*] [*Stays*] *Checks its dark*

145 *What* is clear in E, and (as Freeman noted—"Text," p. 46) is superior to *Who* of 1820-M in light of the spirit's answer. The change might have been Mary's (possibly, of course, with Shelley's approval) or Peacock's.
146 An optional *image* is present, with *shadow* clearly the better choice.
147 Consistency dictates *mine aspect* as against *my* of E-M.

Asia

So much I asked before, and my heart gave
The response thou hast given; and of such truths
Each to itself must be the oracle.
One more demand; and do thou answer me
As my own soul would answer, did it know   125
That which I ask. Prometheus shall arise
Henceforth the Sun of this rejoicing world:
When will the destined hour arrive?

Demogorgon

Behold!

Asia

The rocks are cloven, and through the purple night
I see cars drawn by rainbow-wingèd steeds   130
Which trample the dim winds: in each there stands
A wild-eyed charioteer, urging their flight.
Some look behind, as fiends pursued them there,
And yet I see no shapes but the keen stars;
Others, with burning eyes, lean forth, and drink   135
With eager lips the wind of their own speed,
As if the thing they loved fled on before,
And now, even now, they clasped it. Their bright locks
Stream like a comet's flashing hair: they all
Sweep onward.

Demogorgon

These are the immortal Hours,   140
Of whom thou didst demand. One waits for thee.

Asia

A spirit with a dreadful countenance
Checks its dark chariot by the craggy gulf.
Unlike thy brethren, ghastly charioteer,
What art thou? Whither wouldst thou bear me? Speak!   145

Spirit

I am the shadow of destiny
More dread than is mine aspect: ere yon planet

150 [*That*] *The* although Mary apparently thought the reverse for 1820-M.

151 *as* [*doth*] *may the lurid* [*smoke*] *dust* Freeman assumed that "Shelley got rid of *doth* so he could use *dust*," and he thought that Mary erred in copying ("Text," p. 47). Careful examination of the manuscript suggests a different explanation: *doth* was apparently deleted at once and *may* substituted, giving the line as Mary transcribed it (*dust* and the deletion of *smoke* are in different ink). I believe that Shelley made the change after the transcription was completed, but did not list it in the errata list since, as Locock suggested, he "changed his mind again" with respect to *dust* (Edition, *1*, 615).

152 [*to*] *oer*

153 [*See!*] *Lo!*

154 [*& its path darkens the night*] → received.

155 [*Darkens*] *Darkening* ⟨option: *Blackening*⟩ with the final choice giving the stronger word.

156 First given to Asia with [*See*] *But see*

157 [*Like the*] *An ivory*

158 *Which* [*burns around*] *comes*

159 *the* [*fair*] *young*

160 [*Within it,*] *That guides it,*

162 [*Attracts*] [*Leads*] *Lures*

168, 174 *daughters* in each line of E suggests inclusion of both Asia and Panthea in the invitation. The 1820-M *daughter* places the preferable attention on the main character.

173 *at noon* of 1820-M was possibly an attempt of Mary to avoid the repetition of *Ere* in l. 171, but E must take preference on the basis of sense. They "rest" at the opening of the next scene but it is not yet noon (see II.v.10).

Has set, the Darkness which ascends with me
Shall wrap in lasting night Heaven's kingless throne.

                    Asia

What meanest thou?

                    Panthea

                    The terrible shadow floats   150
Up from its throne, as may the lurid smoke
Of earthquake-ruined cities o'er the sea.
Lo! it ascends the car . . . the coursers fly
Terrified. Watch its path among the stars,
Blackening the night!

                    Asia

                    Thus I am answered . . . strange!   155

                    Panthea

See, near the verge, another chariot stays:
An ivory shell inlaid with crimson fire
Which comes and goes within its sculptured rim
Of delicate strange tracery. The young spirit
That guides it has the dovelike eyes of hope;   160
How its soft smiles attract the soul!—as light
Lures wingèd insects through the lampless air.

                    Spirit

My coursers are fed with the lightning,
    They drink of the whirlwind's stream,
And when the red morning is bright'ning   165
    They bathe in the fresh sunbeam;
    They have strength for their swiftness, I deem:
        Then ascend with me, Daughter of Ocean.

I desire—and their speed makes night kindle;
    I fear—they outstrip the typhoon;   170
Ere the cloud piled on Atlas can dwindle
    We encircle the earth and the moon;
    We shall rest from long labours ere noon:
        Then ascend with me, Daughter of Ocean.

SD E: Names lacking. They were added for 1820-M.

1-97 There are no known drafts of these lines, although occasional analogous passages will be indicated. Manuscript readings below are from E.

4-5 Notebook Bodleian MS Shelley adds. e.6, p. 16 has a suggestion of these lines in an isolated: *Thy swift feet are shod with the speed of desire*

9 Possibly *this cloud* of E was changed to *the cloud* in 1820-M to avoid the duplication and overemphasis that would have resulted at l. 12.

SCENE V

The Car pauses within a Cloud on the Top of a snowy Mountain.
Asia, Panthea *and the* Spirit of the Hour.

Spirit

On the brink of the night and the morning
   My coursers are wont to respire;
But the Earth has just whispered a warning
   That their flight must be swifter than fire:
   They shall drink the hot speed of desire!   5

Asia

Thou breathest on their nostrils, but my breath
Would give them swifter speed.

Spirit

                  Alas! it could not.

Panthea

O Spirit! pause, and tell whence is the light
Which fills the cloud—the sun is yet unrisen.

Spirit

The sun will rise not until noon. Apollo   10
Is held in heaven by wonder; and the light
Which fills this vapour, as the aerial hue
Of fountain-gazing roses fills the water,
Flows from thy mighty sister.

Panthea

              Yes, I feel—

Asia

What is it with thee, sister? Thou art pale.   15

Panthea

How thou art changed! I dare not look on thee;
I feel, but see thee not. I scarce endure
The radiance of thy beauty. Some good change
Is working in the elements, which suffer
Thy presence thus unveiled. The Nereids tell   20
That on the day when the clear hyaline

26 *like* [*a fiery s*⟨un⟩] [*an*] *the atmosphere*

30 [*Earth*] *grief cast   dwells* of 1820-M (rather than *dwell* of E) offers the more exact form in this context.

35 E-M: *Hearest*   See note on I.341.   E-M: *i'*   For the present reading see note on I.745.
    36 [*each*] *all*

43 [*Making*] *It makes*

47 SD: [*Panthea*]   When Shelley decided to use the transitional passage below (see n. on l. 71) he might have intended *list, spirits speak* to go to Asia, and so have deleted *Panthea*   There is no indication in E of restoration of the name, which must have been made while Mary was copying. M: *Spirits,* (See n. on II.i.171.) Following SD: [*Song of an enamoured Spirit*] *Voice in the air*   One must assume that Shelley initiated, or approved, the addition of *singing* for 1820, and so to M.
    48-71 See n. on II.i.110. For Shelley's translation of these lines into Italian, see *Variorum*, pp. 677-78.

Was cloven at thine uprise, and thou didst stand
Within a veinèd shell, which floated on
Over the calm floor of the crystal sea,
Among the Ægean isles, and by the shores   25
Which bear thy name—love, like the atmosphere
Of the sun's fire filling the living world,
Burst from thee, and illumined earth and heaven,
And the deep ocean and the sunless caves,
And all that dwells within them; till grief cast   30
Eclipse upon the soul from which it came:
Such art thou now; nor is it I alone,
Thy sister, thy companion, thine own chosen one,
But the whole world which seeks thy sympathy.
Hearest thou not sounds in the air which speak the love   35
Of all articulate beings? Feelest thou not
The inanimate winds enamoured of thee? List!

                          [*Music.*]

Asia

Thy words are sweeter than aught else but his
Whose echoes they are: yet all love is sweet,
Given or returned. Common as light is love,   40
And its familiar voice wearies not ever.
Like the wide heaven, the all-sustaining air,
It makes the reptile equal to the God:
They who inspire it most are fortunate,
As I am now; but those who feel it most   45
Are happier still, after long sufferings,
As I shall soon become.

Panthea

List! Spirits speak.

Voice (*in the air, singing*)

Life of Life! thy lips enkindle
With their love the breath between them;
And thy smiles before they dwindle   50
Make the cold air fire; then screen them
In those looks, where whoso gazes
Faints, entangled in their mazes.

54 *limbs* of E is acceptably clear, with *lips* of 1820 probably the result of transfer from l. 48 by Mary or the printer, and with the correction in M from the errata (Galignani: 1820).

60-65 Lines 66 to *sou*⟨ls⟩ of line 68 originally opened this stanza.

60-63 One must assume that it is the *atmosphere* (l. 58) and not the *voice* (l. 61) that *folds* ⟨them⟩ *From the sight,* and adjust the punctuation accordingly.

68 *whom* ⟨option: *those*⟩

71 At this point there is an unused but undeleted transitional passage: *Asia | You [say] said that Spirits [speak] spoke but it was thee | Sweet sister, for even now thy curved lips | Tremble as if the sound were dying there | Not dead | Panthea | Alas it [is] was Prometheus [speaks] spoke | Within me, [if I spoke, & even now it] and I know it must be so | I mixed my own weak nature with his [life] love | And ⟨space⟩ And my thoughts | Are like the many forests of a vale | Through which the might of whirlwind & of rain | [Has] Had [past] passed [but] [and] they [glimmer] rest through the evening light | As [I] mine do now in thy beloved smile*

72-84 The following, written in 1817, anticipated these lines (as Locock, *Examination*, p. 63, and Neville Rogers, "Music at Marlow," pp. 22-23, noted): *My spirit like a charmed [boat] bark doth [float] swim | Upon the [lulling] liquid waves of thy [sweet singing] | [Sped] Far far away [amid] into the regions dim | [As] [Even as a rapid boat] Of rapture, as ⟨a⟩ boat with swift sails winging | Its way adown some many-winding river | Speeds thro dark forests oer the waters swinging*

79 *[Between] Upon*

80 *[forests] mountains, woods,*

84 *[flowing] spreading*

Child of Light! thy limbs are burning
Through the vest which seems to hide them,   55
As the radiant lines of morning
Through the clouds ere they divide them;
And this atmosphere divinest
Shrouds thee wheresoe'er thou shinest.

Fair are others; none beholds thee—   60
But thy voice sounds low and tender
Like the fairest—for it folds thee
From the sight, that liquid splendour,
And all feel, yet see thee never,
As I feel now, lost forever!   65

Lamp of Earth! where'er thou movest
Its dim shapes are clad with brightness,
And the souls of whom thou lovest
Walk upon the winds with lightness,
Till they fail, as I am failing,   70
Dizzy, lost, yet unbewailing!

Asia

  My soul is an enchanted boat,
    Which, like a sleeping swan, doth float
Upon the silver waves of thy sweet singing;
    And thine doth like an angel sit   75
    Beside the helm conducting it,
Whilst all the winds with melody are ringing.
    It seems to float ever, forever,
    Upon that many-winding river,
    Between mountains, woods, abysses,   80
    A paradise of wildernesses!
Till, like one in slumber bound,
Borne to the ocean, I float down, around,
Into a sea profound of ever-spreading sound.

  Meanwhile thy spirit lifts its pinions   85
    In music's most serene dominions,

96 Since E is clear, the omission of *and* after *winds* for an inferior reading in 1820-M would appear to be an uncorrected oversight in copying or printing.

98-102 There are two drafts of these lines.

100 (1): *And youth's delusive sea which smiles but to betray*   (2): *And youth's [false sea which smiles but] false waters smiling to betray*
101 (1): *[Into] Beyond the sunny* ⟨space⟩ *we flee*   (2): *Beyond the [sunny] gleaming [isles] we flee*
102 (1): *Of* ⟨space⟩ *glassy Infancy*   (2): *Of [mist] shadow-peopled infancy*
103 Draft: *[And beyond] [And] through death & birth to a serener day*

109 The desirable parenthetical separation of *somewhat like thee* was initiated by Rossetti.
110 Shelley spells the word *chaunt* here, but *chant* at III.iii.27. 1820 has *chaunt* in both positions, while M has *chant* here and *chaunt* in the next act. Possibly errors of the press account for the printed inconsistencies.

Catching the winds that fan that happy heaven.
    And we sail on, away, afar,
    Without a course, without a star,
But by the instinct of sweet music driven,   90
    Till, through Elysian garden islets,
    By thee, most beautiful of pilots,
    Where never mortal pinnace glided,
    The boat of my desire is guided:
Realms where the air we breathe is love,   95
Which in the winds and on the waves doth move,
Harmonizing this earth with what we feel above.

    We have passed Age's icy caves,
    And Manhood's dark and tossing waves,
And Youth's smooth ocean, smiling to betray: 100
    Beyond the glassy gulfs we flee
    Of shadow-peopled Infancy,
Through death and birth to a diviner day—
    A paradise of vaulted bowers
    Lit by downward-gazing flowers,   105
    And watery paths that wind between
    Wildernesses calm and green,
Peopled by shapes too bright to see,
And rest, having beheld—somewhat like thee—
Which walk upon the sea and chant melodiously!   110

END OF THE SECOND ACT.

The drafts for Act III, representing only fifty of the 512 lines in the act, are found in Bodleian MSS Shelley adds. e.11 and e.12. The fair copy is in Bodleian MS E.3.

There are no known drafts for Scene i, and the manuscript readings below are from E.

3 1820-M: *I am* offers a more direct and forceful reading than the *am I* of E.

4 [*had*] *has*   Mary apparently thought the reverse (*had* in 1820-M) but *s* is heavily over *d* and *has* is the correct word in the context of Jupiter's climactic moment.

5 *like an* in 1820 could have been an error in transcription or printing (possibly as an anticipation of *un* in *unextinguished*   Restoration of *like unextinguished* in M was probably from the errata list (Galignani: 1820).

8 [*In tameless*] *insurrection*   →   [*The masks of a rebellion*]   →   received.

13 *night* in E is clear, with *might* of 1820 either Mary's slip or printer's error. The correction in M was probably from the errata list (Galignani: 1820).

14 *climb*[*s*]

15 *wound*[*s*]

18 *begotten* [*the*] *a strange* [*might*] *wonder,*

19 [*That*] [*A*] *That*

20 *Hour*[*s*]   *destined* is clear in E, with *distant* of 1820 chargeable to either Mary or the printer, and corrected in M from the errata list (Galignani: 1820).

22 [*robe*] *might*

23 [*shadowy*] *awful*

24 [*He shall descend &*] *To redescend*   The original *He shall descend* might appear a more accurate description of what Jupiter expects to happen, since neither the fatal child nor the incarnation (l. 46) has previously "descended." Probably, as F. A. Pottle suggested to me, the poet was simply being redundant (a circumstance that would follow from the demands of meter).

27 [*of Heaven*] *divine*

28 [*Let the*] *Ye all*

29 [*the*] *Earth* [*above*] *under*

30 [*living*] *circling*

ACT III

Heaven. Jupiter *on his Throne;* Thetis *and the other Deities as-sembled.*

Jupiter

Ye congregated powers of Heaven, who share
The glory and the strength of him ye serve,
Rejoice! henceforth I am omnipotent.
All else has been subdued to me; alone
The soul of man, like unextinguished fire,   5
Yet burns towards Heaven with fierce reproach, and doubt,
And lamentation, and reluctant prayer—
Hurling up insurrection, which might make
Our antique empire insecure, though built
On eldest faith, and Hell's coeval, fear.   10
And though my curses through the pendulous air,
Like snow on herbless peaks, fall flake by flake
And cling to it; though under my wrath's night
It climb the crags of life, step after step,
Which wound it, as ice wounds unsandalled feet,   15
It yet remains supreme o'er misery,
Aspiring, unrepressed, yet soon to fall:
Even now have I begotten a strange wonder,
That fatal child, the terror of the earth,
Who waits but till the destined Hour arrive,   20
Bearing from Demogorgon's vacant throne
The dreadful might of ever-living limbs
Which clothed that awful spirit unbeheld,
To redescend and trample out the spark.

Pour forth Heaven's wine, Idæan Ganymede,   25
And let it fill the dædal cups like fire;
And from the flower-inwoven soil divine
Ye all-triumphant harmonies arise,
As dew from earth under the twilight stars.
Drink! be the nectar circling through your veins   30

36 [*Shadow*] *Image* with *Image* the superior word in this context. (Cf. II.iv.146.)

39 [*Thy*] *The* and [*frame*] *being* with the latter to avoid the *flames-frame* echo.

44-45 [*Even*] [*Which now unbodied & invisible*] / *Between us, floats,* [*our mighty Progeny*] → received with [*al*]*though* Shelley's intent (E: *unbodied now* / *Between us,*) was changed by the 1820-M punctuation (*unbodied now,* / *Between us floats,*) In [*al*]*though* the deletion line is short and possibly was accidental. Mary either assumed the latter for *although* of 1820-M, or restored the syllable in the interests of meter.

47 [*winds*] *wheels*

49 E-1820: *Feel'st   Feelest* of M strengthens the line without loss of metrical integrity since the trochee is initial to the phrase. See note on I.341.

54 *as thou* [*art*] *wert Saturns* ⟨option: *Rheas*⟩ *child . . .* ⟨sic⟩

55 [*pent*] *together*

The soul of joy, ye ever-living Gods,
Till exultation burst in one wide voice
Like music from Elysian winds. . . .
                    And thou!
Ascend beside me, veilèd in the light
Of the desire which makes thee one with me,   35
Thetis, bright image of eternity!
When thou didst cry, 'Insufferable might!
God! Spare me! I sustain not the quick flames,
The penetrating presence; all my being,
Like him whom the Numidian seps did thaw   40
Into a dew with poison, is dissolved,
Sinking through its foundations'—even then
Two mighty spirits, mingling, made a third
Mightier than either, which, unbodied now
Between us, floats, felt although unbeheld,   45
Waiting the incarnation, which ascends—
Hear ye the thunder of the fiery wheels
Griding the winds?—from Demogorgon's throne.
Victory! victory! Feelest thou not, O World,
The earthquake of his chariot thundering up   50
Olympus?
[*The Car of the* Hour *arrives.* Demogorgon *descends
   and moves towards the Throne of* Jupiter.]
         Awful shape, what art thou? Speak!

          Demogorgon

Eternity. Demand no direr name.
Descend, and follow me down the abyss.
I am thy child, as thou wert Saturn's child,
Mightier than thee; and we must dwell together   55
Henceforth in darkness. Lift thy lightnings not.
The tyranny of Heaven none may retain,
Or reassume, or hold, succeeding thee:
Yet if thou wilt—as 'tis the destiny
Of trodden worms to writhe till they are dead—   60
Put forth thy might.

68 [*mild if he is now*] *dreadless*

69 The omission of E's *then* in 1820 was either Mary's or the printer's error, corrected in M from the errata (Galignani: 1820).

70-71 *No* [*respite*] *refuge, no appeal*— . . . ⟨sic⟩ [*Defiance*] → [*then shall we sink*] → [*Let* [*loose*] *Hell unlock*] → [*Together then / Shall we* [*be drowned in ruin fathomless*] *sink down upon the stream of ruin*] → received.

71 In this context *will* of 1820-M is preferable to *shall* of E, the latter carried over from its more defensible use in the draft (see above). *on* of 1820-M appears to be just that in E, with a dot over a thin *o*, but I believe that the intent was to balance *in* here and *Into* of l. 74, and that the letter is an intended *i*, easily misread by Mary in copying.

72 [*like*] *as*

73 [*Sink*] *Drop*

75 [*Thy*] *Its*

76 [*Swallow*] *And* [*let*] *whelm*

77 The discrepancy between *The* of E and *This* of 1820-M is an important one, and I believe that sense calls for *The* Jupiter is speaking in Heaven, and nowhere in the poem does Shelley confuse *Heaven* and *world* (as earth)— only eight lines above, Jupiter has referred to Prometheus as *The monarch of the world*. If *This* is used, l. 77 would reverse the normal practice and equate *Heaven* with *world*. It seems clear that, beginning with l. 74, Jupiter is making one last effort for final victory, commanding that if he falls all creation shall fall with him—including *the world* for which he and Prometheus (and, finally, Demogorgon) have combated. He fails: *The elements obey me not* (l. 80), and the *enemy above / darkens my fall with victory* (ll. 82-83).   *thee* (l. 77) is ambiguous, but probably refers to Demogorgon as the immediate cause of the overthrow, rather than to Prometheus, who would be included in the *desolated world*. 1820-M corrected the faulty *thou* of E to *thee*.

80 This line is followed by: [*Down down down down dizzily, far & deep / Ever ever*]

82 [*mine*] *the*   Since *the* was apparently not in the errata list it is possible that Shelley reverted to *mine* to balance l. 65.

Only ll. 12-17 of this scene are represented by known drafts, with other manuscript readings below from E.

2 *made* [*pale*] *dim*

3 The E punctuation (*stars.* as against *stars* with the comma pointing of 1820-M) indicates Shelley's intent and assists the reader's comprehension of these lines.

Jupiter

Detested prodigy!
Even thus beneath the deep Titanian prisons
I trample thee! . . . Thou lingerest?
                                 Mercy! mercy!
No pity, no release, no respite! Oh,
That thou wouldst make mine enemy my judge,   65
Even where he hangs, seared by my long revenge,
On Caucasus! He would not doom me thus.
Gentle, and just, and dreadless, is he not
The monarch of the world? What then art thou? . . .
No refuge! no appeal!
                        Sink with me then—   70
We two will sink in the wide waves of ruin,
Even as a vulture and a snake outspent
Drop, twisted in inextricable fight,
Into a shoreless sea. Let Hell unlock
Its mounded oceans of tempestuous fire,   75
And whelm on them into the bottomless void
The desolated world, and thee, and me,
The conqueror and the conquered, and the wreck
Of that for which they combated.
                              Ai! Ai!
The elements obey me not. I sink   80
Dizzily down—ever, forever, down;
And, like a cloud, mine enemy above
Darkens my fall with victory! Ai! Ai!

SCENE II

The Mouth of a great River in the Island Atlantis. Ocean *is discovered reclining near the Shore;* Apollo *stands beside him.*

Ocean

He fell, thou sayest, beneath his conqueror's frown?

Apollo

Aye, when the strife was ended which made dim
The orb I rule, and shook the solid stars.
The terrors of his eye illumined Heaven

5 *With* [*crimson*] *sanguine*

12 Draft: *tempest baffled*   E: *Caucasus*[:][;],
13 E: *Intangled   Entangled* of 1820-M avoided both the obsolescent spelling and the objectionable *in-in-wind* echo.
14 Draft: *Which gazed* [*undazzled*] *on the sun, now* [*saw*] → received.
15 E: [*when*] *while*

22 The hyphen between *many* and *peopled* is present in E but sufficiently
light to have been missed by Mary for 1820-M. It is, of course, essential to
exact meaning.

26 [*unladen*] *light-laden*   At this point the hyphen is clear, and its omission
in 1820-M leads to an unfortunate ambiguity.
27 [*which is*] *its* [*unseen*] *sightless*

32 *and odours* [*sweet*] → received.
33 [*frank*] *free*

With sanguine light through the thick ragged skirts   5
Of the victorious Darkness, as he fell—
Like the last glare of day's red agony,
Which from a rent among the fiery clouds
Burns far along the tempest-wrinkled deep.

Ocean

He sunk to the abyss? to the dark void?   10

Apollo

An eagle so, caught in some bursting cloud
On Caucasus, his thunder-baffled wings
Entangled in the whirlwind, and his eyes,
Which gazed on the undazzling sun, now blinded
By the white lightning, while the ponderous hail   15
Beats on his struggling form, which sinks at length
Prone, and the aerial ice clings over it.

Ocean

Henceforth the fields of heaven-reflecting sea
Which are my realm, will heave, unstained with blood,
Beneath the uplifting winds, like plains of corn   20
Swayed by the summer air; my streams will flow
Round many-peopled continents, and round
Fortunate isles; and from their glassy thrones
Blue Proteus and his humid nymphs shall mark
The shadow of fair ships—as mortals see   25
The floating bark of the light-laden moon
With that white star, its sightless pilot's crest,
Borne down the rapid sunset's ebbing sea—
Tracking their path no more by blood and groans,
And desolation, and the mingled voice   30
Of slavery and command, but by the light
Of wave-reflected flowers, and floating odours,
And music soft, and mild, free, gentle voices,
That sweetest music, such as spirits love.

Apollo

And I shall gaze not on the deeds which make   35
My mind obscure with sorrow, as eclipse

39 *i[n]*   *on* of 1820 could well have been a misreading of the transcript by the printer, especially if Mary gave *in*. For the present reading see note on I.745. The errata list possibly accounted for *i'* of M (Galignani: 1820). With respect to the question mark after *away* in E, it can be assumed that Ocean is in a position to understand the meaning of the lute without asking the question. Either Mary or Shelley might well have noticed this.

40 [*noon* ⟨?⟩] *even*

41 [*Hark the loud Deep calls me home too, to feed it*]   →   received.

45 *Streams* was susceptible of misreading as *stream* by Mary for 1820-M, but I am reasonably sure that the *s* is present. *streams* (currents) better fits the context. It is unusual for Shelley to leave a combination like *streams-streaming* (note the change from *too-to* in l. 41).

48 SD: The change from *The roar* of E to *A sound* of 1820-M must be ascribed to Shelley.

There are no known drafts for this scene, and all manuscript readings below are from E.

SD The full stop after *Spirits* (corresponding to *Spirits—* of E) corrects the misleading *Spirits,* (with comma) of 1820-M since the car probably contained only Asia, Panthea, and the Spirit of the Hour.

8 It can be assumed that Shelley made or approved the change of tense from *make* of E to *made* of 1820-M. The long years of pain are now over.

Darkens the sphere I guide.—But list, I hear
The small, clear, silver lute of the young spirit
That sits in the morning star.

Ocean

Thou must away;
Thy steeds will pause at even—till when, farewell.   40
The loud deep calls me home even now, to feed it
With azure calm out of the emerald urns
Which stand forever full beside my throne.
Behold the Nereids under the green sea—
Their wavering limbs borne on the windlike streams,   45
Their white arms lifted o'er their streaming hair
With garlands pied and starry sea-flower crowns—
Hastening to grace their mighty sister's joy.

> [*A sound of waves is heard.*]

It is the unpastured sea hungering for calm.
Peace, monster! I come now! Farewell.

Apollo

Farewell.   50

SCENE III

Caucasus. Prometheus, Hercules, Ione, *the* Earth, Spirits. Asia *and* Panthea *borne in the Car with the* Spirit of the Hour. Hercules *unbinds* Prometheus, *who descends.*

Hercules

Most glorious among spirits, thus doth strength
To wisdom, courage, and long-suffering love,
And thee, who art the form they animate,
Minister, like a slave.

Prometheus

Thy gentle words
Are sweeter even than freedom long desired   5
And long delayed.
Asia, thou light of life,
Shadow of beauty unbeheld; and ye
Fair sister nymphs, who made long years of pain

10 *let us not* ⟨option: *we will not*⟩

17 *Hang downward,* ⟨option: *Cling pendent*⟩ *raining* [*down*] *forth*   The revision avoided the *downward-down* echo.

25 [*For*] *What*

27 *shall* of E was changed to the conventional *thou . . . shalt* for 1820 but returned to *shall* in M (Galignani: 1820). The M change could have been a printer's error, but it is possible also that considerations of euphony dictated the alteration (from the errata list?) since *shalt chant* is both unharmonious and awkward.

30 *flowers,* [*& make*] *& beams   & make* was recovered for l. 31.

36 [*till,*] *and*   The comma (probably accidentally deleted, and omitted in 1820-M) suggests Shelley's original intent as to the phrasing here.

40 [*For*] *And thither   hither* of 1820-M reestablishes the emphasis on the existing cave and its surroundings (ll. 10-21) after the projection into the future of ll. 22-39.

Sweet to remember, through your love and care:
Henceforth we will not part. There is a cave,   10
All overgrown with trailing odorous plants
Which curtain out the day with leaves and flowers,
And paved with veinèd emerald; and a fountain
Leaps in the midst with an awakening sound.
From its curved roof the mountain's frozen tears,   15
Like snow, or silver, or long diamond spires,
Hang downward, raining forth a doubtful light;
And there is heard the ever-moving air,
Whispering without from tree to tree, and birds,
And bees; and all around are mossy seats,   20
And the rough walls are clothed with long soft grass:
A simple dwelling, which shall be our own,
Where we will sit and talk of time and change
As the world ebbs and flows, ourselves unchanged—
What can hide man from mutability?   25
And if ye sigh, then I will smile; and thou,
Ione, shall chant fragments of sea-music,
Until I weep, when ye shall smile away
The tears she brought, which yet were sweet to shed.
We will entangle buds and flowers, and beams   30
Which twinkle on the fountain's brim, and make
Strange combinations out of common things,
Like human babes in their brief innocence;
And we will search, with looks and words of love,
For hidden thoughts, each lovelier than the last,   35
Our unexhausted spirits, and, like lutes
Touched by the skill of the enamoured wind,
Weave harmonies divine, yet ever new,
From difference sweet where discord cannot be.
And hither come—sped on the charmèd winds   40
Which meet from all the points of heaven, as bees
From every flower aerial Enna feeds
At their known island-homes in Himera—
The echoes of the human world, which tell
Of the low voice of love, almost unheard,   45
And dove-eyed pity's murmured pain, and music,
Itself the echo of the heart, and all

50-53 This difficult and involved passage is made somewhat easier to grasp if *as . . . reality* and *whence . . . phantoms* are set off, as first done by Rossetti. E-M: commas only.

55 *rapt* is clear in E, and *wrapt* might well have been an error of the printer in 1820, corrected in M from the errata list (Galignani: 1820).

59 I have followed Robert Bridges (*The Spirit of Man,* London, 1916, item 68 [see *Variorum,* pp. 238-39]) in the capitalization of *Love,* which here requires the intensification not called for in l. 45. Neville Rogers ("Punctuation," p. 24) has described Bridges' use as a "masterly touch" since it "at once personifies the Power that Prometheus and Asia worship, and who gives back (my lower cases are important) love for love—the winged δαίμων who as an intermediary between divine and mortal can, as shown in the drama, 'bind together the whole universe of things.' "

70 It is possible that Shelley intended the E reading (*this the*) and that it was restored in M from the errata list to correct *this is the* of 1820 (and Galignani). But it is more probable that, as Forman suggested (Edition, 2, 224 n.) the dropping of *is* in M was an accident of the press (where *is* after *this* is "peculiarly liable" to be omitted; he compared IV.554, q.v.). There can be little question that 1820 offers the more natural and effective reading.

That tempers or improves man's life, now free.
And lovely apparitions, dim at first,
Then radiant—as the mind, arising bright   50
From the embrace of beauty (whence the forms
Of which these are the phantoms) casts on them
The gathered rays which are reality—
Shall visit us, the progeny immortal
Of Painting, Sculpture, and rapt Poesy,   55
And arts, though unimagined, yet to be.
The wandering voices and the shadows these
Of all that man becomes, the mediators
Of that best worship, Love, by him and us
Given and returned; swift shapes and sounds which grow   60
More fair and soft as man grows wise and kind,
And veil by veil evil and error fall:
Such virtue has the cave and place around.
                    [*Turning to the* Spirit of the Hour.]
For thee, fair Spirit, one toil remains. Ione,
Give her that curvèd shell which Proteus old   65
Made Asia's nuptial boon, breathing within it
A voice to be accomplished, and which thou
Didst hide in grass under the hollow rock.

Ione

Thou most desired Hour, more loved and lovely
Than all thy sisters, this is the mystic shell;   70
See the pale azure fading into silver,
Lining it with a soft yet glowing light:
Looks it not like lulled music sleeping there?

Spirit

It seems in truth the fairest shell of Ocean;
Its sound must be at once both sweet and strange.   75

Prometheus

Go, borne over the cities of mankind
On whirlwind-footed coursers: once again
Outspeed the sun around the orbèd world;
And as thy chariot cleaves the kindling air,
Thou breathe into the many-folded shell,   80

83-84 Between these lines E has an undeleted but unused SD: *kissing the ground* which is compensated for in l. 85. (See n. on I.106.)

85 *their touch* is clear in E, with *thy touch* of 1820-M possibly the result of transfer and uncorrected in M. The reference is clearly to *lips*

95 [*Sucking*] *Draining*

98 The correctly pointed *wind,* (there is no comma in E-1820) was initiated by Galignani, and so to M.

102 *unwithering* [*colours as they dream*] *hues unwithering* might easily have been misread by Mary as *unwitting* for 1820 since the *t* crossing also crosses the shaft of *h* The M correction was probably from the errata list (Galignani: 1820).

110 [*The*] *It*

Loosening its mighty music; it shall be
As thunder mingled with clear echoes. Then
Return, and thou shalt dwell beside our cave.
And thou, O Mother Earth!—

The Earth

I hear, I feel;
Thy lips are on me, and their touch runs down   85
Even to the adamantine central gloom
Along these marble nerves—'tis life, 'tis joy,
And through my withered, old, and icy frame
The warmth of an immortal youth shoots down,
Circling. Henceforth the many children fair   90
Folded in my sustaining arms—all plants,
And creeping forms, and insects rainbow-winged,
And birds, and beasts, and fish, and human shapes,
Which drew disease and pain from my wan bosom,
Draining the poison of despair—shall take   95
And interchange sweet nutriment; to me
Shall they become like sister-antelopes
By one fair dam, snow-white and swift as wind,
Nursed among lilies near a brimming stream.
The dew-mists of my sunless sleep shall float   100
Under the stars like balm; night-folded flowers
Shall suck unwithering hues in their repose;
And men and beasts in happy dreams shall gather
Strength for the coming day and all its joy;
And death shall be the last embrace of her   105
Who takes the life she gave, even as a mother,
Folding her child, says, 'Leave me not again!'

Asia

O mother! wherefore speak the name of death?
Cease they to love, and move, and breathe, and speak,
Who die?

The Earth

It would avail not to reply: 110
Thou art immortal, and this tongue is known

112 [*Only*] *But*

114 [*Men*] *They*

124 It may be assumed that Mary, or Shelley himself, replaced *cavern whence* of E with the contextually more correct *cavern where* of 1820-M.

126 *those that* of M was introduced by Galignani and uncorrected for M.

131 [*Which now floats upward*] *Which breath*   If Mary replaced *among* of E with *amongst* in 1820-M it was, as Freeman noted ("Text," p. 47), with a loss of euphony.

138 [*Starring*] *Which star*   Before *Which star* (on the facing page) are two words that look like *She dhart* but that have never been satisfactorily identified. Locock's suggestion that each *h* might be a malformed *p* with a resulting *sped past* (for an intended *speed past* as an option for *rain through* in the next line—Edition, *1*, 620) was ingenious, but I doubt that Shelley would omit the downstroke of *p* twice. The words do not appear to have been written at the same time as Earth's speech and may in fact be irrelevant to this passage.

142 I.e. *It* (of l. 135 [the *breath* of l. 131]) also feeds the flowers, etc.

145 [*hum of fountain-gathered dreams*] → received.

147 *that cave* of E is contextually superior to *This cave* of 1820-M (a possible transfer from l. 148?). Shelley's intent seems clear from the parallel use in l. 175.

But to the uncommunicating dead.
Death is the veil which those who live call life:
They sleep, and it is lifted; and meanwhile
In mild variety the seasons mild—   115
With rainbow-skirted showers, and odorous winds,
And long blue meteors cleansing the dull night,
And the life-kindling shafts of the keen sun's
All-piercing bow, and the dew-mingled rain
Of the calm moonbeams, a soft influence mild—   120
Shall clothe the forests and the fields—aye, even
The crag-built deserts of the barren deep—
With ever-living leaves, and fruits, and flowers.
And thou! There is a cavern where my spirit
Was panted forth in anguish whilst thy pain   125
Made my heart mad, and those who did inhale it
Became mad too, and built a temple there,
And spoke, and were oracular, and lured
The erring nations round to mutual war,
And faithless faith, such as Jove kept with thee—   130
Which breath now rises, as among tall weeds
A violet's exhalation, and it fills
With a serener light and crimson air
Intense, yet soft, the rocks and woods around;
It feeds the quick growth of the serpent vine,   135
And the dark linked ivy tangling wild,
And budding, blown, or odour-faded blooms
Which star the winds with points of coloured light
As they rain through them, and bright golden globes
Of fruit, suspended in their own green heaven,   140
And, through their veinèd leaves and amber stems,
The flowers whose purple and translucid bowls
Stand ever mantling with aerial dew,
The drink of spirits. And it circles round,
Like the soft waving wings of noonday dreams,   145
Inspiring calm and happy thoughts, like mine,
Now thou art thus restored. That cave is thine.
Arise! Appear!
                    [*A Spirit rises in the likeness of a winged
                        child.*]

159 Shelley used the currently poetic pronunciation *crystálline*.

161 This line is followed by: [*Which bore thy name ere faith was o⟨ld?⟩*]

163 *capitals* of E was probably made the generic singular in 1820-M to agree
with the similar use of *column* above.

164 It is surprising that the awkward transposition (*most with*) of 1820 was
not corrected in M, but it was probably missed for the errata list.

165-66 Locock (*Examination*, p. 75) first noted the following (a parallel
rather than a draft) in Bodleian MS Shelley E.4: *Praxitelean shapes whose
marble smiles | Filled the mute air*

168 [*and ardent*] *there the emulous*

170 [*when*] *which*

174 [*high*] *far*

175 *Beside* [*it*] *is the destined Cave* ... ⟨sic⟩ [*depart!*]   →   received.

SD E: *Scene*=[*The* [*hut*] *f⟨orest⟩*] *A forest   Ione Panthea Prometheus Asia*
are numbered, respectively, 3   4   1   2   to indicate order.

1-130 There are no known drafts of these lines.

2 [*and*] *how*

    This is my torch-bearer,
Who let his lamp out in old time with gazing
On eyes from which he kindled it anew   150
With love, which is as fire, sweet daughter mine,
For such is that within thine own. Run, wayward!
And guide this company beyond the peak
Of Bacchic Nysa, Mænad-haunted mountain,
And beyond Indus and its tribute rivers,   155
Trampling the torrent streams and glassy lakes
With feet unwet, unwearied, undelaying;
And up the green ravine, across the vale,
Beside the windless and crystalline pool
Where ever lies, on unerasing waves,   160
The image of a temple, built above,
Distinct with column, arch, and architrave,
And palm-like capital, and overwrought,
And populous with most living imagery—
Praxitelean shapes, whose marble smiles   165
Fill the hushed air with everlasting love.
It is deserted now, but once it bore
Thy name, Prometheus: there the emulous youths
Bore to thine honour through the divine gloom
The lamp which was thine emblem—even as those 170
Who bear the untransmitted torch of hope
Into the grave, across the night of life,
As thou hast borne it most triumphantly
To this far goal of time. Depart—farewell.
Beside that temple is the destined cave.   175

SCENE IV

A Forest. In the Background a Cave. Prometheus, Asia, Panthea,
Ione, *and the* Spirit of the Earth.

Ione

Sister, it is not earthly: how it glides
Under the leaves! how on its head there burns
A light, like a green star, whose emerald beams
Are twined with its fair hair! how, as it moves,
The splendour drops in flakes upon the grass!   5
Knowest thou it?

24 SD: *of the Earth* lacking. Opposite is an unused but undeleted SD for which there is no compensation in the text (see n. on I.106): *Asia & the spirit have entered the cave*

27 [W⟨hen⟩] *After*

Panthea

It is the delicate spirit
That guides the earth through heaven. From afar
The populous constellations call that light
The loveliest of the planets; and sometimes
It floats along the spray of the salt sea,   10
Or makes its chariot of a foggy cloud,
Or walks through fields or cities while men sleep,
Or o'er the mountain tops, or down the rivers,
Or through the green waste wilderness, as now,
Wondering at all it sees. Before Jove reigned   15
It loved our sister Asia, and it came
Each leisure hour to drink the liquid light
Out of her eyes, for which it said it thirsted
As one bit by a dipsas; and with her
It made its childish confidence, and told her   20
All it had known or seen, for it saw much,
Yet idly reasoned what it saw; and called her—
For whence it sprung it knew not, nor do I—
'Mother, dear mother.'

The Spirit of the Earth [*running to* Asia]
                    Mother, dearest mother;
May I then talk with thee as I was wont?   25
May I then hide mine eyes in thy soft arms
After thy looks have made them tired of joy?
May I then play beside thee the long noons
When work is none in the bright silent air?

Asia

I love thee, gentlest being, and henceforth   30
Can cherish thee unenvied. Speak, I pray:
Thy simple talk once solaced, now delights.

Spirit of the Earth

Mother, I am grown wiser, though a child
Cannot be wise like thee, within this day;
And happier too: happier and wiser both.   35
Thou knowest that toads, and snakes, and loathly worms,

47-48 Not set off in E, but parentheses supplied in 1820-M.

53 *A sentinel* of 1820-M (probably a slip by Mary or the printer, and missed for the errata list) is less exact in meaning than is *The* of E, even though the latter results in an unfortunate repetition within the line.

56 [*But*] *Than*

60 *heaven* (*Heaven* in E-M) has been preferred here on the assumption that the inhabitants are looking, not towards Jupiter's realm but towards the spheres.

63 [*a*] *the reflex*

71 [*Was* ⟨?⟩] *Were*

And venomous and malicious beasts, and boughs
That bore ill berries in the woods, were ever
A hindrance to my walks o'er the green world;
And that, among the haunts of humankind,   40
Hard-featured men, or with proud, angry looks,
Or cold, staid gait, or false and hollow smiles,
Or the dull sneer of self-loved ignorance,
Or other such foul masks with which ill thoughts
Hide that fair being whom we spirits call man;   45
And women too, ugliest of all things evil—
Though fair, even in a world where thou art fair,
When good and kind, free and sincere like thee—
When false or frowning made me sick at heart
To pass them, though they slept, and I unseen.   50
Well, my path lately lay through a great city
Into the woody hills surrounding it.
The sentinel was sleeping at the gate—
When there was heard a sound, so loud, it shook
The towers amid the moonlight, yet more sweet   55
Than any voice but thine, sweetest of all;
A long, long sound, as it would never end:
And all the inhabitants leapt suddenly
Out of their rest, and gathered in the streets,
Looking in wonder up to heaven, while yet   60
The music pealed along. I hid myself
Within a fountain in the public square,
Where I lay like the reflex of the moon
Seen in a wave under green leaves; and soon
Those ugly human shapes and visages,   65
Of which I spoke as having wrought me pain,
Passed floating through the air, and fading still
Into the winds that scattered them; and those
From whom they passed seemed mild and lovely forms
After some foul disguise had fallen; and all   70
Were somewhat changed; and after brief surprise
And greetings of delighted wonder, all
Went to their sleep again; and when the dawn
Came—wouldst thou think that toads, and snakes, and efts,
Could e'er be beautiful? yet so they were,   75

77 This line is followed by: [*Like an old garment soiled & overworn*]

81 *bunch* ⟨option: *mass*⟩

84 A possible option for *of these* may be present in what Zupitza read as [*those*] *from* (i.e. *full of these happy changes* or *full from happy changes*).

86 [*and*] *till thy* [*cold chaste*] [*cold*] *chaste Sister*

87 *and the inconstant* of E (with *the* inserted) was restored to the superior reading *and inconstant* for 1820-M.

88 *more* [*pure*] *warm*

94 [*lights*] *fires*

95 [*fills*] *trims*

96 [*Why*] *Tis*   An original dash after *darkling* was deleted and transferred to —*Listen*   This line is followed by: *Spirit | I hear & see,* ⟨space⟩ *but I must away*   If the unused line is assigned to the Spirit of the Earth, as it appears to be (the Spirit of the Hour, just arrived, would not say "but I must away"), it would not form a satisfactory transition to the speech of Prometheus, addressed as the latter is to the Spirit of the Hour. With the line omitted, Asia's *Listen! look!* offers a natural clue for the entrance of the Spirit of the Hour, announced by the SD (*Enter, the Spirit of the Hour* in E). The omitted line was clearly designed as a transition to this SD, but is too close in wording to Prometheus' line (97), which it would also make ambiguous.

98 [*thu*⟨nder⟩] *sound*

99 [*air,*] *sky*

And that with little change of shape or hue:
All things had put their evil nature off.
I cannot tell my joy, when o'er a lake,
Upon a drooping bough with nightshade twined,
I saw two azure halcyons clinging downward   80
And thinning one bright bunch of amber berries
With quick, long beaks, and in the deep there lay
Those lovely forms imaged as in a sky.
So, with my thoughts full of these happy changes,
We meet again, the happiest change of all.   85

Asia

And never will we part, till thy chaste sister,
Who guides the frozen and inconstant moon,
Will look on thy more warm and equal light
Till her heart thaw like flakes of April snow,
And love thee.

Spirit of the Earth

What! as Asia loves Prometheus?   90

Asia

Peace, wanton! thou art yet not old enough.
Think ye by gazing on each other's eyes
To multiply your lovely selves, and fill
With spherèd fires the interlunar air?

Spirit of the Earth

Nay, mother, while my sister trims her lamp   95
'Tis hard I should go darkling.

Asia

Listen! look!
[*The* Spirit of the Hour *enters.*]

Prometheus

We feel what thou hast heard and seen: yet speak.

Spirit of the Hour

Soon as the sound had ceased whose thunder filled
The abysses of the sky, and the wide earth,

101 [*The light*] *And*

106-08 E: no end punctuation. 1820-M: *down, plumes,* with a resulting ambiguous referent for *plumes* Since the coursers' flight (II.v.4) and wings
(below, l. 120) are established, Shelley's intent seems clear. With the vigorous
action (III.iii.78) accomplished, the coursers can now relax as they seek their
own utopia. (Moreover, *winnowing* does not suggest *floating* and *languid* is
hardly the word for the spirit's excitement at this moment.)

108 [*pastures*] *birthplace*

111 *And where my moonlike* [*chariot stands*] *within* → *received.*

112-17 *A temple,* [*underneath its* [*fretted*] *hollow dome* / *Poised on twelve
columns of resplendent stone,* ⟨see l. 117⟩ / [*And*] *Around stand Asia & the
Earth & thou* / *Prometheus, and the sisters of the Sea* / *In memory of the
tidings it has borne* ⟨see l. 115⟩ / *And*] *gazed upon by* [*living statues*] *Phidian
forms,* [*around*]   Note that the undeleted *A temple,* picks up *gazed* (following
the general deletion) to give l. 112, followed by the received 113-17 (with ll.
115-117 above repeated).

113 [*thou*] *thee*

114 [*thou*] *you* (not *yon* as Freeman thought).

116 *dome* [*which*] *fretted with* [*carven*] *graven*

118 [*all-surrounding Heaven*] *bright*

119 [*And*] [*Drawn by the likeness of those winged steeds*] → *received.*

121 *flight* is clear in E, and *light* of 1820 was more likely an error of the
press than a slip by Mary. It was corrected in M probably from the errata list
(Galignani: 1820).

123 [*untold*] *unsaid*   The altered word was susceptible of misreading by
Mary as *untold* (1820-M), but was probably restored by Shelley himself for the
transcription since it is not only a superior reading but avoids the *unsaid-said*
echo with l. 124.

131-99 Most of these lines are present in the drafts.

133, 137 Draft: *fawned* in both positions. The transposition of *fawned* and
frowned in these lines for 1820 (as against *frowned* [l. 133] and *fawned* [l. 137]
of E) was almost certainly done consciously to secure consistency in the con-
trasts on which the lines are built.

133 Draft: *trampled;* [*none*] *hate,*

134 Draft: [*No*] *Self love, or self contempt,* [*mid frowning looks*] → *received.*

135 Draft: [*as oer a tyrants*] *as*

137 Draft: *None fawned* and [*fear*] *awe*   E: See n. on ll. 133, 137,
above.

There was a change: the impalpable thin air   100
And the all-circling sunlight were transformed,
As if the sense of love dissolved in them
Had folded itself round the spherèd world.
My vision then grew clear, and I could see
Into the mysteries of the universe: 105
Dizzy as with delight I floated down.
Winnowing the lightsome air with languid plumes,
My coursers sought their birthplace in the sun,
Where they henceforth will live exempt from toil,
Pasturing flowers of vegetable fire;   110
And where my moonlike car will stand within
A temple—gazed upon by Phidian forms
Of thee, and Asia, and the Earth, and me,
And you fair nymphs, looking the love we feel,
In memory of the tidings it has borne—   115
Beneath a dome fretted with graven flowers,
Poised on twelve columns of resplendent stone,
And open to the bright and liquid sky.
Yoked to it by an amphisbænic snake
The likeness of those wingèd steeds will mock   120
The flight from which they find repose. Alas!
Whither has wandered now my partial tongue
When all remains untold which ye would hear?
As I have said, I floated to the earth:
It was, as it is still, the pain of bliss   125
To move, to breathe, to be; I wandering went
Among the haunts and dwellings of mankind,
And first was disappointed not to see
Such mighty change as I had felt within
Expressed in outward things; but soon I looked,   130
And behold! thrones were kingless, and men walked
One with the other even as spirits do:
None fawned, none trampled; hate, disdain, or fear,
Self-love or self-contempt, on human brows
No more inscribed, as o'er the gate of Hell,   135
'All hope abandon, ye who enter here';
None frowned, none trembled, none with eager fear

139-41 Draft lacking.

139 E: *[captive] subject*

140 E: *[subject] abject* (in its substantive use).

145 E: *remained* ⟨option: *creeps*⟩

147 E: *crept* ⟨option: *creeps*⟩

148-49 Draft: *with his own ill; none talked / The common vain false [yet like *ing] bitter hollow cold talk*

150 Draft: *makes the soul*

151 Draft: *the unmeant*

152 Draft: *With such distrust as naught   *   voice*

153 Draft: *[And so they all were lovely, and I] / Thus winged* → received.

154 Draft: *[blue] wide heaven which raining*

155 Draft: *free earth,*

157 Draft: *[Looking] the [knowledge] once they [dared] not think* → received.

158 E: *[Looked] Looking*   Draft: *dared [not [feel] have]* → received.

159 Draft: *[feared to be] dared not be*

160 Draft: *But being so [make] made*   E: *[And] Yet*   Although Shelley was to change to the present tense in the next sentence (ll. 164-72), the context here would confirm *made* (of 1820-M and the draft, as against *make* of E), with *now* an historical present.

161 Draft: *Nor jealousy nor [Shame or the]* → received.

162 Draft: *of [drops] those drops*

163 Draft: *earths* ⟨option: *the*⟩ *nepenthe,*

164-79 E: As Locock noted (Edition, *1*, 622), this difficult passage has led to "tomes of reasoned wrong" (see *Variorum*, pp. 256-57), largely, I believe, because Mary, Peacock or the printer apparently attempted to correct Shelley's loose punctuation, which admittedly needs some clarification. But in key positions Shelley's pointing, in E and the drafts, is the best guide to his intent here.

164 E: *[whereon] wherein*   The passage from *wherein* to *ignorance* (l. 167) is parenthetical, as Rossetti first noted (Edition, *1*, 499.)

165 Draft: *[whom] which*

168 Draft: *those hideous & barbaric [shapes] forms*   E: *those [hideous]* ⟨option: *monstrous*⟩ *secret*

169 Draft: *The [spectres of an un]remembered fame* → received with *[not] no more*

170 Draft: *yet look forth*

172 Draft: *crumbling round;*   E: Here, especially, the comma after *conquerors* (*conquerors:* in 1820-M) gives the surest clue to Shelley's intent. The comma invites the full pause after *round* (suggested in the draft by the semicolon but unpointed in E).

Gazed on another's eye of cold command,
Until the subject of a tyrant's will
Became, worse fate, the abject of his own,   140
Which spurred him, like an outspent horse, to death;
None wrought his lips in truth-entangling lines
Which smiled the lie his tongue disdained to speak;
None, with firm sneer, trod out in his own heart
The sparks of love and hope, till there remained   145
Those bitter ashes, a soul self-consumed,
And the wretch crept, a vampire among men,
Infecting all with his own hideous ill;
None talked that common, false, cold, hollow talk
Which makes the heart deny the *yes* it breathes,   150
Yet question that unmeant hypocrisy
With such a self-mistrust as has no name.
And women, too, frank, beautiful, and kind
As the free heaven which rains fresh light and dew
On the wide earth, passed: gentle, radiant forms,   155
From custom's evil taint exempt and pure;
Speaking the wisdom once they could not think,
Looking emotions once they feared to feel,
And changed to all which once they dared not be,
Yet being now, made earth like heaven; nor pride,   160
Nor jealousy, nor envy, nor ill shame,
The bitterest of those drops of treasured gall,
Spoilt the sweet taste of the nepenthe, love.

Thrones, altars, judgment-seats, and prisons—wherein,
And beside which, by wretched men were borne   165
Sceptres, tiaras, swords, and chains, and tomes
Of reasoned wrong glozed on by ignorance—
Were like those monstrous and barbaric shapes,
The ghosts of a no more remembered fame,
Which, from their unworn obelisks, look forth   170
In triumph o'er the palaces and tombs
Of those who were their conquerors, mouldering round.

173-79 There are three drafts of these lines.

173-79 (1): [*Which Kings & Priests once destined to* *] [*Yet these which*
[*tyrants destined to* * / *This*] [*rulers made this*]] / *A dark yet mighty faith*
[*recorded then*] / *And world wide* [*desolation*] / *Not overthrown, but unregarded, then*

173-78 (2): [*Like these*] / *With which tyrants stamped a seal a* * / [*Ruins
of time*] *That they might mark, to its remotest* [*] *flight* / *A sunless power,
a dark yet mighty faith* / *A ruin wide as* [*where man dwells*] *is the world—
are now* / *But an astonishment, even so they stand* / [*Upon the* *] *Amid the
haunts & dwellings of mankind*

173 (3): [*And those whom they delivered*] *Which once imaged forth* [*a sunless power*] *to priests & kings* →   *They imaged to the* [*Pow⟨er⟩*] *strength of
Kings*   E: *These imaged* It is probable that Mary, or, more likely, Peacock, having arrived at the punctuation of l. 172 (*conquerors:*) for 1820, made
the necessary change to *Those* (l. 173) in that erroneous context, but succeeded
only in aggravating the false pointing of l. 172.

174 (3): [*power*] see (*i.e.,* a religious power).   175 E: *it* ⟨option: * *they*⟩

176-79 (3): *even as they stand* / *Amid the haunts & dwellings of mankind*
/ *Not overthrown, but unregarded, then.* / [*Emblems of fraud and s⟨in?⟩*]

179 E: Shelley's semicolon after *now* might serve, but the long, involved
passage is improved by the full stop of 1820-M.   180-89 Draft lacking.

181-88 The extended passage is clarified if these lines are set off by opening
and closing dashes, as Hutchinson did.   186 E: [*Slain at*] *Dragged to*

187 E: [*among*] *amid* The change was susceptible of misreading by Mary,
who gave *among* for 1820-M.   189 E: [*Stand*] *Frown* and   [*on*] *oer*

192-93 Draft: past tense for all verbs. The change to the present tense in E
was in keeping with the promise of this closing passage.

192 E: It is possible that Mary read *or* as an ampersand for 1820, with the
error (*and hoped*) uncorrected in M.

193-98 E: As at ll. 164-79, this passage too has been much discussed (see
Variorum, pp. 258-59), but again a careful reading of the manuscript offers a
reasonably certain clue as to the poet's intent.

194 E: *uncircumscribed* [*,*]:—*but man:*[—] (cf. l. 197). Shelley's intent was
lost when Mary or Peacock (or the printer?) gave *uncircumscribed* a comma
pause only, and left *man* unpointed.

197 Draft: *just wise sublime—but man*   E: *wise*[*,*]:—*but man:* Again
the unpointed *man* of 1820-M distorted Shelley's intent (see n. on l. 194).

198 Draft: *but free*   E: *Passionless*[*;*]? *no*—[*but*] *yet free from guilt*
[*&*] *or pain*

199 Draft: *suffered them* / [*And walking forth*] [*Erect, Perfect*] *erect the
ornament of Earth*   200-04 Draft lacking.

200 E: [*Though not*] *exempt,* [*yet*] *ruling* →   received.

202 [*Which clog that spirit, else which might outsoar*] →   received.

204 Below this line is *Prometheus* which led Zupitza to inquire if Shelley
intended to close the act with a speech by that character ("Zu . . . Prometheus,"
103, 106).

These imaged to the pride of kings and priests
A dark yet mighty faith, a power as wide
As is the world it wasted, and are now   175
But an astonishment; even so the tools
And emblems of its last captivity
Amid the dwellings of the peopled earth,
Stand, not o'erthrown, but unregarded now.
And those foul shapes, abhorred by God and man—   180
Which, under many a name and many a form,
Strange, savage, ghastly, dark, and execrable,
Were Jupiter, the tyrant of the world;
And which the nations, panic-stricken, served
With blood, and hearts broken by long hope, and love   185
Dragged to his altars soiled and garlandless,
And slain amid men's unreclaiming tears,
Flattering the thing they feared, which fear was hate—
Frown, mouldering fast, o'er their abandoned shrines.
The painted veil, by those who were, called life,   190
Which mimicked, as with colours idly spread,
All men believed or hoped, is torn aside;
The loathsome mask has fallen, the man remains
Sceptreless, free, uncircumscribed—but man:
Equal, unclassed, tribeless and nationless;   195
Exempt from awe, worship, degree; the king
Over himself; just, gentle, wise—but man:
Passionless? no—yet free from guilt or pain,
Which were, for his will made, or suffered them;
Nor yet exempt, though ruling them like slaves,   200
From chance, and death, and mutability,
The clogs of that which else might oversoar
The loftiest star of unascended heaven,
Pinnacled dim in the intense inane.

END OF THE THIRD ACT.

Huntington MS 2177 has the following lines which are suggestive of this scene, especially of ll. 164, 171, and 190: *What hast thou done then . . ⟨sic⟩ Lifted up and torn the [veil] / Which between that which seems & that which is, / Hangs oer the scene of life? with shapes uncertain / [within the pale,] / [Of] [All overwrought with vast tombs] & palaces / And [huts & prisons & heaps] / Confusedly overwrought—tombs palaces / Battles*

The drafts for Act IV are quite full, representing 496 of the 578 lines in the act, plus unused passages, and in many instances offering more than one draft of the same lines. They are found in Bodleian MS Shelley adds. e.12, in Huntington MSS 2176-77, in the *Mask of Anarchy* manuscript, and in a notebook in the Pforzheimer Library. The fair copy is in Bodleian MSS Shelley E.1 and (l. 251 only) E.3.

SD E: *Scene a [beautiful] forest near the cave of Prometheus—Panthea & Ione are [sitting beside a stream]* → received with *sleeping—[dreaming⟨?⟩]—*
SD E: *[Song] Voice of unseen spirits*

1-82 For Shelley's translation of these lines into Italian see *Variorum*, pp. 678-81.   1-8 There are two drafts of these lines.

1-4 (1): *The bright [stars] waves are [flashing] gone / With [Dawn] [the sun] Dawn their [old] [swift] grey shepherd / To the folds them compelling / [Where Arctos is rocking / Constellations to slumber]*

2 (2): *For [dawn] the Sun*

5 (2): *Comes forth in his mantle of light* → *[Has risen &] they flee* → *Comes, in robes of m⟨eteor ?⟩ ⟨space⟩ [array] light* → *Hastes, in [purple] & golden array* → received.

6 (2): *[And the blue [day] sky shuts]* → *To the* ⟨space⟩ *of his dwelling* → received with *[Behind] Beyond*

7 The E punctuation (*leopard . . .* [converted here for consistency to *leopard—*]) is superior in this context to the full stop of 1820 or the comma of M.

8 E: Locock commented: "Although the question is answered . . . by the 'train of dark Forms and Shadows,' it was probably addressed, not to them, but to the present and future Hours, whom the Unseen Spirits had arranged to meet at daybreak, and who answer the repetition of the call [at l. 55]" (Edition, *1*, 624).   SD: An undeleted *Panthea wakens* as part of the SD was undoubtedly omitted because it repeated the opening SD of the act.

11 Draft: *Of the [coffin they* ⟨space⟩ *& the buried] year* → received with [*cancelled*] *buried*

12 Draft: *[Ghosts] Spectres we*

13 Shelley was probably responsible for the change from *Of dead* in E to the superior *Of the dead* in 1820-M since the draft also has the latter.

14 Draft: *[bring] bear*

16 Draft: *[The] Deadly yew* → received.

17 Draft: *[And] wet the [dusty] pall with [cypress] dew* → received with [*dusty*] *grey*

19 Draft: *[Of poison] bowers* → received.

22 Draft: *As [the clouds] shades*

23 Draft: *[By the swift night cloud]* → received with *over Heavens* I agree with Locock that a full stop after *waste* (as in 1820-M; E is unpointed) spoils the sense (Edition, *1*, 624), but feel that his comma leaves an ambiguity that can be avoided by making the line parenthetical. The intent is not "haste . . . as shades are chased" but "As shades are chased ⟨so⟩ we melt away," and the first dash serves as a suspension to indicate this.

ACT IV

Scene: A Part of the Forest near the Cave of Prometheus. **Panthea**
and Ione *are sleeping: they awaken gradually during the first Song.*

Voice of unseen Spirits

The pale stars are gone!
For the sun, their swift shepherd,
To their folds them compelling
In the depths of the dawn,
Hastes, in meteor-eclipsing array, and they flee   5
Beyond his blue dwelling,
As fawns flee the leopard—
But where are ye?

[*A Train of dark Forms and Shadows passes by confusedly,
singing.*]

Here, oh here:
We bear the bier   10
Of the father of many a cancelled year!
Spectres we
Of the dead Hours be,
We bear Time to his tomb in eternity.

Strew, oh strew   15
Hair, not yew!
Wet the dusty pall with tears, not dew!
Be the faded flowers
Of Death's bare bowers
Spread on the corpse of the King of Hours!   20

Haste, oh haste!
As shades are chased—
Trembling, by Day, from heaven's blue waste—

24 Draft: *We [fly we] flee* → *We flee away*   E: *[flee] melt*

25 Draft: *[From the] Like the fleeting spray*

26 Draft: *Of the children of [immortality]* → received.

27-29 Shelley was strongly attracted to this idea. Compare unused lines at IV.116, 135. The same lines are in an unpublished stanza of *The world is dreary* (MS Shelley adds. e.12, p. 149).

28 Draft: *winds that lie*

30 E: SD *Ione [(awakening)]* (See n. on 1.8 SD.)

32 Draft: *[coil] spoil,*

33 Draft: *[Rolled] Raked*

34 Draft: *[which none] but One*

35 Draft: *It is past, it is past* → *They have past, they have past* with the received *Have they passed?* lacking.

36 *[It has outspeeded] They outspeeded*

37 Draft: *[They are gone, they are fled]* → received with *Whilst*

39 Draft: *To the cold, to the [dead] past to the dead* / *[What bright* / *Forms of light]* with the latter possibly an influence on l. 40.   E: *To the [cold, to] dark*

40-45 There are two drafts of these lines, as well as the following unused fragment: *The thin moon is hanging* / *In the whiteness of brightness* / *[As one dying] Weak & waning* / *[With pleasure]*

40-45 (1): *The [stars] clouds are in Heaven* / *The dew is on Earth* / *The waves are in ⟨option: on⟩ Ocean* / *Their legions are showers* / *By the panic of glee* / *[It shakes with emotion]*

40 (2): *[The] clouds [are] in Heaven* → received with *[Swift] Bright*

41 (2): *[The dew is] on Earth* → *Dew [Drops are] on Earth* → received.

42 (2): *[The] waves*

43 (2): *[Their legions are] driven* → received with *and* omitted.

44 (2): *By the blast By the panic of glee* with a tentative *[the storm of delight by]* → received with the deletion recovered for E.

45 (2): *[It] They*

We melt away,
Like dissolving spray,   25
From the children of a diviner day,
With the lullaby
Of winds that die
On the bosom of their own harmony.

Ione

What dark forms were they?   30

Panthea

The past Hours weak and grey,
With the spoil which their toil
    Raked together
From the conquest but One could foil.

Ione

Have they passed?

Panthea

                    They have passed;   35
They outspeeded the blast;
While 'tis said, they are fled—

Ione

Whither, oh whither?

Panthea

To the dark, to the past, to the dead.

Voice of unseen Spirits

Bright clouds float in heaven,   40
Dew-stars gleam on earth,
Waves assemble on ocean—
They are gathered and driven
By the storm of delight, by the panic of glee!
They shake with emotion,   45
They dance in their mirth—
    But where are ye?

49 Draft: [*gladness*] *joyance*   E: [*New*] *Old*

50 Draft: [*And*] *the* [*riv⟨ers⟩*] *fountains & billows*

51 Draft: [*Their*] *Fresh*

53-54 Draft: [*Beams start from their pillows*] → *The streams & the mountains / Are laughing with madness*

54 E: [*Both howl in their*] *With the thunder of*   Rossetti's conjecture (Edition, *1, 5*00) that *gladness* here (cf. 1. 49) was an oversight on Shelley's part for *madness* is supported by the draft. Locock's countering argument perhaps throws light on the reason for the change in E (if indeed it was not an uncorrected oversight): He felt that *madness* "would destroy the force of 'mock,' used here in the sense of 'playfully deceive.' The storms deceive the mountains with thunder which, after all, turns out to be merely 'the thunder of gladness' " (Edition, *1*, 624).

55 The following unused draft lines are relevant here: *The serpent & Dove / Are at play in the cedars / [Entwining enfolding] Their*

56 Draft lacking.   E: [*they*] *these*

57-77 Unused fragmented draft lines possibly relevant at this point include: *The spirits of the imperial / From [desolation] ruin, and thy sobs & Woe / [I am the Present, gathered next to me] / The [living] rapid hours are chainless are kingless / They will but pay [thee] you, * , blood & tears ⟨option: error⟩ / The bitter fruits [of the] uncultured years*

57-58 Draft: [*We are gathering up from the*] → *The voice of the mighty Son of the Earth / Has drawn back [one] the curtain of death & sleep*   E-M: *The voice ⟨. . .⟩ Have*   Although Locock (Edition, *1*, 560) cited ten examples of Shelley's use of a "plural verb with a technically singular but (in some respects) virtually plural subject," there is no reason for a modern edition to perpetuate this mannerism. Rossetti first made the correction silently, but E-M set the general pattern.

57 E: SD: [*Chorus of*] → [*Semichorus 1*] → received. 1820-M: *and of earth* holds closer to the anapestic pattern than does the *& earth* of E.

59 Draft: *our* [*dreamy life in the*] → *our dreamy birth*

60 Galignani initiated the overly forceful *Oh!* which carried into M.

61-62 Draft: [*We were dreaming of one sweet*] → [*For a hundred ages we had dreamed / Of [care] death & ruin & pain & care ⟨?⟩*] → *We had slept / Dreaming of hate & * & care ⟨?⟩*

62 E: [*dreams*] *visions*

64 Draft: [*Worse*] *More dread than* [*the*] *his*

65 Draft: [*She ⟨?⟩ has*] *We have heard the* [*harp*] *lute*

66, 68 E: *dream* is crowded into the margin, but is confirmed by a clear *beam* at l. 68. 1820-M returned to the superior draft reading *dreams-beams*

67 Draft: *felt the touch*   E: This line at first ended with *Power—* (the draft has *Power, & leap*) with the next speaker picking up the suspension with *And leap*, which was then deleted and *and leap—* added after *Power*[—],

      The pine boughs are singing
      Old songs with new gladness,
      The billows and fountains   50
      Fresh music are flinging,
Like the notes of a spirit, from land and from sea;
      The storms mock the mountains
      With the thunder of gladness—
        But where are ye?   55

Ione

What charioteers are these?

Panthea

        Where are their chariots?

Semichorus of Hours I

The voice of the spirits of air and of earth
Has drawn back the figured curtain of sleep
Which covered our being and darkened our birth
In the deep—

A Voice

In the deep?

Semichorus II

        Oh, below the deep.   60

Semichorus I

A hundred ages we had been kept
Cradled in visions of hate and care,
And each one who waked as his brother slept
Found the truth—

Semichorus II

        Worse than his visions were!

Semichorus I

We have heard the lute of Hope in sleep;   65
We have known the voice of Love in dreams;
We have felt the wand of Power, and leap—

68 There are two drafts of unused lines whose echo of ll. 65-67 suggests relevance here: (1): [*The shadow of thy glory mighty Titan*] / *And we dreamed of* [*Love*] *Hope embracing* [*Sorrow*] → *And we dreamed that* [*Love*] [*Hope*] *& Power might meet* → *The* [*dream*] *The* [*cloud*] *shade of thy glory mighty Titan* / *Like a rain cloud* [*which*] *over a frozen dell* / *Descends to soften awaken enlighten*   (2): *For the* [*light*] *blaze of thy glory Titan* / *Like the sunlight upon the vaporous sea* / *Descends to pierce awaken enlighten* / *And the light of our glory* / *Semi*⟨chorus⟩ / *Is thine,* [*or*] *is thee*   E: *beam* (see note on l. 66).

69 Draft: *on azure* [*wind*] *breeze*

70 Draft: [*Lift the*] *song to* [*the sphered*] *light*[*s*] → received with *to Heavens golden light*

71 Draft: [*Delay*] *Enchant*

72 Draft: *To check its* [*car at the cave*] *flight* with a separated *Night* apparently in as a hold for rime.   E: [*soothe*] *check*

73 Draft: *Once indeed, the Hours were hounds*

74 Draft: *chased* [*it*] *the day*   This line was followed by a deleted draft passage: [*Then within Sleep's uncertain bounds* / *It* [*slept*] [*rested*] [*crouched*] *& with eyes all wide with fear* / *But now like a fawn* [*it*] *lingers & listens* / *In the net of the music whose meshes are air* / *It is fed with the chrystal dew that glistens* / *In the flowers that*]

76 Draft: [*From night to night thro the*] *desart year* → received with *nightly* ⟨option: *rugged*⟩

77-78 Draft deleted, but restored with changes in E.

77 Draft: [*But now,* [*o*]—*weave the web of mystic measure*]   (Cf. received l. 129.)

78 Draft: [*Of* [*thot*] *Music & dance & shapes of light*]   This line was followed by: [*In the heart of Man with gladness & might*] / *Till we melt like mist on* ⟨*in?*⟩

79 Draft: *of pleasure*   E: *all Spirits* is clear. It was used, I believe, to relieve the repeated *the* in the preceding and following lines, and to give emphasis to the dominant note of *might and pleasure.* Yet I doubt that Mary would have made the change to *the* for 1820-M without Shelley's approval (the draft has *the*).

80 Draft: *Like the* [*beams of the* *] *cloud & the sun* ⟨option: *stars*⟩ *unite* ⟨?⟩ E: *the sunbeams*   Omission of *the* in 1820-M would, I believe, have been Shelley's change if he made the alteration in l. 79, since 1820 balances the structure in *of might and pleasure* above.

81-82 Draft lacking.

82 E: [*Clothed*] *in sweet* [*song,*] *like radiant* [*garments, come*] → received with *like radiant veils*

83-84 Draft: *We join the* [*dance*] [*song*] / *and the throng*

87 Draft: [*shore* ⟨?⟩] *deep*

89 Draft: *wild & fleet*

90 Draft: [*Like s*⟨*andals*⟩] *For*   92 Draft: *eyes are Love*

Semichorus II

As the billows leap in the morning beams!

Chorus

Weave the dance on the floor of the breeze,
Pierce with song heaven's silent light,   70
Enchant the Day that too swiftly flees,
To check its flight ere the cave of Night.

Once the hungry Hours were hounds
Which chased the Day like a bleeding deer,
And it limped and stumbled with many wounds   75
Through the nightly dells of the desert year.

But now—oh weave the mystic measure
Of music, and dance, and shapes of light;
Let the Hours and the spirits of might and pleasure,
Like the clouds and sunbeams, unite.

A Voice

Unite!   80

Panthea

See, where the Spirits of the human mind,
Wrapped in sweet sounds, as in bright veils, approach.

Chorus of Spirits

We join the throng
Of the dance and the song,
By the whirlwind of gladness borne along—   85
As the flying-fish leap
From the Indian deep,
And mix with the sea birds half asleep.

Chorus of Hours

Whence come ye, so wild and so fleet,
For sandals of lightning are on your feet,   90
And your wings are soft and swift as thought,
And your eyes are as love which is veilèd not?

95 Draft: *so [dark,] & [faint,] & blind* → received.

97 Draft: *Of [gentle] [e]motion] pure emotion*
98 Draft and E: *[Of] A*

99 Draft: fragmented but including: *[From mind to mind]* / *[From the source]* / *[A] deep Abyss* → received.

101 Draft: *[chambers] Caverns*
102-03 Draft: *[We come ⟨space⟩ the bowers]* → *[From the shade of bowers / of Paradise flowers]* → received with *the skiey*

104 Draft: *Are watching*

107 Draft: *catch ye [in woven caresses]* → received with *loose* ⟨option: wild⟩   E: *[loose] sliding* with *loose* then underlined for stet and option. With *sliding* unclear Shelley might well have been consulted for final choice.

110 Draft: *boats*
111-12 Draft: *[From the converse high* / *[Of Philosophy] Of the * & the eye]* → received.
115 Draft: *unsealed* ⟨option: *secret*⟩
116 Draft: *Where Science is dewily Dædal winged* ⟨with *[Is waxing the ba⟨ck⟩ of its]* probably related⟩ → *Where Science bedewily Dædal wings* At this point the draft has unused fragments of similes, including: *[Whose [voices] accents are beams of a]* / *[Like the sphered skies* / *Whose beaming seems clear music]* / *[Like the lullaby* ⟨option: *mixed with the sigh*⟩ / *Of winds that die* / *[On] In the bosom of their own harmony]* (With the last, cf. IV.27-29 and n.)   E: *her* is susceptible of the misreading *his* of 1820-M, and failure to include the change in the errata list was probably an oversight since Shelley elsewhere uses the feminine (e.g. *The Revolt of Islam* 2255, 3681).

118 Draft: *Thro the blood*
119 Draft: *And the Hell of [the hates] thots hatreds*
120 Draft: *[Half wading half flying]* → *[Like] We [flew] waded & flew*
121 Draft: *[islands] islets*
122 Draft: *Where [half]-blighted* → received.

Chorus of Spirits

We come from the mind
Of humankind,
Which was late so dusk, and obscene, and blind;   95
Now 'tis an ocean
Of clear emotion,
A heaven of serene and mighty motion;

From that deep abyss
Of wonder and bliss,   100
Whose caverns are crystal palaces;
From those skiey towers
Where Thought's crowned powers
Sit watching your dance, ye happy Hours;

From the dim recesses   105
Of woven caresses,
Where lovers catch ye by your loose tresses;
From the azure isles
Where sweet Wisdom smiles,
Delaying your ships with her siren wiles;   110

From the temples high
Of man's ear and eye,
Roofed over Sculpture and Poesy;
From the murmurings
Of the unsealed springs,   115
Where Science bedews her dædal wings.

Years after years,
Through blood, and tears,
And a thick hell of hatreds, and hopes, and fears,
We waded and flew,   120
And the islets were few
Where the bud-blighted flowers of happiness grew.

123-25 There are two drafts of these lines: (1): *The swiftness of* / ⟨124 lacking⟩ / *And the speed of its [spirit] [power] might is in our way*   (2): *[Now the speed in our palm]* → *Our feet each* ⟨option: *every*⟩ *palm* / ⟨124-25 received⟩

126 Draft: *[And in our] eyes* → received with *[Within] And*

127 Draft: *The love [lulling] lies* → received.

128 Draft: *all it looks on* ⟨option: *that it looks on* or *all that it looks on*⟩

129 E: This line is followed by: *[Of music & dance & shapes of light]*

130 Draft: *From the ends of the Earth & the depths of the sky*   With *mirth* (l. 132) thus left unrimed and with *by-harmony* present (ll. 133-34), Shelley probably transposed *Earth* and *sky* for E to supply a rime for *mirth*

132 Draft: *Join the dance*

133-34 Draft: *[As] [Like]* and   *rush by* / *[To the Ocean]*

134 Draft: *[With their own light & melody]* → *To an Ocean of light &* *[Music] harmony*

135-36 Transposed in the draft.

135 E: *[Away, away* / *We are]* → received. At this point in the draft the following unused stanza is present: *Away; away!* / *We are melted away* / *Like mist [of] in the warmth of the [widening] [long hot] day* / *[That] Like the lullaby* / *Of winds that die* / *On the bosom of their own harmony* (**Cf.** IV.27-29 and n.)

137 Draft: present but deleted.

138 Draft and E: *[&] or*   E: While susceptible of the 1820 reading *and* (*or* is on *&*), it is more probable that the return to *and* was made to vary the sequence involving *or*

139 Draft: *[The speeding] bound* → received.

140 Draft: *Which [with walls the] clips the world like a wall around*

141 Draft: *We will*   E: *[We've] We'll*

142 Draft: *Of starry skies* → received.

143 Draft: *Into the abyss*   E: *[old] hoar*

144-46 Draft: *And the sound of our flight* / *Will make Chaos & N⟨ight⟩* / *Flee like a * from the Earthquake*

146 E: *[mists] [dust] mist*

147 Draft: *[And the atoms of light]* → *[And of earth & the might]* → received with *[fire] earth*

149 Draft: *[aery] fiery*

150 Draft: *[And the shadows of mind]* → *[Hope Desire fear Love]* → *[And like the atoms of breath* → received with *And the love,*

151 Draft: *[Of [the] life change, & death]* → *Of all that scorns death* E: *[And] the*

152 Draft: *we float shall assemble [behind] beneath*

Our feet now, every palm,
Are sandalled with calm,
And the dew of our wings is a rain of balm;   125
And beyond our eyes
The human love lies
Which makes all it gazes on, paradise.

Chorus of Spirits and Hours

Then weave the web of the mystic measure:
From the depths of the sky and the ends of the earth,   130
Come, swift Spirits of might and of pleasure,
Fill the dance and the music of mirth—
As the waves of a thousand streams rush by
To an ocean of splendour and harmony!

Chorus of Spirits

Our spoil is won,   135
Our task is done,
We are free to dive, or soar, or run
Beyond and around,
Or within the bound
Which clips the world with darkness round.   140

We'll pass the eyes
Of the starry skies
Into the hoar deep to colonize;
Death, Chaos, and Night,
From the sound of our flight   145
Shall flee, like mist from a tempest's might;

And Earth, Air, and Light,
And the Spirit of Might
Which drives round the stars in their fiery flight;
And Love, Thought, and Breath,   150
The powers that quell Death,
Wherever we soar shall assemble beneath;

153-54 Draft: *Our singing shall build* / *On the Void's grey field*

155 Draft: *the Spirit of love*

158 Draft: *And [the] our*

160 Draft: *[remain] depart*

161 Draft: fragmented, but including: *[We with the spirits will haste along]* / *Us [the desart will]* / *[We will encompass]* / *We [with the [Spirits] Genii] are driven along* → received.

162 E: *[We] Us*

163 Draft: *[Ceaseless] & rapid, & [wild] fierce & free*
164 Draft: *that build*
165 Draft: *where till now [it] one*

169 Draft: *[We churn up the sea, & thro the]* → *[[We] let us sing [eer] [and] as we whirl]* → received with *[ball] sphere*
170-71 Transposed in the draft.
170 Draft: *[And the waves & the rocks & the]* → received with *And the trees*
171 Draft: *[And the atoms of chaos]* → *And the waves of its chaos are calm with love & fear*
172 Draft: *earth* / *Singing to* / *As*   E: *Oceans* (the plural undoubtedly intended) is clear, and *ocean* of 1820-M could have resulted either from overlooked faulty copy or error of the printer.
173-74 Draft lacking.

175 Draft: *Break* ⟨option: *Lead*⟩

    And our singing shall build,
    In the void's loose field,
A world for the Spirit of Wisdom to wield;   155
    We will take our plan
    From the new world of man,
And our work shall be called the Promethean.

Chorus of Hours

Break the dance, and scatter the song;
Let some depart and some remain.   160

Semichorus I

We, beyond heaven, are driven along—

Semichorus II

Us the enchantments of earth retain—

Semichorus I

Ceaseless, and rapid, and fierce, and free,
With the spirits which build a new earth and sea,
And a heaven where yet heaven could never be—   165

Semichorus II

Solemn, and slow, and serene, and bright,
Leading the day and outspeeding the night
With the powers of a world of perfect light—

Semichorus I

We whirl, singing loud, round the gathering sphere,
Till the trees, and the beasts, and the clouds appear   170
From its chaos made calm by love, not fear—

Semichorus II

We encircle the oceans and mountains of earth,
And the happy forms of its death and birth
Change to the music of our sweet mirth.

Chorus of Hours and Spirits

Break the dance, and scatter the song;   175

178 Draft: *In leashes of light, soft yet strong*

179 A partly-fragmented unused draft is present, probably intended for this context: [*Some remain, &*] / *As one swarm of populous bees* / *In a mossy islet* [*flower-*] *violet-paven* / *Sick with sweetness, on the breeze* / [*Wandering*] *seek another haven* / [*Wandering on the plains*] / *Others meanwhile,* [*golden stars*] / [*In a heaven of leaves*] *& flowers* / [*Build*] *their waxen citadels* / [*Under their*] *Among* [*those*] *ancestral bowers* / *In the* [*base*] [*stump*] *of the old pine tree* / *Which* [*murmurs*] *sings them*   E: An unused but unde-leted SD: *they depart* follows l. 179 and is compensated for in the next line.

180-84 Draft lacking.

180 E: First SD: [*Ione*] *Pan*⟨thea⟩

181 E: [*dry*] *green*

182 E: *cloud* [*of*] [*has loosed its*] → received.

183 E: [*orbed*] *sunny*

184 E: [*To the pale sky, my*] → received.

185 Draft: *Hark to* [*that*] *the awful sweetness of that sound*

186 Draft: [*It is*] *Tis*

187 Draft: [*Made living*] *Fathomless* → received.

189 Draft: *is* [*broken into*] *notes* → received.

191 Draft: *Which* [*Such as*] *pierce* [*into the spirit,*] *even to the inmost* → received.

192 Draft: *As the* [*clear*] *sharp starbeams pierce the wintry air* → received with *chrystal sky*

194 Draft: *And see*   E: [*And see*] *But see*

Let some depart, and some remain;
Wherever we fly we lead along
In leashes, like starbeams, soft yet strong,
The clouds that are heavy with love's sweet rain.

Panthea

Ha! they are gone!

Ione

            Yet feel you no delight   180
From the past sweetness?

Panthea

              As the bare green hill,
When some soft cloud vanishes into rain,
Laughs with a thousand drops of sunny water
To the unpavilioned sky!

Ione

              Even whilst we speak
New notes arise. What is that awful sound?   185

Panthea

'Tis the deep music of the rolling world,
Kindling within the strings of the waved air
Æolian modulations.

Ione

            Listen too,
How every pause is filled with under-notes,
Clear, silver, icy, keen, awakening tones,   190
Which pierce the sense, and live within the soul,
As the sharp stars pierce winter's crystal air
And gaze upon themselves within the sea.

Panthea

But see where, through two openings in the forest
Which hanging branches overcanopy,   195

196 Draft: *two [bra⟨nches⟩] runnels of the rivulet*

197 Draft: *[Among] Between*

198 Draft: *of [music] melody, like [friends] sisters,*   E: *[friends] sisters*

199 Draft: *Which part [awhile] that they may meet [again]* → received with *Which part* and *with smiles*

200-01 Draft: *their [sweet] dear disunion to an isle / [Which] [Of talk, [whose shades were] whose sweet shade remains with boughs entwined forever]* → *[Of [gen⟨tle⟩] talk, whose * oer each other]* → *a labyrinth of sweets, and* → *Of lovely [talk] grief, [whose sobs were sweet] thoughts,* → received.

203 Draft: *The [billowy] Oceanlike*

204 E: *[calmer] keener*

206 Draft: *the [delicate] thin ⟨option: pointed⟩ boat*

207 Draft: *[Of the young Mother of the Moon, [golden] whose hollow horns appear / To flow [in] & [fade] mingle with the livid [air] sky;]* → received with *Where[in] By which the [young] mother*

208-09 Transposed in the draft.

208 Draft: *Into [the] her western cave, by ebbing light / [Which leaps around]*   E: Mary probably took the *li* of *light* for a poorly formed *n* with a dot over the body of the latter (it could be so read). The superior *light* (confirmed by the draft) apparently did not find its way into the errata list.

209 Draft: *interlunar sleep*

210 Draft: *[Leave] Oer which there is*   M: *curbed* was clearly a typographical error, uncorrected in M².

211 Draft: *hills & [caverns] [trees] forests*

212 Draft: *Seen [through that] more distinctly thro that [from the] mist* E: *aery* is clear, and an acceptable poetic spelling, but *airy* of 1820-M avoids a possible ambiguity.

214 Draft: *[A chariot] Its wheels*

217 Draft: *[sails] rushes*

218 Draft: *wind / [And scarcely bend]*

219 Draft: *And in it sits a [winged child] Infant, [fairer than] white*   E: *[br⟨ight⟩] white*

221 Shelley apparently, and surprisingly, did not notice that a natural reading results in a tetrameter for this (and probably for the next) line.

221 Draft: *like ⟨option: as⟩*   E: *[like] as*

222-223 Draft: *[And its] Its* and *folds / [Of vapours] Of its [pink] white robe,*

225 (first half) Draft: *in [finest] strings*   E: *strings* is clear, with *string* of 1820 the result of poor copy or printer's error, and with the correction in M probably from the errata list (Galignani: 1820).

And where two runnels of a rivulet,
Between the close moss, violet-inwoven,
Have made their path of melody—like sisters
Who part with sighs that they may meet in smiles,
Turning their dear disunion to an isle   200
Of lovely grief, a wood of sweet sad thoughts—
Two visions of strange radiance float upon
The ocean-like enchantment of strong sound,
Which flows intenser, keener, deeper yet
Under the ground and through the windless air.   205

      Ione

I see a chariot—like that thinnest boat
In which the mother of the months is borne
By ebbing light into her western cave
When she upsprings from interlunar dreams—
O'er which is curved an orblike canopy   210
Of gentle darkness, and the hills and woods,
Distinctly seen through that dusk airy veil,
Regard like shapes in an enchanter's glass;
Its wheels are solid clouds, azure and gold,
Such as the genii of the thunderstorm   215
Pile on the floor of the illumined sea
When the sun rushes under it; they roll
And move and grow as with an inward wind.
Within it sits a wingèd infant: white
Its countenance, like the whiteness of bright snow;   220
Its plumes are as feathers of sunny frost;
Its limbs gleam white through the wind-flowing folds
Of its white robe, woof of æthereal pearl;
Its hair is white—the brightness of white light
Scattered in strings; yet its two eyes are heavens   225

---

225 (last half)-228 There are two drafts of these lines: (1): [*like gentle gos-
samer*] → [*its scattered*] → [*and on its delicate brow* | *It bears a gleam-
ing moonbeam for a wand* ⟨cf. l. 231⟩] → *its eyes seem * spread* → *but*
[*its*] *eyes* [*are like*] | *Two Heavens of* [*azure*] *liquid darkness* [*&*] *which they*
[*roll*] *pour* | [*Under*] *From forth their arrowy lashes,* [*black & keen*] *wide &
deep*   225 (2): *her* [*two*] *eyes are like two Heavens*

227 (2): *a [sea] storm*

229 Draft: *[And] tempering*

230 Draft: *brightness* ⟨option: *light*⟩   E: *which* is clear, and the change
to *that* for 1820-M could have been Mary's or Peacock's. Euphony gives a
slight preference to *which*

231-35 E was drawn from a complex draft effort which included the follow-
ing: *It [bears] sways a [gleaming] quivering moonbeam & whereer | It points,
the prow of its keen chariot [rides | Upon] cleaves | The stream of clouds,
[which oer the [waters] [earth] rivulets wan] which bears it & [amid] upon |
And [oer] through waters & amid the flowers & grass [& rocks & leaves] |
Wakes as it rolls [Æolian symphony] [a silver] a sound | [Like a] Sweet as
a rain of singing* ⟨option: *clanging*⟩ *Yet silver dew*

234 E: *[bending] grass*

236 Draft: *in the forest*

238 Draft: *[A sphere whose [green] beams | Like the [green] bright spokes
of some invisible wheel | Pierce thousands]* → received with *is as twen*⟨ty⟩
a thousand spheres

239, 241 Transposed in the draft.

240 Draft: *Music & light flow[ed] as thro empty air*

241 Draft: *A thousand*

242 Draft: *[W*⟨hite⟩*] [Azure] Purple & [green] azure golden & [grey] white
green*   E: *Purple & azure, golden [white] [& green & white]* → received. The ampersand after *white* in the received change is partly obscured,
which might account for Mary's oversight and the inferior reading (*white,
green*) of 1820-M.

243 Draft: *Sphere [soars] within sphere, [& enclosing shapes] [and Many the
spaces between]* → received.

245 Draft: *[Such as seem] Such as we dream [inhabit the] dwell in the lampless [earth] deep [centre]*

246 E-M: *intertranspicuous,* A stop stronger than the comma is needed
(the draft has a dash) to show that it is not the *shapes* but the *orbs* that whirl,
as Locock noted (Edition, *1*, 626).

248-49 Transposed in the draft.

248 Draft: *[Spinning upon]* → *[Oer] Upon a thousand [magnetic] sightless axles spinning.*

249 Draft: *of [their] conflicting swiftness* → *of self conflicting swiftness*

250 Draft: *Whirl solemnly intensely slowly on*

251-52 Draft: *Kindling with many tones & many sounds | Intelligible words*
⟨option: *songs*⟩ *& music soft | [And in its progress]*   E: *Kindling with
many* ⟨space⟩ *Intelligible words & music wild* → received with *[min-
gled] [many] mingled* In the received version the changes only are in Shelley's hand, with the remainder in a vertical script unusual to either the poet,
Mary, or Clare Clairmont.

Of liquid darkness, which the Deity
Within seems pouring, as a storm is poured
From jagged clouds, out of their arrowy lashes,
Tempering the cold and radiant air around
With fire which is not brightness; in its hand   230
It sways a quivering moonbeam, from whose point
A guiding power directs the chariot's prow
Over its wheelèd clouds, which, as they roll
Over the grass, and flowers, and waves, wake sounds
Sweet as a singing rain of silver dew.   235

Panthea

And from the other opening in the wood
Rushes, with loud and whirlwind harmony,
A sphere, which is as many thousand spheres,
Solid as crystal, yet through all its mass
Flow, as through empty space, music and light: 240
Ten thousand orbs involving and involved,
Purple and azure, white, and green, and golden,
Sphere within sphere; and every space between
Peopled with unimaginable shapes,
Such as ghosts dream dwell in the lampless deep,   245
Yet each intertranspicuous; and they whirl
Over each other with a thousand motions,
Upon a thousand sightless axles spinning,
And, with the force of self-destroying swiftness,
Intensely, slowly, solemnly roll on,   250
Kindling with mingled sounds, and many tones,
Intelligible words and music wild.
With mighty whirl the multidinous orb
Grinds the bright brook into an azure mist
Of elemental subtlety, like light;   255

---

253 Draft: *that multitudinous*
254 Draft: *Grinds the [blue rivulet] to a [green] [crimson] mist* → received with *brooklet to an*
255 Draft: *elemental [thinness] subtlety,*

256 Draft: *And [then] the [sweet smell] wild odour*

257 Draft: *the [breathing] living earth & air*

258 Draft (possibly): *The emerald tinted [sunbeams of a far wood]* →
(clearly): *The emerald splendour of the wood sunbeams*

259 Draft: *[Seem kneaded and underneath its solemn speed]* → *[Into one
mass of]* → *[And with keen beams]* → *Beneath around its intense [sol-
emn] yet self delaying speed*

261 Draft: Only an isolated *in the mist* is present as a possible line end.

263 Draft: *[Like] As a*   E: Although E (followed here) offers some metrical difficulties in reading, it seems superior in its naturalness to *Like to a
child o'erwearied* of 1820-M. Possibly Mary or (more likely) Peacock, finding
the meter irregular, made the change, but it is surprising that it was overlooked for the errata list.

264 Draft: *[On] Within* ⟨option: *In*⟩ *its folded wings & scattered* ⟨option:
wavy⟩ *hair*   E: *[Within] On*

267 E: *ch[il]anging* Freeman suggested a start on *childish* or *childlike*
("Text," p. 258).

268 Draft: *[As] Like*   and   *it loves*

269 Draft lacking.

270 Draft: *the star*

271 Draft: *[&] or*

273 Draft: *[For they are Heaven & Earth]* → *received.*   E: The
phrase, *united now,* indicates that this is the Heaven of Jupiter, freed of the
evil influence that set it against earth.

274 Draft: *some* ⟨space⟩ *wheel*   1820: *spoke* was clearly a typographical error, probably corrected in M from the errata list (Galignani: 1820).

276 Draft: *[flashing] sunlike*   E: *lightenings* is clear, and *lightnings* of
1820-M could have resulted from a slip in transcription or an attempted "correction" by Mary, Peacock, or the printer, overlooked for the errata list.

277 Draft and E: *[Which] And*

278 Draft: *[black earth,] dark soil,*

279 *deep heart* / *[Show the black cen*⟨tre⟩*]*

280 Draft: *[Wide caverned] [mighty] Infinite* ⟨?⟩ *mines*   E: *mines* is
clear, and *mine* of 1820-M could have resulted from poor copy or printer's
error.

281 Draft: *[And] Valueless*

282 Draft: *And caverns of columnar stone, like jet*   E: *[of columnar
stone like jet] on chrystalline columns poised poised* is susceptible of the
misreading *poured* in 1820, and was probably corrected in M from the errata
list (Galignani: 1820). Shelley used the current poetic pronunciation *crystálline.*

283 Draft: *overspread* / *[Which mocks the frost]*

284 Draft: *[And] Fountains of glowing fire,*   E: *[Fount*⟨ains⟩*] Wells*

286 Draft: *the Earths*

And the wild odour of the forest flowers,
The music of the living grass and air,
The emerald light of leaf-entangled beams
Round its intense, yet self-conflicting speed,
Seem kneaded into one aerial mass   260
Which drowns the sense. Within the orb itself,
Pillowed upon its alabaster arms
Like a child overwearied with sweet toil,
On its own folded wings and wavy hair
The Spirit of the Earth is laid asleep,   265
And you can see its little lips are moving
Amid the changing light of their own smiles,
Like one who talks of what he loves in dream—

      Ione

'Tis only mocking the orb's harmony . . .

      Panthea

And from a star upon its forehead, shoot—   270
Like swords of azure fire, or golden spears
With tyrant-quelling myrtle overtwined,
Embleming Heaven and earth united now—
Vast beams like spokes of some invisible wheel
Which whirl as the orb whirls, swifter than thought, 275
Filling the abyss with sunlike lightenings;
And perpendicular now, and now transverse,
Pierce the dark soil, and, as they pierce and pass,
Make bare the secrets of the earth's deep heart:
Infinite mines of adamant and gold,   280
Valueless stones, and unimagined gems,
And caverns on crystalline columns poised
With vegetable silver overspread;
Wells of unfathomed fire, and water-springs
Whence the great sea, even as a child, is fed,   285
Whose vapours clothe earth's monarch mountain-tops
With kingly, ermine snow. The beams flash on

287-88 Draft: *With [regal] kingly ermine snow; see as they [pass ⟨?⟩] flash /*
They make   E: *snow; [see, as they flash] [as] the beams flash [deep] on /*
[They] And make

289 Draft: *Of [unremembered] cancelled ⟨option: buried⟩ cycles, mighty cities ⟨option: vast metropolis⟩ ⟨cf. l. 296⟩ / [Jammed in the clay] ⟨cf. l. 302⟩ [ships] anchors, [&] beaks of ships*

290 Draft: *turned into marble, quivers ⟨option: trophies⟩*

292 Draft: *Of [shattered] battle scythed chariots*

293 Draft: *Of [beasts which were armorial, [buried emblems]] standards once* → *received.*

294 Draft: *[buried] sepulchral emblems*   E: A natural reading gives a tetrameter for this line, but Shelley probably (as Locock suggested—Edition, *1*, 627) pronounced *emblems* as a trisyllable. He compared *tremb[e]lingly* (*On the Medusa*, 3) and *ramb[e]ling* (tr. of *The Cyclops*, 58). (Cf. n. on I.15.)

295 Draft: *ruin [over] within*

296 Draft: *[And deeper still]* → *[And wrecks]* → *received with [many] a city vast [a vast Metrop⟨olis⟩]* (Cf. n. on l. 289.)

297-98 Draft: *[With all their mortal population, forms / Unlike the]* → *[Whose population ⟨space⟩ were mortal, but not human]* → *received with Earth [drank up] grew oer / [Were] Was* and *[and] see*

299 Draft: *See their [last] works & uncouth skeletons swallowed up*

300 Draft: *[And around heaven] cleaving* → *Sky cleaving pyramids & domes*   E: *Their [once Heaven-cleaving pyramids & domes]* → *received with [fan⟨es⟩] homes*

301 Draft: *See them Huddled in [black] grey*

302 Draft: *Jammed in[to] the hard [grey] deep*

304 Draft: *And fish, which moved as islands in the sea*   E: *[islands] isles*

305 Draft: *[whose] twisted around*

306 Draft: *or around heaps*   E: *[around] within*

307-08 Draft: *To which they crushed the crags in their last pangs*

309 Draft: *The [cor⟨rugated?⟩] jagged*

310-11 Draft: *Of [dark behemoth, who] earth convulsing mammoth which were once / [The monarch] The Imperial beasts, & on the slimy [earth] shores*

312 Draft: *rank forests ⟨option: of Earth⟩*

313 Draft: *summer [flies] worms*

314 Draft: *this [green globe] blue ⟨option: cold⟩ world*

315 Draft: *Was clothed with waters, or [some Spirit] [Monarch Spirit] [a god]* → *Wore deluge like a robe [or some swift Spirit] [angel]* → *received.*

And make appear the melancholy ruins
Of cancelled cycles—anchors, beaks of ships,
Planks turned to marble, quivers, helms, and spears,   290
And gorgon-headed targes, and the wheels
Of scythèd chariots, and the emblazonry
Of trophies, standards, and armorial beasts—
Round which Death laughed: sepulchred emblems
Of dead Destruction, ruin within ruin!   295
The wrecks beside of many a city vast,
Whose population which the earth grew over
Was mortal, but not human—see, they lie,
Their monstrous works and uncouth skeletons,
Their statues, homes, and fanes; prodigious shapes   300
Huddled in grey annihilation, split,
Jammed in the hard, black deep; and over these
The anatomies of unknown wingèd things,
And fishes which were isles of living scale,
And serpents, bony chains, twisted around   305
The iron crags, or within heaps of dust
To which the tortuous strength of their last pangs
Had crushed the iron crags; and over these
The jagged alligator, and the might
Of earth-convulsing behemoth, which once   310
Were monarch beasts, and on the slimy shores
And weed-overgrown continents of earth
Increased and multiplied like summer worms
On an abandoned corpse, till the blue globe
Wrapped deluge round it like a cloak, and they   315
Yelled, gasped, and were abolished—or some God
Whose throne was in a comet, passed, and cried,
'Be not!'—and like my words they were no more.

---

316 Draft: [*Were suddenly*] *abolished* → *Gasped, yelled & ⟨were⟩ abolished—or some* [*Spirit*] *God*   E: [*Gasped*] *Yelled*
   317 Draft: *Whose* [*chariot is a*] *comet, cried aloud* → received followed
by: *Like icy winds that crawl oer a cold shore*

319-22 There are three drafts of these lines, the third of which is part of a clean draft copy of ll. 319-55.

319 E: [*gladness!*] *madness*

320 (1): *Boundless and* ⟨space⟩ *gladness*

321 (1): *Glory and transport, not to be contained*   (2): *The fire of* [*bursting joy not to be*] *confined*   (3): *The* [*unconquerable*] ⟨space⟩ *not to be confined* with *uncount* ⟨a false start on *uncontainable*?⟩ above [*unconquerable*]

322 (1) has a fragment only: *Ha! ha! 'tis life, 'tis*

323-24 There are two drafts of these lines, with only one variant.

323 (1): [*as*] *like*

325-27 There are three drafts of these lines, with (3) part of the clean draft copy of ll. 319-55.

325-27 The following might have been intended for this context but is probably more pertinent at about IV.470: [*A Green world mid many a star* | *None of which more happy are* | *Th*⟨an⟩ *I am spinning round*]   The specific drafts for 325-27 are (1): *Green & azure wanderer* | *Happy globe of land & air* | [*Glide*] *A Spirit is*   (2): *Sister mine calm* → [*Green & azure Wanderer* | *Happy globe of land & air* | *Who latest born of all the*] → [*Though youngest*] → [*What is this awakens me* | [*As*] *Which stain thy sea, like an embowered well*] → [*Beyond*] *Some Spirit wraps thine atmosphere & thee*

327 (3): as in (2).   E: as in (2) with [*thy*] *thine* → received.

328-55 There are two drafts of these lines, with (2) a part of the clean draft copy of ll. 319-55.

328 (1): [*mine icy axis*] *my frozen* [*breast*] *frame*   (2): [*thy*] *my*

330 (1): [*And*] *With* and *strange melody*

333 (1): *Thy cloud of wrath* → *My mouthed fire-hills,* [*thunder*] *sound-exulting fountains* → *The* [*breathless* ⟨?⟩] *mouth of my* [*volcanoes,*] [*thu*⟨nder⟩] *fire hills,* → received.   (2): *sound-exulting*

334 (1): *Laugh with an inextinguishable laughter* → *with a* [*long*] [*loud &*] *vast & inextinguishable*

335-36 (1): [*My caverns*] → [*My Oceans*] → [*The wildernesses of*] → received.

336 (2): *unmeasured* ⟨option: *unfathomed*⟩   E: *Of* is clear and forms an image superior to *And* of 1820-M, which probably resulted when l. 335 was punctuated. With a comma after *abysses* (as in 1820-M) the parallel structure would be called for. Omission from the errata list was probably an oversight. E has also [*thy*] *thee* and [*unfathomed*] *unmeasured*

337 (1): *From all* → *Answer from all* to form the hexameter.

338 (1): *Ha ha* → [*What didst thou dr*⟨ead⟩] → [*Though dread*] → [*Jupiter* ⟨?⟩ *hear,*] *thou sceptre bearing Curse* → *They cry aloud* [*where art thou*] → received.

339 (1): *Who all* ⟨option: *oer*⟩ [*this*] *our*

The Earth

The joy, the triumph, the delight, the madness!
The boundless, overflowing, bursting gladness!   320
The vaporous exultation, not to be confined!
  Ha! ha! the animation of delight
  Which wraps me, like an atmosphere of light,
And bears me as a cloud is borne by its own wind!

The Moon

  Brother mine, calm wanderer,   325
    Happy globe of land and air,
Some spirit is darted like a beam from thee,
    Which penetrates my frozen frame,
    And passes with the warmth of flame,
With love, and odour, and deep melody   330
    Through me, through me!

The Earth

Ha! ha! the caverns of my hollow mountains,
My cloven fire-crags, sound-exulting fountains,
Laugh with a vast and inextinguishable laughter:
  The oceans, and the deserts, and the abysses   335
  Of the deep air's unmeasured wildernesses,
Answer from all their clouds and billows, echoing after.

  They cry aloud as I do: Sceptred Curse,
  Who all our green and azure universe
Threatenedst to muffle round with black destruction,
    sending   340
  A solid cloud to rain hot thunderstones,
  And splinter and knead down my children's bones,
All I bring forth, to one void mass battering and blending;

---

  340 (1): [*Threatened*] *Threatenedst* [*to*] [*out of the sky* ⟨?⟩] →   received.
(2): *Threatenest*
  341-42 (1): [*raining*] *to rain hot thunder stones* / [*Splintering & kneading
down my*] → [*To*] *splinter* → received.
  343 (1): [*Battering into one dark*] → received with [*to*] *in one dark mass*
(2): [*black*] *void mass*

344 (1): *Until each [mountainous] craglike tower, & [spirelike] [spiry] sto-ried column* / *[And sculptured]*

346 (1): *[With my fire]* → *[And old [each] heaven-cleaving [fane] dome, each pyramid]* → *My [monarch] Imperial mountains crowned with light & snow & stillness* → received.   (2): *[Each] My*

347-48 (1): *My [mighty] forests . . . ⟨sic⟩ [every blossom / Of life that feeds from my fond bosom]* → received with *& cradle*   (2): *& cradle on [thy] my*

348 E: *on* is clear, but sense gives a slight preference to *in* of 1820-M, as Mary or Shelley probably decided.

349 (1): *Were stamped [into a mire of lifeless] by thy strong wrath into a [blank &] lifeless mire*   E: *[my] thy*

350 (1): *How [are] art* and *drunken up*

351-52 (1): *the [half drained] [unreplenished] cup* / *[A ⟨One?⟩ little drop]* → received with *a desart tribe* ⟨option: *the desart wandering Band*⟩

352 (2): *desart-[tribe] troop*

353 (1): *beneath within, above around*

355 (1): *[Like sunlight fills] As sunlight on a prison which sudden earth-quake rends* → *[Fills it, as light]* → *[As lightning fills a [cave ⟨?⟩] prison cloven] by the thunderball* → received with *on [prisons] caves*   E: *the* is clear, and *by thunderball* of 1820 was probably an oversight by Mary or a printer's error, corrected in M from the errata list (Galignani: 1820).

356-62 There are two drafts of these lines.

356 (1): *[the] my*

357 (1): *Is melting*   (2): *Is melted*

358 (1): *My [cra⟨dled ?⟩] solid [Oceans] [seas & lakes flow] & shine* → re-ceived with, as also in (2): *flow & leap & shine*

360 (1): *And [clothes] fills*   (2): *It fills*

361 (1): *My cold hard bosom [dark breast] [I feel that] it is thine* → re-ceived with *cold hard* ⟨option: *void*⟩   (2): *cold void bosom*

363 Draft: After the received Shelley also tried: *[For as I gaze on thee, I know]*

364 Draft: *[A thousand leaves]* → received with *flowers glow* ⟨sic⟩

365-66 Draft: *[Upon my dark & wrinkled countenance]* → received. After the received Shelley also tried: *[And there is music on the ⟨option: my⟩ winds & billows]* → *[Sweet sound is in the water & the air]*

367 Draft: *[And winged clouds walk through my atmosphere]* → *[Wind-walking] clouds [are wandering] here & there* → received.

368 *Full of the rain* → *[Laden with bright rain]* → received.

370-75 There are two drafts of these lines, with the second an unvaried clean draft copy.

371 (1): *[And] through hard* ⟨option: *tangled*⟩ *roots & lifeless* ⟨option: *trod-den*⟩   372 E: *[inmost] utmost*

Until each craglike tower, and storied column,
Palace, and obelisk, and temple solemn,   345
My imperial mountains crowned with cloud, and snow,
    and fire,
My sea-like forests, every blade and blossom
Which finds a grave or cradle in my bosom,
Were stamped by thy strong hate into a lifeless mire:

How art thou sunk, withdrawn, covered, drunk up   350
By thirsty nothing, as the brackish cup
Drained by a desert-troop, a little drop for all;
And from beneath, around, within, above,
Filling thy void annihilation, love
Bursts in like light on caves cloven by the thunderball.   355

The Moon

The snow upon my lifeless mountains
Is loosened into living fountains,
My solid oceans flow, and sing, and shine;
A spirit from my heart bursts forth,
It clothes with unexpected birth   360
My cold bare bosom: Oh! it must be thine
    On mine, on mine!

Gazing on thee I feel, I know
Green stalks burst forth, and bright flowers grow,
And living shapes upon my bosom move;   365
Music is in the sea and air,
Wingèd clouds soar here and there,
Dark with the rain new buds are dreaming of:
    'Tis love, all love!

The Earth

It interpenetrates my granite mass,   370
Through tangled roots and trodden clay doth pass
Into the utmost leaves and delicatest flowers;

374 (1): *It gives a life to*

375 E: [*powers*] *bowers*   In order to sustain the principal emphasis on *It* (love) of l. 370, and carry it with minimal interruption to the next stanza (l. 377: ⟨*it*⟩ *has arisen*), this line should be more fully subordinated than in E-M (E is unpointed; 1820-M have *dead, . . . bowers.*).

376-77 There are four drafts of these lines.

376 (1): [*And*] *like a* [*whirlwind*] *bursting its* [*craggy*] *prison* → received with [*And*] *like a* [*swift*] *storm*   (2): *a wind* and *rocky prison*   (3) and (4): *Which like*

377 (1): [*Under the*] *lightning* → *With* [*earthquake*] *& with whirlwind it has risen* → received with *it has risen*   (2): *With earthquakes and with lightning it has risen*   (3): received with [*it*] *has* [*risen*] *arisen* (4): *received.*

378-81 There are three drafts of these lines.

378 (1): *Out of the* [*caverns of the caves* ⟨*cave ?*⟩ *of thought*] → *Out of the secret caves of mans* [*imagined*] *unimagined being*   (2): *Out of the* [*secret*] *lampless caves of mans* [*imagined*] *unimagined being*   (3): received.

379 (2) and (3): *making quiver*

380 (1): [*The base*] [*Thoughts craglike bases* ⟨*basis ?*⟩] [*chaos*] → *The* [*worlds deep*] *base, immoveable forever* → received.

381 (1): only the fragment *Till, like* is present.   (2): [*And its Hate,*] → [*Dull*] *Hate, & Ignorance like* → *Till ignorance & hate, like sha*⟨*des*⟩ *from* [*the morning planets*] *sunrise fleeing*   (3): *Till Hate &* [*Death*] *F*⟨*ear*⟩ *& Pain,* [*like wind-*] *vanquished* [*vapours*] *fleeting* → received with *fleeting*

382-83 There are two drafts of these lines.

382 (1): *Leave Man, my latest born* → *Leave Man, the likeness of my inmost soul* / [*The centre of my circumference, the which,*] / *The sea to which all else* [*is*] *are unremaining waves* → (abstract): *Leave Man* [*the loveliest*] *My latest born, the* [*cloudy*] [*cloudiest*] *mirror* / *Of* [*thy*] [*thee*] *his* [*Thou mightiest*] [*perfect man* ⟨*?*⟩]   (2): *Leave man my latest born* [*my most beloved* / *The image of the Power by*] *which is moved* → received with *Leaves*   E: [*Leaves*] *Leave*

383 (1): [*at whose feet Pain & Hate & Error*] → *Through whom* [*I conquer*] *forever* ⟨*?*⟩ *fear & error* / [*Are like slaves chained*] / *The image of* [*thy*] *his like thy patience & thy* [*glory*] *boldness* / [*In d*⟨*efeat*⟩ *in victory*]   (2): [*Reflecting*] *Which imaged many a monstrous shape of error* → received with *could* ⟨option: *did*⟩

384 Draft: [*Like*] *As* [*the*] *calm* [*lake*] *the* [*Heavens,*] *reflecting* [*thee great Titan*] → *As a calm sea the sky reflecting Love, bright love* → received with *This true* [*& lovely*] *fair*

Upon the winds, among the clouds 'tis spread;
It wakes a life in the forgotten dead—
They breathe a spirit up from their obscurest bowers—   375

And like a storm, bursting its cloudy prison
With thunder and with whirlwind, has arisen
Out of the lampless caves of unimagined being,
  With earthquake shock and swiftness making shiver
  Thought's stagnant chaos, unremoved forever,   380
Till hate, and fear, and pain, light-vanquished shadows,
      fleeing,

Leave Man—who was a many-sided mirror
Which could distort to many a shape of error
This true fair world of things—a sea reflecting love;
  Which over all his kind, as the sun's heaven   385
  Gliding o'er ocean, smooth, serene, and even,
Darting from starry depths radiance and life, doth move:

385-86 Draft: *[And] Which like a cloud melodious sounds* ⟨option: *winds*⟩ *embolden | To scale [the] steep with wings purple & golden* → *To scale [steep] Dawn* → *To scale the Dawn with wings [azure & white] [purple] [obscure] shadowy & golden* → received with *[like] as the [great] Sun's Heaven | [Over the sea,] Oer ocean glides with pace serene & even*
386 1820-M: The lack of punctuation after *even* leads to ambiguity. E, with the comma, clarifies the intent.
387 Draft: *[Radiance & Light & life] [Darting [Shooting] from its lampy depth]* → received with *[From sphere] Darting from* E: *life* (the superior word) is loosely written, but not likely to be confused with *light* as in 1820-M. 1820 was probably an unconscious slip stemming from the context of the stanza, surprisingly not corrected in M, and first noted in Mathilde Blind's review of Rossetti ("Shelley," p. 80). M: *move* with a comma resulted from an uncorrected typographical error in Galignani.

388 There are two drafts of this line: (1): [*Even as a leprous child*] →
[*As*] *Like some sweet child* [*covered*] *masked in a leprous* / *Who*   (2): received with *Leaves*   E: [*Leaves*] *leave*

389 Draft: *Who* [*gathers*] *follows* [*some*] *a sick* [*child*] *beast, to some warm
cleft*   E: [*some*] *a sick beast to* [*a*] *some warm cleft*

391 Draft: [[*She*] *It went*] → received with [*returns*] *wanders*

392 Draft: *Unconsciously*

394 Draft: [*Leaves man,*] *not men,* [*an union*] → received.

396 Draft: [*Which this re*⟨bellious⟩] [*By which the rebellious shapes of this*]
→ received with [*Binding*] *Compelling* and [*sway*] *stress*

397-99 There are five drafts of these lines: (1): *The unquiet Republic of
the spheres* / *Of ever wandering planets, whom* / *The great Sun rules as with
a tyrant*⟨s⟩ *gaze*   (2): *Yon sun, who rules as with a tyrants gaze* ⟨option:
frown⟩ / *The unquiet republic of the spheres* / *Of ever wandering Planets* /
comets are his ministers   (3): [*As the sun rules*] *The great Sun rules as
with a tyrants gaze* / *The unquiet republic of the maze* / *Of ever wandering
Planets—*   (4): [*So*] *As the Sun rules,* [*as*] *even with a tyrants gaze* / *The
unquiet republic of the maze* / *Of ever wandering Planets,* [*round*] *revolving
in their spheres*   (5): received ll. 397-98, with l. 399: *Of* [*ever wandering*]
world [*wandering Planets*] *whilst struggling to seek Heaven*⟨s⟩ *keepless wilderness*

400 Draft: [*And his own heart is*] → [*My sons are as*] *one soul of many
a soul* → received with [*The earth*] *Man*

401 Draft: [*Subject to one*] [*Conscious*] → *Whose Love is* [*their*] *its own
law, & one controul*

402 Draft: [*And all the forms of life*] → [*And all things flow to*] → received with *To which*

403 Draft: *Familiar* [*Sweet*] [*things*] *acts*   E: [*thro*] [*by*] *thro*

404 Draft: [*And Toil, & Thought*] *thro life's green grove* → received
with *grief* [*with solemn*] *thro life's*   E: [*through*] *in*

405 Draft: [*Like beasts that once were wild*] → [*Wander like beasts made*]
tame—how gentle they can be → received with *Walk like* and [*know*]
knew and [*can*] *could*

406 Draft: [*ill*] *bad*

407 Draft: [*With low cares, its terror mailed*] *satellites* → received with
And sceptred cares,

408 Draft: [*Is* [*a spirit*] *as a*] *spirit ill to* [*serve*] *rule but mighty to obey*

409 Draft: [*A tempest winged* [*boat*] *ship, a chariot speeding* / *With winds
for steeds*] → received.

410 Draft: *Love* [*rules*] *guides,*

411 Draft: *Forcing remotest shores to own its sovereign's sway*   With *sovereign's* in the draft and *sovereigns* in E, Shelley's original intent is clear, and
suggests a possible confusion in his mind as to the antecedent of *its*   The pas-

Leave Man, even as a leprous child is left
Who follows a sick beast to some warm cleft
Of rocks, through which the might of healing springs is
    poured;   390
  Then when it wanders home with rosy smile,
  Unconscious, and its mother fears awhile
It is a spirit, then weeps on her child restored:

Man, oh, not men! a chain of linkèd thought,
  Of love and might to be divided not,   395
Compelling the elements, with adamantine stress,
  As the sun rules, even with a tyrant's gaze,
  The unquiet republic of the maze
Of planets, struggling fierce towards heaven's free
    wilderness:

Man, one harmonious soul of many a soul,   400
  Whose nature is its own divine controul,
Where all things flow to all, as rivers to the sea;
  Familiar acts are beautiful through love;
  Labour, and Pain, and Grief, in life's green grove
Sport like tame beasts—none knew how gentle they
    could be!   405

His will—with all mean passions, bad delights,
  And selfish cares, its trembling satellites,
A spirit ill to guide, but mighty to obey—
  Is as a tempest-wingèd ship, whose helm
  Love rules through waves which dare not overwhelm,   410
Forcing life's wildest shores to own its sovereign sway:

---

sage is sufficiently complex to suggest that Mary might have consulted with the
poet for the 1820-M reading (*sovereign*). The sense appears to be that man's
will, formerly guided by destructive passions (ll. 406-07), has been in itself
faulty as a guide, though powerful (tyrannical?) in exacting obedience. But
now that the creative force of Love is its pilot, man's sovereign will is benefi-
cent, and exacts obedience of a kind detailed in the following stanzas.

412 Draft: [*And from the mass*] → [*And*] *all things* [*own*] *his* [*power;*]
→ received with *from the cold mass*   E: [*From*] *through*

413 Draft: *Of* [*white &*] *silent marble,* [*such forms pass / At his command*]
→ received with *Of silent marble,*

414 Draft: [*And mothers gaze & love & children*] → *And* ⟨option:
Whence⟩ *mothers gazing* [*wove*] *weave* [*the light*] *the robes their children wear*
E: [*And mothers gazing*] *Bright threads, whence mothers* (Cf. II.iv.83.)

415 Draft: [*Language*] *is* [*a music*] → [*Language*] *is a*[*s*] [*an Orphic*]
⟨space⟩ [*strong*] → [*Language*] *is as a perpetual*[*ly*] *Orphic song*

416 Draft: [*Which* [*builds*] *rules*] *Ruling with mighty harmony, the throng*
E: [*Which rules*] *Ruling*   Locock thought that Shelley rejected *Ruling* for
Which rules of 1820-M to avoid a "second trochaic commencement" (Edition,
1, 629). But *Ruling* (added in pencil before the line) was probably a return to
the final draft reading after Mary had completed the transcription, and was
overlooked for the errata list. I believe that Shelley would find the "second
trochaic commencement" less objectionable than the awkwardness of the
Which rules . . . which else (l. 417) construction. E also has [*the*] *a*

417 Draft: *Of* [*feelings &*] *of forms,* → received with *thoughts of forms*

418 Draft: [*his*] *slave, Heavens* [*blue*] [*Abyss*] *Abysm* → received with
mans slave

421 Draft: [*rides*] *strides*

422-23 Draft: [*The World within the World tears off its veil*] → [*The
elem*⟨*ents*⟩] ⟨space⟩ *is laid all bare*] → [*The world within*] *shouts from
her depth laid bare / To Heaven* → *And The Abyss* ⟨space⟩ *laid bare /*
[*Shouts what are now thy secrets*] → received with *What are thy secrets,*
[*Heaven?*] → *secrets? man unveils*   E: [*What secrets hast thou Heaven?*]
Heaven, hast thou

424-25 Draft: *Death* [*has past*] *at last*   and   *Heaven has past*   The structure was strengthened by the transposition in 1820-M.

424 E: [*has*] *hath*   In spite of *hath-path* and the inducement to lisp on *past*
the word is clear. If Mary noted this problem, Shelley would have been quick
to agree on the change to *has past* for 1820-M (note *has* in the draft).

426 Draft: *The cold still shadow of an icy sleep / Which made the* → *A*
[*solid*] *shroud of clinging* [*snow*] → received with *solid frost & nought /*
Whi⟨ch⟩   The seemingly irrelevant *nought* might have been intended to go
with the following *Whi*⟨ch⟩

427-30 Draft lacking.

431-36 There are two drafts of these lines.

431 (1): *As the* ⟨space⟩ *dissolving* [*warmth*] *light* → [*And*] *as the*
[*spirit*] *of* [*the*] *Dawn, may fold* → received with *light* [*warmth*]   (2):
[*light*] *warmth*

432 E: *unfrozen* is clear, and *infrozen* of 1820 probably resulted from poorly
written copy or printer's error, with M corrected from the errata list (Galignani: 1820).

All things confess his strength. Through the cold mass
Of marble and of colour his dreams pass—
Bright threads whence mothers weave the robes their
　　　children wear;
　　Language is a perpetual Orphic song,   415
　　Ruling with dædal harmony a throng
Of thoughts and forms, which else senseless and shape-
　　less were:

　　The lightning is his slave; heaven's utmost deep
　　Gives up her stars, and like a flock of sheep
They pass before his eye, are numbered, and roll on!   420
　　The tempest is his steed—he strides the air;
　　And the abyss shouts from her depth laid bare,
'Heaven, hast thou secrets? Man unveils me; I have none.'

The Moon

　　The shadow of white Death has passed
　　From my path in heaven at last,   425
A clinging shroud of solid frost and sleep;
　　And through my newly-woven bowers
　　Wander happy paramours,
Less mighty, but as mild as those who keep
　　Thy vales more deep.   430

The Earth

　　As the dissolving warmth of dawn may fold
　　A half-unfrozen dewglobe, green, and gold,
And crystalline, till it becomes a wingèd mist,
　　And wanders up the vault of the blue day,
　　Outlives the noon, and on the sun's last ray   435
Hangs o'er the sea, a fleece of fire and amethyst—

---

433 (1): *a winged [purple] [wandering] [beamy] mist*
434 E: *[path] vault*
435 (1): *on the [evenings] ray* → received.   E: *[in] on*
436 See p. 222

436 (1): *[gold] & amethyst*   E: With respect to the change from the dash after *amethyst* to the period in 1820-M, Locock commented: "It is possible that the Earth may have intended to apply its simile to the newly vitalized Moon rather than to itself; but it seems to me that the Earth's attitude throughout is intended to be that of one so wild with joy that it takes no notice of the calmer strains of the moon; yielding only to its 'soft influence mild' at the conclusion of its final song (cf. 499). The Moon's lyrics abound in sympathetic references to the Earth, which seems to be reserving its reply until the full confession of the Moon has fulfilled Asia's prediction [III.iv.86-90]. From this point the Moon is intended to have its full share of the verse. Accordingly it takes up the strain of the Earth's simile and, however it was intended to be applied, applies it to the Earth" (Edition, *1*, 629).

437 Draft: *Thou art [lying] folded*   This was probably an accidental anticipation of the rime word.

439 Draft: *& the [sweet] smile [of Heaven]* → received with *divin[est]*

440 Draft: *The [Sun & Constellation⟨s⟩]* → *All [Heaven] Constellations [power]* → received with *hour* present as a possible hold for rime.

442 Draft: *[But] In which [thou movest, bright—]* → received with *In which*

444-48   There are two drafts of these lines.

444 (1): *I [lay] [spin] roll*   (2): *I [roll] [lie] spin*

445-47 E: Locock commented on the commas after *heavens* and *love-dreams* (both unpointed in 1820-M): "The first makes it clear that 'dreaming delight' refers to the Earth; the second that 'faintly sighing' goes with 'youth' rather than with 'love-dreams,' the faint sighs of the youth being analogous to the spinning of the sleeping Earth. The line below may be taken quite literally: the youth is lying under the shadow, or halo, cast by the light of his own beauty into the air above" (Edition, *1*, 629).

446 (1): *[And murmuring in ⟨option: to⟩ my dreams wild notes of joy & exultation]* → *my dreams the fond [sweet wild exultation]* → *in my sleep [melodious] harmonious exultation*   (2): *[And] murmuring [in my sleep, the]* → received with *[melodious] victorious*

447 (1): *[Even like a love]* → *[Like] And ⟨for As?⟩ a nymph lulled in love dreams, faintly sighing*   (2): received with *[maid] youth ⟨option: boy⟩*

448 (1): *[Wrapt] Under the shadow of her beauty lying* / *[Mingling]* (2): *[her] his*

449 Draft: *o'er his rest*   E: *[a]round*

450 Draft: *[And like] As in*

451 E: *[darkens] meets*

452 Draft: *And brightest ⟨option: dark⟩ eyes are dull, [& highest hearts are calm]* → received.

453 Draft: *[Though] So*

454 Draft: *Then am I dark & [calm], by thee* → received.

The Moon

Thou art folded, thou art lying
In the light which is undying
Of thine own joy, and heaven's smile divine;
  All suns and constellations shower   440
  On thee a light, a life, a power
Which doth array thy sphere; thou pourest thine
     On mine, on mine!

The Earth

I spin beneath my pyramid of night,
  Which points into the heavens, dreaming delight,   445
Murmuring victorious joy in my enchanted sleep—
  As a youth lulled in love-dreams, faintly sighing,
  Under the shadow of his beauty lying,
Which round his rest a watch of light and warmth doth
    keep.

The Moon

  As in the soft and sweet eclipse   450
  When soul meets soul on lovers' lips,
High hearts are calm, and brightest eyes are dull—
  So when thy shadow falls on me,
  Then am I mute and still, by thee
Covered; of thy love, Orb most beautiful,   455
  Full, oh, too full!

  Thou art speeding round the sun,
  Brightest world of many a one,
  Green and azure sphere, which shinest
  With a light which is divinest   460

---

455 Draft: [*thine*] *thy*
456 Draft: [*So*] *full, too full* → received.
458 Draft: [*Thou green*] [*Fairest*] *Brightest world of many a one* / [*Swifter calmer is thy motion* / *Finless cleaver of the* ⟨option: *an*⟩ *Ocean*]
459 Draft: *azure orb* ⟨option: *moon*⟩

462 Draft: [*life*] *love & light*   E: The verb is defensible here since it follows a compound subject whose sense is singular.

463 Draft: [*chrystal*] *icy*   E: [*thine*] *thy* [*icy*] *chrystal*

465-66 Draft: *Like the* [*magnet*] *Paradise* / [*Which there is in*] *lovers eyes* → *received with* [*of*] *in lovers eyes*

467 Draft: [*Like a most*] *enamoured maiden* → *And I,* [*like*] *as an enamoured maiden*   E: *I,* [*like*] *a*

470 Draft: *around thee moving* / [*A Green world mid many a star* / *None of which more happy are* / *Th*⟨*an*⟩ *I am spinning round*] (See n. on IV.325-27.)

471-80 Draft lacking.

472 E: *thy* [*sweet*] *form*

478 E: [*Caverns*] *Heavens*

483 Draft: *or* [*a*] *cameleon*   E: The question of an *a* before *cameleon* is difficult to answer. Shelley first wrote *As a lover or cameleon* and then inserted the article above the line, heavily and indistinctly (note that it was deleted in the draft). But a careful analysis of this heavy *a* leads me to wonder if it is not actually more than that. I do not believe that an evident lower part of the looped body was made with the same stroke as what I take to be overwriting, but rather that an original *a* was deleted and rewritten heavily, suggesting uncertainty on Shelley's part. However, a more certain choice of a final text reading can now be made in the light of the M dependence on Galignani for printer's copy. It would appear that Mary assumed the *a* for the 1820 transcription, but that, since Galignani followed 1820, M (without the *a*) was corrected from the errata list and represents the poet's final choice.

484 Draft: *Grows* [*with*] *like what he gazes on*   E: The change from *gazes on* of E to *looks upon* of 1820-M would be necessary when the next ten lines (with *Gazes on*) were added later. It can be assumed that Shelley was responsible for the change.

485-94 Lacking in E, although drafts of ll. 485-92 are extant (see below). There is also an unused draft passage relevant here: *As a strain of sweetest sound* / *Wraps itself the wind around* / [*Until*] *Till the* [*voiceless*] *void wind* [*be*] *itself grow music too—* / *As aught dark & vain* ⟨&⟩ *dull* / [*Movi*⟨*ng*⟩] *Basking* [*near*] *in what is beautiful* / *Is full of light & love* [*& dew* ⟨?⟩]

485-87 There are two drafts of these lines, with no variants in the second.

485 (1): *As the*

487 (1): fragment only: [*Till* [*he*] *it*] *Till*

488 Draft: *empty mist*

489 Draft: *Lies like*

490 Draft: *Over the western mountain*

492 The line is not in E, but the draft reading (*snow—*), indicating suspension of sense, should be given precedence over the period ending in 1820-M. (Cf. n. on IV.67.)

493-99 Draft lacking.

Among all the lamps of heaven
To whom life and light is given;
I, thy crystal paramour,
Borne beside thee by a power
Like the polar paradise,   465
Magnet-like, of lovers' eyes;
I, a most enamoured maiden,
Whose weak brain is overladen
With the pleasure of her love,
Maniac-like around thee move,   470
Gazing, an insatiate bride,
On thy form from every side,
Like a Mænad round the cup
Which Agave lifted up
In the weird Cadmæan forest.   475
Brother, wheresoe'er thou soarest
I must hurry, whirl and follow
Through the heavens wide and hollow,
Sheltered, by the warm embrace
Of thy soul, from hungry space;   480
Drinking, from thy sense and sight,
Beauty, majesty, and might,
As a lover or chameleon
Grows like what it looks upon;
As a violet's gentle eye   485
Gazes on the azure sky
Until its hue grows like what it beholds;
As a grey and watery mist
Glows like solid amethyst
Athwart the western mountains it enfolds   490
When the sunset sleeps
Upon its snow—

The Earth

And the weak day weeps
That it should be so.
O gentle Moon, the voice of thy delight   495

500 Draft: [*The solid heart of my glad universe*] → received.

501 Draft: [*Soothing the eagle*] *tyger* [*joy, which g**] *whose trampling fierce*

502 Draft: *Makes wounds*

504 Draft: [*Among*] *In the deep hollows of the sunless rocks*

505 (first half): E: Although Shelley might have intended suspension by *sound*— the context supports the period of 1820-M.

505 (last half): Draft: [*Ha ha*] *Ah, me!*

506 Draft: *from you*   E: *sound[s]*

507 For this shift from *thou* to *you* see Intro., n. 25, above.

508-09 Draft lacking.

508 E: [*are*] *fall*

510 Draft: *a Darkness*

511 Draft: [*from*] *out o' the Earth*

514 Draft: *of light—and the*

515 Draft lacking.

516 The draft has only the fragment: *Gleam like two meteors*   E: *mist* was probably changed to *night* in 1820-M to avoid the rime with *list* below, as Locock first suggested (Edition, *1*, 630).

517-18 Draft lacking, but there are two unused passages (the second fragmented) relevant to the Demogorgon apostrophes following l. 518: (1): [*Ye Hours, that speed or linger as ye* [*will*] *wist* / *Chainless as winds,* [*rich as*] *bright as illumined bees* / *Which flee from flower to flower to seek their fill*] / *Whose life is one long dream of*   (2): *Ye spirits who kept watch beside* [*within that deep*] / [*The*] *Of* ⟨the⟩ *human heart, until its* [*bars*] *frozen* [*bars*] [*gates*] *prison* / *Were* / *Who make* [*their*] *life, with the instinct of their sleep*

520 [*Home*] *Sphere*

Falls on me like thy clear and tender light
Soothing the seaman, borne the summer night
   Through isles forever calm:
O gentle Moon, thy crystal accents pierce
The caverns of my pride's deep universe,   500
Charming the tiger joy, whose tramplings fierce
   Made wounds which need thy balm.

Panthea

I rise as from a bath of sparkling water,
A bath of azure light, among dark rocks,
Out of the stream of sound.

Ione

                Ah me! sweet sister,   505
The stream of sound has ebbed away from us,
And you pretend to rise out of its wave
Because your words fall like the clear soft dew
Shaken from a bathing wood-nypmh's limbs and hair.

Panthea

Peace! peace! a mighty Power, which is as darkness,   510
Is rising out of earth, and from the sky
Is showered like night, and from within the air
Bursts, like eclipse which had been gathered up
Into the pores of sunlight: the bright visions,
Wherein the singing spirits rode and shone,   515
Gleam like pale meteors through a watery night.

Ione

There is a sense of words upon mine ear—

Panthea

A universal sound like words: O list!

Demogorgon

Thou Earth, calm empire of a happy soul,
   Sphere of divinest shapes and harmonies;   520

521 Draft: *Attractive* ⟨option: *Beautiful*⟩ [*spirit*] *orb*
522 Draft: [*along*] *thro the Void skies*

523 Draft: *I am a dew drop, trembling ere it dies!* / [*To thy strong*]

524-28 Draft lacking.
524 E: [*of*] *on*

529 Draft: [*O* G⟨*ods*⟩ *Demons & elemental Spirits,*] → received with *Kings* [*&*] *of*
530-32 Draft: [*Powers of those Elysian windless*] → received 1. 530 / *Thou people* [*of*] *the* / [*The world beyond*]

533 Draft: *We hear* [*thee—We*] → *We hear,—Kingless we are blest & bless*

534 Draft: [*Ghosts*] [*O unimagined People of the dead*] → *Ye* [*People of the dead, on whom even my words*] → received.
535 Draft: [*but*] *not*
536 Draft: [*fills*] *the Universe* → received with *that* ⟨option: *the*⟩ *universe*
537 Draft: *Which* [*living ye beheld & felt*]*—as they* → received with [*felt*] *suffered—or as they* (with *or as they* given to Demogorgon).   E: [*like*] *as*

538 E: *Whom we hither haste* → *Who*[*m we*] *hither haste* → received (as originally in the draft).

539-78 Draft lacking, with all manuscript readings below from E.

Beautiful orb! gathering as thou dost roll
   The love which paves thy path along the skies:

The Earth

I hear: I am as a drop of dew that dies.

Demogorgon

Thou Moon, which gazest on the nightly Earth
   With wonder, as it gazes upon thee, 525
Whilst each to men, and beasts, and the swift birth
   Of birds, is beauty, love, **calm,** harmony:

The Moon

I hear: I am a leaf shaken by thee.

Demogorgon

Ye kings of suns and stars, Dæmons and Gods,
   Ætherial Dominations, who possess 530
Elysian, windless, fortunate abodes
   Beyond heaven's constellated wilderness:

A Voice: *from above*

Our great Republic hears: we are blest, and bless.

Demogorgon

Ye happy dead, whom beams of brightest verse
   Are clouds to hide, not colours to portray, 535
Whether your nature is that universe
   Which once ye saw and suffered—

A Voice: *from beneath*

               Or as they
Whom we have left, we change and pass away.

Demogorgon

Ye elemental Genii, who have homes
   From man's high mind even to the central stone 540
Of sullen lead; from heaven's star-fretted domes
   To the dull weed some sea-worm battens on:

547 [*who*] *which* and [*throng*] *feed* The change back to *throng* for 1820-M probably resulted from Shelley's realization that *feed* was ambiguous in this context.

550 *or* is slightly blotted and could have been read as an ampersand by Mary; or Shelley might finally have preferred the parallelism in this minor choice.

554 In this instance I am inclined to agree with Forman that the dropping of *is* in M (uncorrected in M² however) was an accident of the press (see n. on III.iii.70). Demogorgon's "strong words" (l. 553) lose much of their opening force with the verb omitted.

557 *home* is clear, and the much stronger *throne* of 1820-M was almost certainly Shelley's change.

559 *dread* is clear, and *dead* of 1820 was either a lapse in transcription or an error of the press, corrected in M from the errata list (Galignani: 1820).

562 [*Virtue & Love &*] *Gentleness, Virtue*

566 [*would*] *should*

569 The change from *that* of E to *the* of 1820-M prevented a third use of *that* in this stanza, where the force of the third occurrence would be lost through repetition.

A confused Voice

We hear: thy words waken Oblivion.

Demogorgon

Spirits whose homes are flesh; ye beasts and birds;
   Ye worms and fish; ye living leaves and buds;   545
Lightning and wind; and ye untameable herds,
   Meteors and mists, which throng air's solitudes:

A Voice

Thy voice to us is wind among still woods.

Demogorgon

Man, who wert once a despot and a slave;
   A dupe and a deceiver; a decay;   550
A traveller from the cradle to the grave
   Through the dim night of this immortal day:

All

Speak: thy strong words may never pass away.

Demogorgon

This is the day, which down the void abysm
At the Earth-born's spell yawns for Heaven's despotism,   555
And Conquest is dragged captive through the deep:
Love, from its awful throne of patient power
In the wise heart, from the last giddy hour
Of dread endurance, from the slippery, steep,
And narrow verge of crag-like agony, springs   560
And folds over the world its healing wings.

Gentleness, Virtue, Wisdom, and Endurance:
These are the seals of that most firm assurance
Which bars the pit over Destruction's strength;
And if, with infirm hand, Eternity,   565
Mother of many acts and hours, should free
The serpent that would clasp her with his length,
These are the spells by which to reassume
An empire o'er the disentangled Doom.

575 *falter* is clear in E, and *flatter* of 1820 probably resulted from a slip by Mary or an error of the press, corrected in M from the errata list (Galignani: 1820).

578 *This is alone [Peace,] Life, [Peace,] Joy, Empire & Victory*

To suffer woes which Hope thinks infinite; 570
To forgive wrongs darker than death or night;
To defy power which seems omnipotent;
To love, and bear; to hope, till Hope creates
From its own wreck the thing it contemplates;
Neither to change, nor falter, nor repent: 575
This, like thy glory, Titan, is to be
Good, great and joyous, beautiful and free;
This is alone Life, Joy, Empire, and Victory.

Appendixes

Appendix A

Hyphenation of E-M is inclusive and indicates that the variant is found
in all three of the test items (E, 1820 and M). Angle brackets represent
editorial comment.

Variant readings as between the present text and E-M are given in
detail, with the following exceptions: The use, in all but forty-two instances, of medial ampersands in E, and the consistently unmarked but
pronounced final -*ed* in E-M, can be assumed, to avoid inconsequential
repetition. Mary Shelley's second edition (M²) readings agree with M
unless separately identified, in which case if they parallel the received
reading they are given in parentheses.

All verbal variants, and those in punctuation that have an important
bearing on textual interpretation, have been discussed in textual notes.

TITLE PAGE

in four acts ⟨and epigraph⟩ ⟨lacking⟩ E

PREFACE

Heading: Preface E   1 writers E   5 interpretation 1820   6
story, as in title, M   7 wᵈ E   9 Agamenmonian ⟨sic⟩ E   12 li-
cense—E   13 "Prometheus unbound" of Æschylus, E   "Prometheus
Unbound" M   17 subject E   18 Pelias, ⟨sic⟩ & Prometheus E   19
Jupiter E   Hercules.— E   20 model E   22 ambition, E-M   25
challenge, E   26 But in truth E   29 fable E   30 the endurance
E   32 language, E   32-33 perfidious & successful E   34 Satan:
M²   35 judgment, M   36 Satan E   courage E   37 majesty E
39 envy E   40 which   E   41 Hero of Paradise Lost, 1820-M   Paradise lost E   perpetually interfere E   44 wrongs E   46 feeling 1820

51 Poem E-M   53 trees E   54 ever winding E-1820   57 awakening spring 1820   61 found E   62 instances E   65 Poetry; E
Shakspeare 1820-M   67 poet E   70 power, E   71 it is from the
study E   works, ⟨since 1820   72 me,⟩ 1820   me⟩, M   73 singu-
lartity ⟨sic⟩ E   One ⟨no indention⟩ E   75 composition; E   77 and
indeed E-1820   78 popular E   81 himself, E   84 true, E-M
85 due, E   86 minds, E   89 have the form, E   90 imitate, E
94 The peculiar ⟨no indention⟩ E   96 England, E-M   power E

101 republics each æqual E   105 Shakspeare) 1820-M   109 Religion. E   110 developement E-1820   111 spirit; E   112 Repub-

lican E   enquirer E   114 age, E   suppose E   115 or forerunners E
116 condition, & in the E   condition 1820   118-119 is is ⟨sic⟩ E
120 imitation; Poetry E   124 man, M   127-28 thought. One great
Poet E ⟨and with . . . them *lacking*⟩ E   128 them: one 1820-M
129 nature, E M   132 lovely— E   136 greatest, the effect even
in him E   137 strained unnatural E   Poet, E   139 others; 1820-M
141 is in this respect E   142 art, E   146-47 philosophers or painters sculptors or musicians, E   are, in one sense, 1820-M   148 creators
E   and, in another, 1820-M   creations E   150 similarity, E   Hesiod E

153 Shakspeare 1820-M   Fletcher E   Pope;— E   157 imitated.— E
160 "a E-M   161 world." E   world:" what 1820-M   162 explain.
— E   part 1820   164 heaven M   166 inforcement E   of of ⟨sic⟩ E
169 equally well be E   172 familiarise M   174 excellence; E-M
175 ⟨no punctuation⟩ E   177 life, M   180 systematical developement E   182 sources of our human E   184 model.— E   186 candid; 1820-M   187 me, E   188 minds, by misrepresentation;— E
189 amuse and 1820-M   191 them; E   ineffectual E   193 sufficient, E   194 efforts.— E   195 grave E-1820

Dramatis Personae

D.P. E   Demogorgon / Ocean / Apollo / The Spirit of the Moon
⟨lacking⟩ E   The Spirit of the Moon ⟨lacking⟩ 1820   The Spirits of the
Hours E   The Echoes E   Fawns E-M (Fauns M²)

Act I

SD Act 1. E   SD Scene—Night A Ravine of Icy E   Scene, a 1820-M
Icy 1820-M   precipice— E   feet. E, M   scene morning slowly breaks E
1 Dæmons E   2 Worlds E   3 Thou E-M   4 eyes, E   eyes! 1820-
M   Earth E-M   6 prayer E   8 fear & self contempt E   fear and
self-contempt 1820-M   hope. 1820-M   11 Oer E   revenge. . . . E
12 hours, 1820-M   13 moments, E   moments 1820-M   14 seem E
years, E-M   15 despair,— 1820-M   empire. E-M   17 throne o E
O, 1820-M   20 eagle baffling mountain E   21 herb E   22 Insect E
life. 1820-M   23 me! 1820   me, alas! M   ever E   for ever! 1820-M
24 hope! Yet 1820-M   endure E   26 Heaven, 1820-M   Sun E   Sun,
1820-M   27 The 1820-M   calm E   calm, 1820-M   28 ever changing Shadow, E   Shadow, 1820-M   below, 1820-M   29 it's ⟨sic⟩ E
30 ⟨no punctuation⟩ E   me! 1820-M   for ever! 1820-M   32 chrystals
E-1820   33 bones, E   bones. 1820-M   35 it's ⟨sic⟩ own, E   36 by
E   37 dream E   38 me E   me: 1820-M   40 behind: 1820-M

41 While E-M   abysses E-M   44 ⟨option⟩: And even E   day and
night, 1820-M   46 slow E   47 East; E   48 Thier ⟨sic⟩ wingless E
The 1820-M   Hours, E   whom E-M   49 —As E-M   Priest E-M
53 Disdain! 1820-M   ah no E   thee—what E   ruin 1820-M   54
thro E   thro' the 1820   through the M   55 terror E   56 Hell E
grief E   57 Exultation, E   more, 1820-M   58 then 1820-M   wise
—the Curse E   59 mountains E   60 Echoes thro E   61 spell; E
62 Springs E   frost E   64 thro' 1820   India; thou E   Air E   65
Thro' 1820   beams, E   66 Whirlwinds E   67 oer E   abyss E
68 ⟨no punctuation⟩ E   69 world—if E   power, E-M   70 —Though
E   71 within, E   72 hate, 1820-M   73 speak E   74 SD 1ˢᵗ
Voice, from the Mountains E   75 Oe'r ⟨sic⟩ the Earthquakes E
stood: 1820-M   76 Oft E   fears E   78 SD 2ᵈ Voice from the
Springs E   Thunder-bolts 1820   79 blood E   80 had ran ⟨sic⟩
mute E   slaugter ⟨sic⟩ E   81 Thro' E-1820   solitude! E   82 SD 3ᵈ
Voice from the Air E   clothed E   uprose E   83 own, E-1820   85
groan E   86 SD 4ᵗʰ Voice from the Whirlwinds E   87 ages;— E
thunder E   88 Volcano's E   fountains E   90 wonder! E   91 SD
1ˢᵗ Voice E   92 unrest— E   93 SD 2ᵈ E   94 bore.— E   96
agony E   97 cried—ah woe is me! E   98 be E   99 SD 3 E
99 Earth E-M   100 riven E
102 oer E   Day E   103 SD 4 E   103 shank ⟨sic⟩ back— E   back:
1820-M   106 a hell 1820   us E   SD they pass with a terrible
sound E   107 SD ⟨option for *The Earth*⟩: A Voice E   107 Caverns 1820-M   108 Misery, then, E   Cried, 1820-M   "Misery!" M
Heaven E-M   replied E   109 Misery! E   "Misery!" M   And 1820-
M   Oceans E   Ocean's 1820-M   110 land E   winds. E   111 it,—
Misery! E   it, "Misery!" M   it, M   112 voices: 1820-M   113 forth.
—Mother E   114 him, E-M   115 Jove, 1820-M   116 vanished,
1820-M   117 wind!— E   me E   118 Titan, E   He 1820-M
119 all conquering E   120 Oh, 1820-M   lawns, 1820-M   streams,
1820-M   121 vapours E   122 Thro E   Thro' 1820   oer-shadow-
ing E   123 eyes, E   eyes; 1820-M   125 me— E   check'd, 1820
checked, M   126 chariteer, 1820-M   127 falshood ⟨sic⟩ E   Him E
129 wildernesses: 1820-M   130 brethren! E   Theydare ⟨sic⟩ 1820
not E   131 again. 1820-M   132 Ha! M   133 sound, E   thro E
thro' 1820   134 strike— E   135 Speak E   137 hear, M   139
spirit; 1820-M   they E   142 roll.— E   143 good, E-1820   tho' E-
1820   144 voice— E   God E-M   145 kind— E   now— E   146
thro' 1820   brain E   dim E   147 thoughts E   thick— E   148
love, E   149 pleasure E   hear E

151 die . . . E thou E   152 O, 1820 Earth E   153 mother, E
veins E   155 air E   156 frame E   157-58 like a beam / From
sunrise, leap— E   158 arise, E-M   160 Thier ⟨sic⟩ E dust E
162 pale— E here— E   163 Then, 1820-M   164 us; E   165
⟨option for sphered⟩: moonlike E Heaven, E Heaven; 1820-M
166 with strange E   169 Inundation E-M   171 crawled; E, M
crawled: 1820   172 Plague E-M man, and beast, 1820-M worm E
worm, 1820-M   173 Famine, E Famine; 1820-M tree, E   174
⟨no punctuation⟩ E meadow-grass, 1820-M   176 growth, E-M   177
grief, E grief; 1820-M   178 mothers E   179 destroyer—aye, E
destroyer; aye, 1820-M   180 which E not E   181 streams E
182 Mountains & caves E Air E   183 dead E   185 words E-M
186 them E Mother! E   188 comfort; E-M flowers & fruits E
sounds E   189 fleeting; these E-M mine E mine. 1820-M   190
not E   191 told—. ⟨sic⟩ E dust E   192 child E   193 garden, E
195 know E-M death E   196 beholdest, E   198 live E-M   199
them 1820-M more, E   200 men E

201 creates 1820-M desires, E-M   203 shade, 1820-M   204
whirlwind-shaken E gods 1820-M   205 Powers E worlds E worlds,
1820-M   206 sceptered Phantoms; E beasts E   207 Gloom E
gloom; 1820-M   208 Supreme Tyrant E   209 throned / on burning Gold. Son E   212 Hades 1820-M Typhon E   213 evil, E Evil,
1820-M   214 sons— E   215 Ask E reply— E   216 supreme E
thro' 1820 shades, 1820-M   217 thro' 1820   218 palace E   219
evil, E-M   220 me— E   221 Jupiter arise E   222 oer mine ears,
E ears: 1820-M   223 o'er mine eyes: 1820-M eyes, E   224 thro E
thro' 1820 appears E   225 thro' 1820 arise, 1820-M   226 Shape,
E-M sounds; 1820-M   227 be, E   228 wounds E   229 whom E
sake E   230 wake E   231 underground E   232 Earthquake E
cloven, E   233 Shape is awful E awful 1820-M   234 purple star-
inwoven E   235 gold E-M   236 proud, E-M oer E cloud E-M
237 ⟨option for *His*⟩: Its E hold E   238 ⟨option for *he*⟩: it E looks
E strong E   239 wrong E   240 **SD** Phantasm E   241 phantom E   243 lips E   245 and E sufferer, 1820-M   246 image, E
Image, 1820   247 Him E foe E   248 hear E   249 voice E
250 And 1820-M tho' 1820 mute E

251-52 ⟨no punctuation⟩ E   253 ye dare not speak E   254 me
1820-M within E   255 thunder-cloud. 1820-M   256 See, 1820-M
looks, E-M Heaven E-M   257 me— E   258 cold E   260 smiles
E   261 scroll: yet speak: Oh, 1820-M o speak . . E   262 Fiend I
defy thee, E calm fixed mind E   263 do E do; 1820-M   264

Humankind E   Human-kind, 1820-M   265 subdue E   266 here E
267 disease, 1820-M (disease M²)   fear E   270 ⟨no punctuation⟩ E
272 Aye E   Ay, M   Omnipotent. E   273 Oer E   power E   274
my E-M   275 mankind E   etherial tower E   277 In darkness
1820-M   279 hate E   hate; 1820-M   280 agony, 1820-M   281
high E   282 thou, 1820-M (thou M²)   Lord: O, thou, 1820-M
(thou M²)   283 woe E   woe, 1820-M   284 Earth E-M   285 worship: 1820-M   287 remorse; 1820   remorse! M   288 'Till E-1820
289 agony E   290 pain, 1820-M   292 soul E   Curse E   Curse,
1820   293 deeds, E-M   good; 1820-M   294 this Universe E   295
self torturing E   solitude M²   296 Image E   299 internally E   internally. 1820-M   300 crime, M

   301 thro' 1820   SD the Phantasm vanishes E   302 words o E   O,
1820   thine E   304 mine E   306 Misery o E   Oh 1820-M   me E
307 thee E   308 aloud E   Sea E   309 Earths E   ye E   310
Howl E   Spirits 1820-M   dead E   312 SD 1ˢᵗ Echo E   ⟨First Echo⟩:
Fallen E   ⟨First Echo⟩: vanquished! 1820   313 SD 2ᵈ Echo E   314
not: 1820-M   tis E   spasm E   spasm, 1820-M   316 see, where E-M
thro E   thro' 1820   317 hill E-M   319 feet, E-M   320 dye,
1820-M   321 ivory E   322 Shape E-M   now E   324 wand E
325 Tis E   Herald, Mercury E   327 wind E   wind, 1820-M   328
represses E-M   330 crowd E   crowd— 1820-M   331 Joves hounds
E   332 gluts on E   blood, 1820-M   333 When E-M   cloud E-M
334 bounds E   335 led, 1820-M   dead E-M   337 ever E   338 SD
1ˢᵗ Fury E   Ha E   SD 2ᵈ E   in E   339 SD 3ᵈ E   340 corpses, 1820-
M   To E   battle. 1820-M   341 SD 1ˢᵗ E   delay o E   Herald! 1820-
M   cheer E   342 Hell: 1820-M   343 sport—who 1820-M   344
iron E   345 gnash 1820-M   fire . . E   fire, M   wail E-M   346
teeth! . . E   teeth. 1820-M   Geryon arise & Gorgon E   347 Chimæra
& thou Spinx ⟨sic⟩ E   Chimæra, 1820-M   fiends E-1820   348 wine E
wine, 1820-M   349 love, 1820-M   hate E   350 task E   SD 1ˢᵗ E
mercy mercy E   Oh, 1820-M

   351 desire: 1820-M   352 silence.— E   Sufferer E-1820   Sufferer;
M²   354 down, 1820-M   356 Alas E   357 do more ⟨sic⟩ —aye E
more: aye 1820-M   more; aye M²   358 heaven seems hell E   heaven
seems hell, 1820-M   360 thou E   good E   362 Omnipotent; 1820-
M   364 taught, M   365 teach—even E   Torturer E-M   366
with E   367 hell, E   368 is, E   here E   369 subtle foul & savage E   foul M²   371 so . . . there E   so! there 1820-M   372 thee E
things E   373 Heaven E   374 Supreme . . . E   Supreme: 1820-M
Supreme; M²   376 prayer E   377 fane, 1820-M   378 heart:

1820-M   382 has; 1820-M   383 ages E   day, E   day: 1820-M
day; M² Sun E-M   385 chrystal-winged E-1820   hair: 1820-M
386 trodden E   388 tyrants E   tyrants' 1820   tyrant's M   recompense—'tis E   recompense: 'tis 1820-M   389 good E   390 bestowed E   lost E   391 Can E   shame; 1820-M   gratitude E   392
misdeed E   393 reproach E   395 know 1820-M   try; M   396
word E   397 captivity, E-M   398 Sicilians E   sword, 1820-M
399 oer E   crown, E-M   accept E   400 yield?—which E

401 Crime, 1820-M   thrond ⟨sic⟩ E   402 Omnipotence; E, M²
Omnipotence: 1820-M   they E   they: 1820-M   403 Justice when triumphant E   404 ⟨no punctuation⟩ E   405 wait E   406 thus E
407 now— E   408 hark E   hark, 1820-M   hell-hounds clamour, E
hell-hounds clamour: fear delay: 1820   409 Behold E   frown E
410 Oh, 1820-M   spared— E   inflict, M   411 once E, M²   me E
412 Joves E   413 come E   alas, E   415 reign, E   reign: 1820
more, 1820-M   416 pause M²   417 Eternity, E-M   time E   418
age on age E   420 Flags, M²   it's ⟨sic⟩ E   flight E, M²   421 shelterless; E-M   423 unreprieved? 1820-M   424 them, 1820-M   pass E
425 gods M²   while E-1820   426 joy?— E   427 pains E   428
Alas E   thee E   429 Heaven E   430 serene, 1820-M   431
throned ... how E   throned: how 1820-M   432 fiends E   O, 1820-M
sister look, white E   433 Cedar E   cedar; 1820-M   435 thine:
1820-M   alas E   437 Heaven, 1820-M   feet, 1820-M   438 dawn E
439 sister E   440 die—they come E   die: they come: 1820-M   441
wings E   442 underneath like death E   SD 1ˢᵗ Fury E   443 SD 2ᵈ
E   SD 3ᵈ E   444 invokes, E   here, E-M   445 Titan.— E   forms E
447 thro E   thro' 1820   448 Jove; E-M   449 shapes E   450 contemplate E

451 sympathy E   452 SD 1ˢᵗ Fury E   452 ⟨no punctuation⟩ E
pain M   453 ⟨no punctuation⟩ E   dissappointment ⟨sic⟩ E   455
Thro' 1820   fawn E   456 ⟨no punctuation⟩ E   457 will E   458
Oh! 1820-M   name! E   459 ye, E   463 SD 2ᵈ Fury E   that—Sisters rejoice E   465 SD 2ᵈ E   465 glad E   466 another— E   we,
M²   469 cheek, 1820-M   471 round E   round, 1820-M   472 we
are 1820-M   Mother Night E   473 power E   here E   474 scorn.
—pour E   pain E   475 SD 1ˢᵗ Fury E   bone from bone? E   477
element E   thine E   478 now, E   not— E   SD 2ᵈ Fury E   480
suffer E   481 evil—cruel E   power 1820-M   482 light E   483
SD 3ᵈ Fury   thinkest E   thro' 1820   by one E   484 life E   life,
1820-M   tho' 1820   485 within E   487 men— E   men: 1820-M
488 brain E   489 heart E   491 agony E   agony. 1820-M   now E

492 myself E   493 within E   494 mutinous E   495 Earth, from
yͤ ends of the Earth E   496 birth E   497 Come, Come, Come E
498 Oh, 1820-M   mirth, 1820-M   499 ruin; 1820-M   500 Sea E
   501 Famines E   track, 1820-M   502 wreck E   wreck; 1820-M
503 Come, Come, Come E   504 low cold & red E   506 hatred— E
507 burning,— E   509 it E   returning: 1820-M   510 self contempt E   511 spirits E   sense enchanted, M²   512 fuel: 1820-M
513 Hells' E   half-unchanted E   unchanted, M   unchanted M²
514 dreamer; 1820-M (dreamer: M²)   515 hate 1820-M   517 Come,
Come, come! E   518 Hells E   gate E-1820   519 atmosphere E
520 here E   521 Sister E   wings E   523 air—thier ⟨sic⟩ E   525
SD 1ˢᵗ E   car, M   526 far E   527 gulphs E-1820   war E   war.
1820-M   528 SD 2ᵈ E   cities E   famine-wasted— E   529 SD 3 E
untasted— E   530 SD 4 E   conclaves, M   cold E   531 was bought
E   sold E   532 SD 5 E   furnace E   hot E   533 SD a Fury E
Speak not—whisper not E   Speak not; M   whisper not: 1820-M   534
tell E   536 Invincible E   537 thought E   538 Hell E   SD a
Fury rushing from the crowd E   539 SD Fury. 1820-M   veil— E
SD ⟨following veil—⟩: The Furies having mingld ⟨sic⟩ in a strange
dance divide, & in the background is seen a plain covered with burning
cities E   ⟨Another Fury⟩: torn. 1820-M   540 misery, 1820-M   borne
E   541 faint E   Titan! M²   scorn E   542 waken'dst 1820-M
man! M²   544 waters, E   fever E   545 hope love doubt E   desire,
1820-M   for ever 1820-M   546 forth, E   worth E-1820   547 earth,
E   earth: M²   549 truth peace & pity E   550 Look E
   552 air— E   553 Mark 1820-M   despair E   554 Tis E   555
kindled E   kindled: 1820-M   556 again, E-1820   557 dwindled E
559 dread E   560 Joy, Joy, Joy, E   561 thee E   remembers; M
562 dark E   563 head E   565 brow, E   566 now: 1820-M
567 See E-1820, M²   Nation E   568 desolation E   569 truth E-
1820, M²   state, E   dedicate; E   571 brothers, M   572 SD Semichorus 2 E   another's: 1820   another's M   573 kin E   kin: 1820
574 Tis E   vintage time M²   death and sin: 1820   death and sin. M
Sin E   575 within E   within: 1820-M   576 'Till 1820   577
World— E   win E   SD All the Furies depart but one E   578 Hark
sister, E   580 Titan— E   deep E   583 Alas, E   twice E   more E
584 sight— E   585 crucifix E   586 The Heaven around the Earth
E   587 death E, M²   588 hands E   hands, 1820-M   589 Tho E
And some 1820-M   hearts E   hearts. M²   590 smiles: E-M   592
by—let E   593 forth— E   594 Behold, an emblem— E   595
scorn E   596 Thousand-fold E   SD a darkness floats slowly across

the scene E   597 stare— E   598 lips— E   lips: M²   599 blood;
1820-M   600 Fix fix E   death E

601 crucifix E   602 gore— E   603 O, 1820-M   thy E   speak E
speak, 1820-M   605 ⟨no punctuation⟩ E   606 thee E   thee, 1820-M
607 hearts E   608 home; 1820-M (home, M²)   610 unwholeesome
⟨sic⟩ cells E   cells: 1820-M   611 Hear 1820-M   loud? E   613 feet
E   isles E   615 homes— E   616 see E   groans E   groans; 1820-M
(groans: M²)   617 ⟨no punctuation⟩ E   things M   619 The ruin
1820   gorged: E-M   623 mans estate E   625 tears: E   tears. 1820-
M   626 them E   them. 1820-M   627 love; 1820-M   628 ill E
629 rich,— E   just— E   630 fellow-men 1820-M   631 felt— E
632 snakes E   633 yet, E   not E   634 SD Exit E   ah woe E
635 pain pain ever E   for ever! 1820-M   637 woe-illumined M
mind E   638 tyrant . . . . peace E   tyrant! 1820-M   grave— E
639 good— E   640 there— E   there, 1820-M   641 it: for, 1820-M
revenge E   642 defeat Fierce King E   king, 1820   king! M   victory. 1820-M   644 endurence, ⟨sic⟩ E   645 are E   646 sawest
thou? 1820-M   woes E   woes; 1820   647 speak, 1820   one E   648
watchwords— E   watch-words, 1820-M   they, M²   649 emblazonry
E   emblazonry; 1820-M   650 And nations E   aloud E

651 voice—truth liberty & love— E   Truth, liberty, and love! 1820-M
652 heaven 1820-M   653 them— E   strife deceit E   fear: 1820-M
654 spoil E   655 saw— E   656 torture Son, E   657 Virtue give— E
658 spirits, 1820-M   659 thought E   661 Its' ⟨sic⟩ E   ether: 1820-M
and they see E   662 glass E   663 future— E   thee E   664 Look
Sister E   gather, 1820-M   665 delighful ⟨sic⟩ weather E   666 air—
E   see more come E   667 dumb E   668 lines E   669 And, hark?
1820   670 lake? Is 1820-M   water fall? E   674 heaven-oppressed
1820-M   mortality— E   mortality! M²   677 ⟨no punctuation⟩ E
678 day, 1820-M   679 oer E   gleams: M²   681 streans ⟨sic⟩ E
682 Silent liquid & serene— E   serene; 1820-M   683 wind E   684
wave E   686 thro' 1820   grave E   grave; 1820-M   grave: M²   687
We make these 1820   there, E   688 cloud like E   689 Thro E
Thro' 1820   element— E   692 one by one, E   693 radiant like E
star E   694 SD 1ˢᵗ Spirit E   695 ⟨no punctuation⟩ E   696 Mid E
cast— E   697 outworn E   698 tyrants E   torn E   699 'round
1820   borne E   700 cry E

701 Freedom, Hope, Death Victory! E   Freedom! 1820-M   Victory!
1820-M   702 thro E   thro' 1820   sky E   703 sound, E-1820
above around E   704 ⟨no punctuation⟩ E   705 moving; E-M
twas E   love E   706 ⟨no punctuation⟩ E   Twas E   707 thee E

708 SD 2ᵈ Spirit E   rainbows E   sea E   **709** rock'd M (rocked M²)
710 Storm E   flee E   **711** conqueror, 1820-M   **712** Between 1820-
M   cloud E-M   **713** ⟨no punctuation⟩ E   dark 1820-M   **714** half
— E   half: 1820-M   **715** laugh— E   laugh: 1820-M   **717** beneath, E   **718** Oer E   waters— E   **719** ship lightning-split E
ship 1820-M   **722** plank, 1820-M   die E-1820   **723 SD** 3ᵈ E
sate E-M   bed E   **725** fed E   **726** dream E   flame, 1820-M   **727**
came E   **730** ⟨no punctuation⟩ E   **732** shade, E-1820   made E
733 born ⟨sic⟩ 1820   **734** Desires E   feet E   **735** morrow E   **736**
sorrow E   **737 SD** 4ᵗʰ E   Poets E   **740** blisses E   **741** aërial M
742 thoughts wildernesses E   **745** i the ivy-bloom E   **746** see, E-M
be E   **748** man E   **749** immortality!— E   **750** me E
　751 thee E   **752** Beholdst ⟨sic⟩ E   East E   **753** Come M²   nest E
754 all sustaining E   air E-M   **755** atmosphere E   **756** And, 1820-M
hark—their sweet sad voices, tis E   sweet M²   **757** love 1820-M   sound
—E   **758** speak E   drowned E   **760** grain E   **761** azure, E   deepning ⟨sic⟩ E   gold E   **762** Thier ⟨sic⟩ E   fire E   **763 SD** 5ᵗʰ Spirit
E   **764** wildernesses E   **765** pinions E   **767** light— E   light;
1820-M   past 1820-M   fading E   **768** behind—great Sages E   behind: great 1820-M   madness E   **769** patriots, 1820-M   perished un-
upbraiding E   **770** Night E   night. 1820-M   o'er—till thou o E
o'er, 1820-M   sadness E   sadness, 1820-M   **771** gladness E   **772**
SD 6ᵗʰ Spirit E   Ah sister, E   thing E   **773** Earth E   air E   **774**
silent footstep, 1820-M   **775** bear E   **776** Who E   above 1820
778 aërial 1820-M   monster, E-M   Love E   **779** their shadow Pain—
E Pain, 1820-M   his ⟨?⟩ E   greet E   **780** Tho' 1820   Loves E   be E
781 him, destroyingly, 1820-M   **782** death's M²   steed E   **783**
flee, 1820-M   **784** weed E   **785** beast E   fair E   **786** thro E
thro' 1820   air; E-M   **787** Horseman grim E   **788** limb.— E
789 Spirits E   be E   **790** breathe E   breathe, 1820-M   **791** when
the snow-storms flee, 1820-M   **792** beneath E   **793** shake, E   elder-
brake, M²   brake E   **795** blow: 1820-M   **796** ⟨no punctuation⟩ E
797 increase E   **799** shepherd-boys— E   shepherd boys, 1820-M
800 thee E   **SD** They vanish E
　801 Spirits 1820-M   **802** Omnipotence E   **803** music, 1820-M
804 reponses ⟨sic⟩ E   mute, 1820-M   **805** thro E   thro' 1820   soul E,
M²   **806** thro' 1820   caverns E   roll E   **807** shapes; E   **808** love,
E   far E   **809** who E   overflowed E   **811** dust E   **812** still—
alas E   still: alas! 1820-M   **813** heart; E-M   **814** Tho' 1820
dream 1820-M   grief, M   **815** not .. E   **816** to be E   **817** man E
818 gulph E   things: 1820-M   **819** agony, 1820-M   left E   **820**

more E   **824** love—thou lovest . . . E   **825** In truth— E   Eastern
E   looks wan E   **826** vale E-M   **827** exile; 1820-M   once E-M
828 frozen E   ravine; E-M   **829** herbs E   **831** waters: E   **832**
presence— E   **333** thine—farewell E   **SD** ⟨lacking⟩ E

ACT II, SCENE I

SD Act 2. E   **SD** Scene Morning—a lovely vale in the Indian Caucasus—. Asia alone E   lonely vale M   **1** Heaven E   descended— E
2 Yes E   thought, 1820-M   **3** eyes E   **4** heart, 1820-M   **5** repose— E   repose: 1820-M   **6** tempests E   wake o Spring E   **7**
winds . . E   **8** dream, 1820-M   **10** genius E   **11** Earth E   **12**
desart E   life. 1820-M   **13** season E   day E   hour, E   **14** come E
mine . . . E   **15** desired E   delaying come . . . E   **19** mountains:
1820-M   thro' 1820   **21** Reflects it: 1820   it; M   wanes: 1820
wanes; M   **23** air. . . . E   **24** Tis E   thro' 1820   **25** sunrise E
sun-light quivers: 1820-M   **26** eolian E   seagreen E   **27 SD** Panthea enters E   **28** thro E   thro' 1820   tears E   **29** half-quenched
M   dew— E   **31** live E   **32** art; E   **33** sea; 1820-M   **35** Great
Sister! E   Sister! 1820-M   **36** dream E   **37** noon-tide 1820-M
38 calm E-M   **40** fall, E-M   and thy 1820-M   **41** love, E-M   made
E   thro' 1820   pity E   **43** yours . . . erewhile E   thine: erewhile
1820-M   **44** Ocean E-M   **45** moss; E   **47** then as now E   dark
moist hair E   **49** bosom . . . E   **50** now E

54 sweet— E   sweet; 1820-M   **55** eyes, 1820-M   **56** dream— E
said E-M (said, M²)   **57** slept E   **58** mountain-mists E   **59**
flakes E   **60** sheilding ⟨sic⟩ E   sleep . . . E   **61** One, 1820-M   **62**
⟨no punctuation⟩ 1820-M   **66** makes dizzy E   brain, 1820-M   **68**
"Sister 1820-M   **69** "With 1820   her, 1820-M   **70** "Whose 1820
me! E   me." 1820-M   **71** them— E   **72** oer E   **73** love; E-M
limbs E   **74** keen E   eyes E   **75** Steam'd E   fire; E-M   **76**
wrapt E-1820   power, 1820-M   **79** not—heard not—moved not— E
onlv ⟨sic⟩ 1820   **80** thro E   thro' 1820   **81** life E   mine E   **82**
absorb'd, 1820   absorbed, M   past E   past, 1820   **83** down E   **84**
pines E   **86** condensed, E   **88** as they died E   **89** weak melody:
thy name 1820-M   melody thy E   **90** sounds 1820-M   **91** tho'
1820   **93** me E   **94-106** ⟨double quotes precede each line except
104 and 106 E; precede each line 1820⟩   **94** to-night? E, M   to night?
1820   **95** before E   **96** vain E   **97** seek E   seek; 1820-M   **98**
not; 1820-M   sweet E   **99** desire—it E   desire; it 1820-M   sport
false Sister! E   sister; 1820-M   **100** inchantment old E

102 thine;— E   thine: 1820-M   **104** me, E-M   **105** life-blood,

1820-M faint, 1820-M   **106** arms" E   arms." 1820-M   **107** Eastern E-M pale E   **108** thee E   **109** air E   not: Oh, 1820-M   oh E
110 eyes E   soul. E   **111** them tho' 1820   **112** express— E   **113**
there E   **114** deep blue E   Heaven E   **115** Contracted in E
116 long E   lashes— E   measureless,— E   measureless, 1820-M
117 thro' 1820 inwoven— E   **118** past? E-1820   **119** change, E
change; M   **120** shade—a shape— E   He, E-M   **121** smiles E
122 moon E   morn. 1820-M   **123** Prometheus it is thou— E   it is
thine! 1820-M yet E   **125** Pavilion E   **126** oer E   build on 1820-
M world? E-M   the dream is told E   **127** its E   **128** it, E-M
129 quick, E-M air E-M   **130** thro' 1820   **131** quench'd 1820
Follow, Follow! 1820-M   **132** dream— E   dissappears. ⟨sic⟩ E   **134**
sate E-M here, 1820-M   **135** almond-tree E   almond-tree, 1820
tree, M   **136** swift, E   wilderness, E   **137** forth E-M   Earth E-M
frost . . . E   frost: 1820-M   **138** down E   **139** stamped, 1820-M
140 Apollos E   grief, 1820-M   **141** O, E-M   **142** pause mine E
my own 1820-M   **143** shapes . . . methought E   the lawns 1820-M
144 dawn E   **146** mountains E-M   **147** slow E   **148** new bladed
1820 grass E   **149** silently— E   silently; 1820-M   **150** not: 1820-M
     151 But, E   morning clouds, 1820-M   **152** slope, 1820-M   **153**
Follow, o follow E   O, 1820-M   As 1820-M   by, E-M   **154** herb,
1820-M Heaven's E-M   fallen, 1820-M   **155** stamped, 1820-M   fire
E fire, 1820-M   **156** pines— E   **158** ⟨no punctuation⟩ E   **159**
heard—Oh, E   Oh, 1820-M   me ⟨underlined⟩ E   **160** ⟨no punctua-
tion⟩ E   said: 1820 ⟨double quotes⟩ 1820-M   **162** saw follow, follow.
E   **163** crags E   morning E   voices E-1820   **164** spirit-tongued E
165 crags—what E   sounds—o list E   O, 1820-M   **166 SD** Echoes unseen E   we—listen E   **167** stay E   **169** away— E-M   **171** Hark
spirits speak! the E   Spirits, M   speak. 1820-M   **172** aërial M
sound— E   **173** O follow follow E   O, 1820   **175** Thro E   Thro'
1820 hollow, 1820-M   **176** spreadeth E   **SD** More distant E   **177**
O follow follow E   O, 1820   follow, follow! 1820-M   **178** Thro'
1820 hollow E   hollow, 1820-M   **179** floats 1820-M   pursue E
180 wild-bee E   flew E   **181** Thro' 1820   noon-tide 1820-M   deep
E   **182** odour breathing E   **183** night flowers, 1820   **184** caves
E   **185** music E   **186** gently falling 1820-M   feet E   **188** sound?
—it E   **189** distant E   list— E   now E   **190 SD** Echo E   **191**
unspoken E   **193** broken E   broken; 1820-M   **194** Ocean E   **195**
wind E   win ⟨sic⟩ 1820 ⟨second issue⟩   **196 SD** Echo E   O, 1820   follow follow E   follow, follow! 1820-M   **197** Thro E   Thro' 1820
hollow E   hollow, 1820-M   **198** floats, E   pursue E   **199** wood

land E   noon-tide dew; 1820-M   dew E   200 ⟨no punctuation⟩ E
fountains 1820

201 Thro E   Thro' 1820   mountains E   mountains; 1820-M   **202**
⟨no punctuation⟩ E   gulphs E   gulphs, 1820   chasms, 1820-M   **203**
spasms, 1820-M   **204** He E-M   **205** Parted— E   now E   now;
1820-M   **206** Ocean E   **207** Come E   Panthea— E   thine E
mine E   **208** away E

ACT II, SCENE II

SD Scene 2. A forest intermingled with rocks & caverns. Asia & Panthea pass into it—2 young fawns are sitting on a rock listening E   **1**
SD Semi-Chorus of Spirits—1 E   thro' 1820   **2** past, E-M   pine &
yew E   **3** grew E   **4** Heaven's E-M   blue E   **5** no punctuation
E   **6** bowers, 1820-M   **7** aught E   where 1820-M   dew E   **8**
breeze, 1820-M   **9** trees E   **11** anew; E-M   **12** bends E   silently
E   **13** anemone: E-M   **15** climb & wander E   thro' 1820   Night E
16 thro E   thro' 1820   **17** upon 1820-M   **19** Heavens E-M   stay—
E   stay, 1820-M   **20** glolden ⟨sic⟩ light E   **21** unite: E-M   **22**
around E   around; 1820-M   **23** ground E   **24 SD** Semichorus 2. E
nightingales, 1820-M   **25** thro' 1820   noonday E   noon-day, 1820-M
26 fails E   fails, 1820-M   **27** thro' 1820   ivy-boughs E   **29** mates
E   bosom; 1820-M   **30** blossom E   **33** melody E   **34** 'Till 1820
new strain 1820-M   **35** Thesong, ⟨sic⟩ M (The song, M²)   **36** thro'
E-1820   **38** lake-surrounding 1820   flute E   **39** listeners E   **40**
sweet, E-M   pain E   **41 SD** Semichorus 1. E   inchanted E   **42**
echoes E   draw E   **43** Demogorgons E   law E   **44** rapture, or
sweet awe, 1820-M   **45** way; 1820-M   **46** Ocean E-M   **47** mountain-thaw: 1820   mountain thaw; M²   **49** bound E   **50** destined—
E   destined soft emotion, 1820   destined, M²

51 them: those E-1820   them; those M   **52** Earth E   **53** streams
M²   **54** while, E   **56** within, obey E   obey: 1820-M   **57** way E
58 ⟨no punctuation⟩ E   sweet, 1820-M   **59** along E   **60** hurrying—
E   hurrying 1820   **61** Behind E   **63** air E   **64 SD** 1ˢᵗ Faun E
68 meet them E   tho' 1820   oft, E   **69 SD** 2ᵈ Faun E   tell— E
70 say E   **71** bubbles E   Which enchantment M   **72** water-flowers,
E   **73** pools E   **74** dwell, E   **76** which the noontide E   noontide 1820-M   thro' 1820   leaves E   **77** air E   **78** ⟨options⟩: lucent
homes ⟨or⟩ shining homes E   **79** thro' 1820   **80** ride on them,
1820-M   it E   **81** crests E   **82** Earth again E   **83 SD** 1ˢᵗ E
lives E   **85** deep E   **86** die E   die? M²   **87** Or on 1820-M

88 SD 2ᵈ E   Ay, M   more 1820-M   divine E   89 But, 1820-M   wᵈ E
90 undrawn E   92 fate & chance E   93 love E   Love, 1820-M
Titans E   doom E   dooms, 1820   doom. M   94 Earth E   95
brotherhood— E   97 nightingales . . E

ACT II, SCENE III

SD Scene 3. A pinnacle of rock among Mountains—Asia & Panthea E
2 portal E   3 chasm E   4 breathed up E   5 youth E   6 genius
or joy E   joy, 1820-M   8 intoxication; 1820-M   uplift E   9 loud E
11 Power! 1820-M   Magnificent: E   12 thou Earth! E   And 1820-M
beest E   13 Spirit E   still E   14 work E   15 beautiful E   16
thee— E   17 adoreth— E   adoreth: 1820-M   18 Look Sister— E
brain; E   19 mist E   21 light E   22 vale . . . behold E   24
stand, 1820-M   around, 1820-M   25 forests E   26 twilight-lawns,
1820-M (twilight lawns M²) stream-illumined 1820-M   caves E   27
wind-inchanted E   mist E   28 mountains, M²   29 sun-like 1820-
M   30 Oceans E   Ocean's 1820-M   spray E   31 up E   32 water
drops E   33 walls— E   walls, 1820-M   34 thaw-clovén ⟨sic⟩ E
36 silence—hark! E   snow E   37 avalanche, whose mass E   38
storm E   39 flake: E   in heaven-defying 1820-M   41 round E
42 roots: E   43 Look 1820-M   44 foam E   feet— E   45 Ocean
E-M   inchantment E   46 on an E   isle E   47 up— E   48
which E   hair— E   49 It's ⟨sic⟩ E   oer my eyes— E   50 dizzy— E
I see thin shapes 1820   I see shapes M   mist. 1820-M

51 smiles— E   52 locks— E   53 another—hark E   another:
1820-M   54 To the Deep, to the Deep E   55 Down, Down! E
56 Sleep E   58 life E   59 viel ⟨sic⟩ E   60 are E-1820   61
Throne E   62 Down, Down! E   63 sound, E   64 Down, Down!
E   65 hound E   66 vapour E   67 taper E   68 Death Despair,
Love Sorrow E   69 both, To-day E   to day, to morrow; 1820   70
Spirit E   stone E   71 Down, Down E   Down, down. 1820   72
grey E   Abysm E   73 Down, Down! E   74 prism E   75 not E
77 Heaven, E-M   78 Earth E-M   given, 1820-M   79 one pervading, one 1820-M   80 Down, Down! E   81 Deep E   deep 1820-M
82 Down, Down! E   83 veil'd Lightning E   84 the 1820-M   embers E   86 diamond, 1820-M   87 mines E   mines. M²   88 hidden, but from thee alone,— E   treasur'd 1820   89 Down Down! E
90 bound thee; 1820-M   91 Down Down! E   92 thee— E   thee;
1820-M   93 weakness— E   weakness, 1820-M   94 meekness— E
95 Eternal the Immortal E   96 thro E   98 alone. 1820-M

ACT II, SCENE IV

SD Scene 4 the Cave of Demogorgon Asia, Panthea, E   1 throne.
E   2 fallen! . . E   fallen. 1820-M Darkness E   3 power; E
4 Sun E   5 shapeless— . . E shapeless; 1820-M limb E   6 ⟨no
punctuation⟩ E   7 Spirit E   Spirit. 1820-M ⟨spirit. M²⟩   know E
8 dar'st 1820-M   demand E   10 contains? 1820-M   11 God, Almighty E   12 which E   sping ⟨sic⟩ E   13 visitation M²   14
alone E   15 tears, E   16 flowers E   18 more E   God E   19
remorse E   20 things, 1820-M   22 heavily— E   24 hate E   25
self-contempt M²   26 Pain E   27 howling E   day after day, E
28 reigns E   29 name: 1820-M   30 name; E   31 reigns E   it—
E   32 there E   first E   33 Love;— E   34 shadow: 1820-M
35 earth ⟨option: world's⟩ E   sway E   37 have E   them E-M   38
semivital E-1820   39 birthrights E   being, E-M   knowledge E   41
pieerces ⟨sic⟩ E   Universe E   42 Self-empire E   love, E   43
fainted; then E   44 Jupiter E   45 alone: E   "Let man be free,"
M   let E   ⟨no quotes⟩ E   47 faith nor love nor law, E   48 friendless 1820-M   reign; E-M   49 man, E   50 ⟨no punctuation⟩ E

   51 before E   52 Fell, E   drove E-1820   53 fire E   54 shelterless E   caves E   caves: 1820-M   55 desart E   sent E   61 blooms;
E   63 death, and love E   66 fire which, 1820-M   beast of prey,
1820-M   68 man, E   69 power; E   71 waves E   72 thought E
73 Universe E   74 Earth & Heaven E   heaven, 1820-M   75 shook,
1820-M   76 song; 1820-M   80 mocked E   81 own E   82 ⟨op-
tion for *till*⟩: until E   divine; 1820   divine M   84 race, 1820-M
perish— E   85 spings ⟨sic⟩ E   86 slept— E   sleep,— E   88
stars; 1820-M   Sun E   89 lair,— E   91 sea; E   sea: 1820-M   93
Ocean E   Ocean, 1820-M   94 Indian: E   95 thro E   snowlike E
96 æther E-M   shone E   97 seen . . . E   98 Such E   state E   99
man— E   100 pain— E   reigns 1820

   101 which E   103 on E-M   104 Earth, E   105 alone?— E
106 Jove, E   heaven, 1820-M   aye E-1820   107 adversary, E   108
slave: E   109 is he E   110 evil E   112 called'st 1820-M   speak E
114 —If the Abysm E   115 secrets:—but E   secrets. But 1820-M
118 What 1820-M   119 Change:— E   120 love. E   123 oracle.—
E   124 demand . . . E   126 ask— E   127 sun 1820-M   world E
128 When shall 1820-M   130 Cars E   131 winds— E   132 charioteer 1820-M   133 there E   134 stars E   stars: 1820-M   135
Others E   eyes E   136 speed E   137 before E   138 now—even
now E   it; their bright hair E   139 Streams E   comets & all E
140 onward— E   Hours E   141 demand—one E   thee E   142

Spirit E   143 gulph E   gulph. 1820   144 brethren— E   charioteer E   145 Who 1820-M   speak E   146 ⟨option for *shadow*⟩:
image E   147 my E-M   aspect— E   148 darkness 1820-M   149
heaven's 1820-M   throne E   150 That 1820-M

151 lurid dust E   152 earthquake ruined cities oer the sea— E
153 Car . . . E   car; 1820-M   154 Terrified; watch E   Terrified:
watch 1820-M   stars E-M   155 ⟨option for *Blackening*⟩: Darkening E
night E   answered—strange.! ⟨sic⟩ E   answered: 1820-M   156 verge
E   stays E   stays; 1820-M   157 fire, 1820-M   159 tracery—the E
tracery; the 1820-M   Spirit E   160 it, E   dove-like 1820-M   hope.
E   161 soul! 1820-M   162 thro E   thro' 1820   163 lightning E
164 stream E   165 brightning ⟨sic⟩ E-1820   167 swiftness E-M
deem E   deem, 1820-M   168 me E   daughters E   daughter 1820-M
Ocean E   169 desire: 1820-M   170 fear: 1820-M   Typhoon; E-M
172 moon, E   moon: 1820-M   173 at noon: 1820-M   noon— E
174 me daughters of Ocean E   daughter 1820-M

ACT II, SCENE V

SD Scene—the Car pauses within a cloud on the top of a snowy
mountain E   ⟨names lacking⟩ E   2 respire, E   4 fire E   6 nostrils— E   7 speed E   Alas, E   8 Oh 1820-M   Spirit pause E   9
this cloud— E   cloud? 1820-M   unrisen E   10 noon— E   11
Heaven by wonder— E   13 water E   14 sister E   feel . . . E   15
thou art pale E   16 changd! ⟨sic⟩ E   thee E   17 feel 1820-M
19 elements E   20 unveiled—the E   22 thy uprise, 1820-M   24
chrystal E   25 Egean E-M   26 name, E   name; 1820-M   27
world E   28 Earth & Heaven E   heaven 1820-M   29 caves E-M
30 dwell E   32 now, E   alone E   33 sister E   one E   35 i the
air E   i' 1820-M   36 feelest E   37 thee?—list E   39 are— E
sweet E   40 returned; common E   love E   41 ever E   42 Heav-
en, E   air E   43 God . . . E   44 most, are fortunate E   46 sufferings E   47 become E   list, spirits speak E   Spirits, M   48 SD
Voice in the Air E   Life of life! E   49 them E

52 looks E   53 mazes E   54 thy lips 1820   55 Thro E   Thro'
1820   them E   them; 1820-M   57 Thro' 1820   clouds, M   them E
59 whereso'er ⟨sic⟩ thou shinest E   60 others;— E   thee, E-M   62
fairest, 1820-M   63 sight E   splendour E   64 never E   65 for
ever! 1820-M   67 brightness E-1820   68 ⟨option for whom⟩: those
E   69 lightness E   71 lost . . . yet unbewailing E   72 Boat E
74 singing, E   75 Angel E   76 it E   77 ringing E   78 ever—
forever— E   for ever, 1820-M   79 many winding River E   80 Be-

tweens ⟨sic⟩ E   81 Paradise E   wildernesses, E   82 Till E   bound
E   83 Ocean, E   float, E   84 Sea E   profound, E-M   sound E
sound: 1820   85 ⟨no stanza division⟩ 1820   Spirit E   86 Music's E
dominions E   dominions; 1820-M   87 Heaven E   89 course— E
star— E   90 But, 1820-M   Music driven E   driven; 1820-M   91
Till 1820-M   islets E-M   93 glided E   94 guided— E   95 Love
E   96 winds on 1820-M   move E   97 Earth E   above E   98
past E   pass'd 1820   99 waves E   100 betray; E

      101 gulphs E-1820   102 infancy, E   103 Thro E   Death and
Birth, 1820-M   day; E-M   104 Paradise E   bowers, 1820   105
down ward-gazing ⟨sic⟩ flowers E   107 green E   108 see E   109
beheld; E-M   thee E   thee; 1820-M   110 sea, E-M   chaunt melodiously E   chaunt 1820   SD ⟨lacking⟩ E

ACT III, SCENE I

SD Act 3ᵈ E   SD Scene—Heaven. Jupiter on his throne Thetis &
The other Deities assembled— E   1 Powers of Heaven E   heaven,
1820-M   2 serve E   3 am I omnipotent E   4 had been 1820-M
me— E   5 like an unextinguished 1820   fire E   6 heaven 1820-M
reproach & doubt E   7 lamentation E   prayer E   prayer, 1820-M
10 hell's 1820-M   fear; E-M   11 tho' 1820   thro E   thro' 1820   air
E   12 by flake, 1820-M   13 it— E   tho' 1820   wrath's might 1820
15 feet E   16 misery E   17 Aspiring . . unrepressed; E   19
Child, E   Earth, E   20 distant hour 1820   hour M   arrive E   21
Demogorgons E   22 ever living E   23 unbeheld— E   24 redescend, 1820-M   spark . . . E   25 ⟨no punctuation⟩ E   heaven's
1820-M   26 Dædal 1820-M   fire E   fire, 1820-M   27 divine, M
28 all triumphant E   arise E   29 Earth E   stars; E   stars: 1820-M
30 Drink, E   thro E   thro' 1820   31 everliving Gods E   33 winds.
—& thou E   winds. / And thou 1820-M   35 me E   36 Image of
Eternity— E   37 cry— E   ⟨initial quotes each line⟩ 1820   might E
38 spare E   39 presence, E   being E   41 dissolved— E   42 thro
E   thro' 1820   foundations"— E   foundations:" 1820-M   43 spirits
mingling E   mingling M   44 either—which E   now, 1820-M   45
us 1820-M   felt, 1820-M   though ⟨?⟩ unbeheld E   46 ascends, 1820-
M   47 (Hear 1820-M   48 winds? E   winds?) 1820-M   throne— E
49 Victory! Victory!; ⟨sic⟩ feel'st thou not o World E   Feel'st 1820
world! M   50 Earthquake E

      51 SD The Car of the Hour arrives, Demogorgon descends & moves
toward the throne of Jupiter. E   descends, 1820   Shape, E   Speak E
52 Eternity—demand E   53 abyss; E   54 Saturns child . . . E

child; 1820-M   55 thee E   thee: 1820-M   56 darkness— E   not—
E   57 heaven 1820-M   retain E   58 hold E   thee . . . E   59 wilt,
1820-M   tis E   60 dead, 1820-M   61 might E   63 thou E-M
(Thou M²)   Mercy, mercy E   64 pity— E   respite! . . oh E   65
judge— E   66 revenge E   67 Caucasus—he E   he 1820-M   thus—
E   68 ⟨no punctuation⟩ E   69 world?—what E   What art thou?
1820   thou? E   70 refuge, no appeal— . . . E   then, 1820-M   71
shall E   on 1820-M   ruin E   73 fight; E   74 sea.— E   hell 1820-
M   75 Oceans E   fire E   77 ⟨no punctuation⟩ E   This 1820-M
thou E   79 combated . . . Ai, ai, E   80 not . . . I sink . . . E   81
down, ever, for ever, down. 1820-M   forever, down E   82 And like a
cloud the enemy above . . . E   83 victory—ai! ai! E   Ai, Ai! M

ACT III, SCENE II

SD Scene The mouth of a great River in the island Atlantis—Ocean
is discovered reclining near the shore—Apollo stands beside him— E
Shore; 1820-M   1 fell thou sayest E   Conquerors E   2 Ay, M
3 stars, 1820-M   4 heaven 1820-M   5 light, 1820-M   thro E   6
Darkness E   darkness, 1820-M   fell; E   fell: 1820-M   7 agony E   8
Which, 1820-M   clouds, 1820-M   9 Deep E   10 abyss? To 1820-M
11 so 1820-M   13 Intangled E   eyes E-M   16 form E   17 aërial
M   it— E   18 Heaven-reflecting E-M   19 unstain'd E-1820   blood
E   blood. M (blood, M²)   20 winds— E   22 many peopled 1820-M
continents E   24 Nymphs E   26 light laden 1820-M   27 crest E
28 sunsets E   sea; E-M   29 groans E   31 command— E   command; 1820-M   33 mild free gentle voices E   34 music,— E   36
Eclipse E   37 guide—but E   guide; but 1820-M   38 small clear E
Spirit E-M   39 i the Morning star— E   on 1820   i' M   away? E
40 even, till when farewell: 1820-M   farewell E   41 Deep E   now
1820-M   43 for ever 1820-M   throne . . . E   44 sea E   sea, 1820-M
45 wind-like stream, 1820-M   streams E   46 oer E   47 crowns, E-M
48 Sisters joy E   SD The roar of waves is heard— E   49 Sea hun-
gring ⟨sic⟩ for Calm E   50 Peace Monster— E   monster; 1820-M
now! farewell E   now. 1820-M   ⟨after *Apollo*⟩: Farewell!— E

ACT III, SCENE III

SD Scene Caucasus, Prometheus, Hercules, Asia Panthea Ione, the
Earth. ⟨sic⟩ borne by the spirit of the Hour   Spirits— Hercules unbinds Prometheus who descends E   Spirits, Asia, and Panthea, 1820-M
1 Spirits, E   spirits! M   2 ⟨no punctuation⟩ E   3 animate E   4
Minister 1820-M   7 unbeheld, E   unbeheld: 1820   ye, 1820-M   8

sister-nymphs who make E   9 remember E   thro' 1820   care E
care; M   10 ⟨option⟩: let us not E   Cave E   11 plants, 1820-M
12 flowers E   13 emerald, E-M   fountain, M   14 sound; E   15
tears E-1820   16 ⟨no punctuation⟩ E   17 ⟨option⟩: Cling pendent E
light: 1820-M   18 air E   20 seats E   21 grass E   grass; 1820-M
22 own E   own; 1820-M   23 change, 1820-M   24 unchanged.
1820-M   25 Mutability?— E   26 smile, E   thou E   27 shalt
chaunt 1820   shall chaunt M   29 brought; E   shed; E   30 flowers 1820-M   31 brim E   32 things E   33 innocence E   34
search M   love E   35 thoughts E   last E   36 spirits; 1820-M
and E-M   37 wind E   39 be . . E   40 thither E   come, E-M
winds, 1820-M   41 Heaven, E   42 aërial M   feeds, 1820-M   43
Himera, E-M   45 unheard E   46 music E   48 free E   free;
1820-M   49 apparitions E   first E   50 radiant, E-M

53 reality E   reality, 1820-M   55 ⟨no punctuation⟩ E   wrapt 1820
56 tho' 1820   be E   59 worship love, E-1820   worship, love M
60 returned, E   sounds, 1820-M   61 kind E   62 by veil, 1820-M
fall . . . E   63 around E   SD turning to the Spirit of the Hour E
64 thee fair Spirit E   Ione E   65 shell, E-M   old, M   68 rock E
70 sisters E   this the E, M   shell E   71 silver E-M   72 light. E
74 Ocean E   Ocean: 1820-M   75 It's ⟨sic⟩ E   strange E   77 coursers! E   78 world E   79 air E   80 Shell E   81 music . . . E
82 echoes—then E   echoes: then 1820-M   83 Return E   Return;
1820-M   cave E   SD kissing the ground E   84 thou o E   Earth— E
O, 1820   I hear—I feel— E   85 thy touch 1820-M   87 nerves;
1820-M   life 'tis joy E   88 And, M   thro' 1820   withered old E
89 down E-M   90 Circling—henceforth E   91 arms; E-M   plants
E   92 rainbow-winged E   93 ⟨no punctuation⟩ E   94 bosom E
95 despair, E-M   98 snow white E   wind E-1820   99 stream; E
100 dew mists E

101 balm, E   balm: 1820-M   102 unwitting 1820   repose E   repose: 1820-M   104 day, 1820-M   joy E   joy: 1820-M   106 mother
E-1820   107 leave E   "Leave 1820-M   again! E   again." 1820-M
108 Oh, 1820-M   mother E   109 ⟨no punctuation⟩ E   110 reply E
111 immortal E   112 dead— E   113 life E   114 sleep— E
lifted . . . E   lifted: 1820-M   mild E-M   116 winds E   118 Sun's
E   120 mild; E   mild, 1820-M   121 fields, 1820-M   aye E   122
desarts E-1820   deep E   deep, 1820-M   123 ⟨no punctuation⟩ E
124 Thou . . . there E   Cavern whence E   126 those that M   127
Temple there E   128 spoke E   129 war E   130 thee; E-M   131
rises E   amongst 1820-M   132 violets E   134 Intense yet soft E

135 vine E   **136** wild E   **138** light, 1820-M   **139** thro' 1820
bright, E   **140** heaven; E   **141** And 1820-M   thro' 1820   stems E-M
143 aërial 1820-M   **144** spirits; and E   spirits: and 1820-M   round E
145 dreams E   **146** mine E   **147** restored . . . that Cave is thine E
This cave 1820-M   **148** appear! E   **SD** a spirit rises in the likeness
of a winged child E   this E   torch-bearer E   torch-bearer; 1820-M
149 time, E

151 ⟨no punctuation⟩ E   Daughter E   **152** own—run Wayward! E
wayward, 1820-M   **154** mountain E   **155** Indus, E   **157** undelaying, 1820-M   **158** vale E   **159** chrystálline E   pool, 1820-M
160 waves E   **161** temple built above. E   **162** ⟨no punctuation⟩ E
163 capitals, E   over wrought, E   over-wrought, 1820-M   **164** populous most with 1820-M   imagery E   imagery, 1820-M   **168** name
Prometheus, E   Prometheus; 1820-M   **169** thy 1820-M   thro E
thro' 1820   **170** lamp, E   emblem . . . E   emblem; 1820-M   **172**
grave E   life . . . E   **174** Time . . . depart, farewell! E   Time. 1820-
M   Depart, 1820-M   **175** Temple E   Cave . . . E

ACT III, SCENE IV

SD Scene=A forest—in the background a Cavern—Prometheus Asia
Ione Panthea the Spirit of the Earth— E   Back-ground M   **1** Sister
E   Earthly . . . E   **3** light E   **4** moves E   **7** thro Heaven. E
thro' 1820   **9** planets, E   **10** sea E   **11** cloud E   **12** thro E
thro' 1820   sleep E   **13** oer E   **14** thro' 1820   **19** dipsas, 1820-
M   **21** much E   **22** saw— E   her, 1820-M   **23** not E   I, 1820-M
24 Mother dear Mother E   **SD** Asia & the spirit have entered the cave
E   **SD** The Spirit running to Asia E   **24** ⟨no quotes⟩ E-M   ⟨follow-
ing the SD⟩: Mother dearest Mother! E   **26** my eyes 1820-M   arms,
1820-M   **28** noons, 1820-M   **30** thee E   being! M   **31** unenvied
—speak I pray E   unenvied: speak, 1820   **32** solaced . . . E   **33 SD**
Spirit E   wiser E   **34** day E   **35** too, E   too; 1820-M   **36** ⟨no
punctuation⟩ E   **37** venemous ⟨sic⟩ E   **39** An hindrance E-1820
oer E   world E   world: 1820-M   **40** humankind E   **41** Hard fea-
tured E   proud angry looks E   **42** cold E   smiles E   **43** ignorance
E   **44** masks, 1820-M   **45** man E   **46** evil E   evil, 1820-M   **47**
(Tho' 1820   (Though M   art fair E   **48** kind E   thee; E   thee,)
1820   thee), M   **50** tho' 1820

51 Well— E   thro' 1820   City E   **52** it: 1820-M   **53** A sentinel
1820-M   gate. E   gate: 1820-M   **56** all E   **57** A long E   end E
59 streets E   **60** Heaven, E-M   **61** along; E   **62** square E   **64**
leaves— E   **65** visages E-M   **66** pain E   **67** Past 1820-M   thro'

E-1820   68 them, E   69 past 1820-M   70 fallen— E   fallen,
1820-M   71 changed— E   changed, 1820-M   73 again— E   again:
1820-M   74 Came, 1820-M   would'st 1820   toads & snakes & efts E
75 beautiful?— E   were E   76 hue E   77 off E   off: 1820-M   78
oer E   lake 1820-M   79 nighshade ⟨sic⟩ twined E   night-shade 1820
81 ⟨option for *bunch*⟩: mass E   berries, 1820-M   82 quick E-M   83
sky— E   sky; 1820-M   84 So E-M   ⟨option for *of*⟩: from ⟨?⟩ E
changes E   86 Sister E   sister 1820-M   87 and the inconstant
moon E   moon 1820-M   89 snow E-1820   90 thee E   What, E
What; 1820-M   What! M²   Prometheus E   91 Peace Wanton— E
wanton, 1820-M (wanton! M²)   enough E   92 ye, E   others E   95
Nay Mother E   96 Tis E   darkling E   —Listen! E   Listen; 1820-M
SD Enter, the Spirit of the Hour E   97 seen— E   speak E   99 sky
1820-M   earth; E   100 change . . . E

101 transformed E   102 love, M   them, M   103 world E   104
clear E   105 Universe E   106 down E   down, 1820-M   107
plumes E   108 birth-place 1820-M   sun E   109 toil E-1820   110
fire— E   fire. 1820-M   112 temple, E-M   forms, E   113 Asia E
me E   114 nymphs 1820   feel E   feel; 1820-M   115 borne E
borne; 1820-M   116 flowers E   117 stone E   118 sky E   119
amphisbenic 1820-M (amphisbænic M²)   121 The light 1820   repose—alas E   Alas, 1820-M   123 unsaid E   w^d hear!— E   124
said E-1820   Earth E   127 mankind E   128 dissappointed ⟨sic⟩ E
129 change, M   within, M   130 looked E   131 behold, 1820-M
132 do, E-M   133 None frowned, E   trampled, hate disdain or fear
E   fear M²   134 self-contempt E   brows, E   135 oer E   hell, E-M
136 "All E-M   abandon 1820-M   here" E   here;" 1820-M   137
fawned, E   frown'd, M   138 anothers E   command E   139 tyrants E   140 own E   141 death— E   death. 1820-M   142 truth
entangling E   143 speak E   144 ⟨no punctuation⟩ E   145 hope
1820-M   147 ⟨option⟩: creeps E   crept 1820-M   men E   148 ill. E
150 breathes E

153 ⟨no punctuation⟩ E   155 past; E-M   gentle 1820-M   forms E
156 customs E   pure. E   157 think E   158 feel E   159 be E
160 make Earth like Heaven—nor pride E   161 ⟨no punctuation⟩ E
ill-shame, M   162 gall— E   163 nepenthe E   164 Thrones
altars E   judgement-seats, E-1820   prisons; E-M   wherein E   166
Sceptres tiaras swords E   167 wrong, 1820-M   ignorance, E-M
168 ⟨option for *monstrous*⟩: secret E   shapes E   169 fame E   170
⟨no punctuation⟩ E   171 oer E   172 conquerors: mouldering
round 1820-M   round E   173 Those 1820-M   Kings & Priests E

175 ⟨option for *it*⟩: they E   **177** it's ⟨sic⟩ E   captivity, 1820-M   **178**
Earth, E   **179** now; E   **180** god 1820-M   man E   **181** Which E
form E-1820   **182** dark & execrable E   **183** world E   **184** ⟨no
punctuation⟩ E   **186** garlandless E   **187** slain among 1820-M
tears E   **188** hate E   hate, 1820-M   **189** oer E   shrines E   shrines:
1820-M   **190** veil E   **191** mimick'd, M   **192** and hoped, 1820-M
aside— E   **194** Scepterless, E   uncircumscribed:— E   uncircumscribed, 1820-M   man 1820-M   **195** tribeless, 1820-M   nationless E
nationless, 1820-M   **196** degree,— E   degree, 1820-M   King E
197 wise:— E   wise: but man 1820-M   **198** Passionless; no, 1820-M
pain E   **199** made 1820-M   them, E-M   **200** tho' 1820   **201** ⟨no
punctuation⟩ E   **203** Heaven E   **SD** ⟨lacking⟩ E

ACT IV

SD Act 4 E   **SD** Scene a part of forest ⟨sic⟩ near the cave of Prometheus—Panthea & Ione are sleeping—they awaken gradually during
the first song. E   Scene, 1820   Scene,— M   **1** Stars are gone,— E
2 Sun thier ⟨sic⟩ swift Shepherd E   shepherd M   **3** compelling,
1820-M   **4** Dawn E   **7** leopard . . . E   leopard. 1820   leopard, M
8 SD A train of dark forms & shadows passes by confusedly, singing—
Panthea wakens E   confusedly M   **9** Here oh here. E   oh! M   **11**
Father 1820-M   year E   **13** Of dead hours be E   **14** time M²
eternity E   **15** Strew E   Strew, oh, 1820   oh! M   **19** Deaths E
21 oh, 1820-M   **22** chased E   chased, 1820-M   **23** day, 1820-M
Heaven's E   waste E   waste. 1820-M   **24** away E   **25** spray E
29 harmony E   harmony! 1820-M   **SD** they vanish E   **30 SD** Ione, E
forns ⟨sic⟩ E   **31** grey E   **32** spoil, E   **34** foil E   **35** they past?
E-M   have past E   have past; 1820-M   **36** blast, E-M   **37** tis E
fled: 1820-M   **38** oh, 1820   oh! M   **40 SD** Voice of unseen Spirits
E-M   Heaven, E   **41** Earth, E   **42** Ocean, E   ocean, 1820-M
44 Storm E   glee E   **45** emotion— E   **46** mirth. 1820-M   **48**
pine-boughs E
       51 flinging E   **52** spirit E-M   sea E   **54** gladness. E-M   glad-
ness, M²   **56** these E   **57 SD** Semichorus of Hours. 1. E   Semichorus of Hours 1820-M   Spirits E-M   air & earth E   Air and of
Earth 1820-M   **58** Have E-M   **60** ⟨first occurrence⟩: deep. 1820-M
SD a Voice E   **SD** Semichorus 2. E   Oh below the deep E   Oh! M
61 SD Semichorus 1. E   An hundred E-1820   **62** care E   **63** slept,
1820-M   **64 SD** Semichorus 2. E   were E   **65 SD** Semichorus 1. E
sleep E   **66** love in dream E   dreams, 1820-M   **SD** Semichorus 2 E
68 beam E   **70** Heaven's E   **71** day 1820-M   flees E   **72** flight, E

Night; E night. 1820-M   74 Day, E day 1820-M deer E   76
desart E-1820   year E   77 now, 1820-M oh! M   78 music & dance
E   79 Hours, 1820-M all Spirits E pleasure E   80 the sunbeams unite E **SD** a Voice E Unite. M   81 See E mind 1820-M
82 Wrapt E-M like radiant veils, approach E   84 song E   **85**
along; E-M   88 sea-birds, 1820-M half-asleep. M   89 ⟨no punc-
tuation⟩ E   **90** feet E   **92** Love E   **94** human kind E-1820
kind, M   **95** dusk & obscene E blind, 1820   **96** tis an Ocean, E
97 emotion E   **98** Heaven E motion. E-M   **99** Abyss E   **100**
bliss E

101 chrystal palaces, E   **103** Thoughts crowned Powers E   **104**
Hours E Hours! 1820-M   **106** caresses E   **107** ⟨option for *loose*⟩:
sliding E tresses— E   **108** isles, 1820-M   **109** smiles E   **110**
syren E-M wiles ⟨sic⟩ 1820 wiles. M   **112** Man's 1820-M eye E
113 Poesy E   **115** springs E-M   **116** his Dædal 1820-M Dædal E
wings E   **117** after years E   **118** blood & tears E   **119** hatreds &
hopes E fears; 1820-M   **120** flew E   **122** grew E   **126** And,
1820-M eyes, 1820-M   **128** on Paradise. 1820-M Paradise E   **129**
measure; E-M   **130** Earth E   **132** mirth, E-M   **134** Ocean E
135 won E   **136** done E   **137** dive or soar or run . . . E run;
1820-M   **138** or around E   **140** round E   **141** Eyes E   **143**
Deep to colonize E colonize: 1820-M   **144** Death Chaos E   **145**
flight, 1820-M   **146** Tempests might E might. 1820-M   **147** ⟨no
punctuation⟩ E   **148** Might, 1820-M   **149** Stars E   **150** love,
thought, & breath E

151 the E death, E   **152** beneath! E beneath. 1820-M   **153**
build E-M   **154** Void's E field 1820-M   **155** weild; ⟨sic⟩ E   **157**
man E, M²   **158** Promethean E   **159** song E   **160** remain, E
161 SD Semichorus 1. E Heaven, E along: 1820-M   **162 SD** Semichorus 2. E inchantments of Earth E retain: 1820-M   **163 SD**
Semichorus 1. E ⟨no punctuation⟩ E   **164** Spirits E-M sea E
165 Heaven where yet Heaven cᵈ never E be. 1820-M   **166 SD**
Semichorus 2. E ⟨no punctuation⟩ E   **167** Day 1820 Day, M
Night, 1820-M   **168** Powers E light. 1820-M   **169 SD** Semichorus
1. E sphere E   **170** trees E   **171** fear. 1820-M   **172 SD** Semichorus E Oceans & Mountains of Earth E   **174** mirth E   **175**
dance E song— E song, 1820-M   **176** depart E remain E remain, 1820-M   **178** star-beams, M strong E   **179** Loves sweet rain
E **SD** they depart E   **180 SD** Pan ⟨sic⟩ E Ha, E   **181** hill E-M
182 rain E   **185** arise . . . E sound E   **186** Tis E world E-1820
187 air, 1820   **188** modulations E too E   **189** under notes E

190 keen 1820-M   tones E   191 sense E   192 Winter's chrystal E
194 see, E   where 1820   196 rivulet E   197 moss violet-inwoven E
moss 1820   198 melody, E-M   199 smiles E

201 thoughts E   thoughts; 1820-M   203 Ocean-like inchantment E
sound E   204 intenser keener E   205 air E   206 chariot E-M
boat, 1820   207 Mother of the Months E   208 ebbing night 1820-
M cave, 1820-M   209 inter lunar E   dreams, E-M   210 Oer E
curbed M   211 woods E-M   212 aery veil E   213 enchanters E
215 thunder-storm, 1820-M   217 Sun E   it, E   218 wind; 1820-M
219 Infant, E   infant, 1820-M   220 countenance E   snow, E-M
221 frost, E-M   222 white, thro E   white, 1820-M   223 ætherial
E-M   pearl— E   pearl. 1820-M   224 is white,— E   white, 1820-M
225 strings, E   string; 1820   Heavens E   227 Within, E   228
lashes E   229 around, 1820-M   230 fire that 1820-M   brightness,
E   231 moon-beam, 1820-M   232 chariots E   233 which E-M
234 grass & flowers E   sounds, 1820-M   237 ⟨no punctuation⟩ E
239 chrystal, E-1820   240 light E   241 involved E   242 white &
green & golden E   white, green 1820-M   243 sphere, E   244 shapes
E   245 deep— E   246 intertranspicuous, E   inter-transpicuous,
1820-M   247 motions E   248 spinning E   249 And E-M   self
destroying swiftness E   250 Intensely slowly E   solemnly, M   on— E

251 tones E   252 wild— E   253 Orb E   255 light, E   256
flowers E   257 air E   259 intense 1820-M   260 aërial M   261
sense . . within the Orb E   262 arms, E-M   263 Like to a child o'erwearied 1820-M   264 wings, and wavy hair, 1820-M   265 asleep E
266 moving, 1820-M   267 ther ⟨sic⟩ own smiles E   268 dream. 1820-M
269 Orb's E   harmony. 1820-M   270 shoot, E-M   273 heaven
1820-M   now, E-M   274 spoke 1820   275 Orb E   276 sun-like
lightnings, 1820-M   lightenings E   277 transverse E   278 and E-M
pass E   279 Earths E   heart; E-M   280 mine 1820-M   gold E
281 ⟨no punctuation⟩ E   282 chrystalline E   columns poured 1820
poized M (poised M²) 283 overspread E   284 watersprings E   water
springs 1820-M   285 Sea, E   child 1820-M   fed E   286 Earth's E
287 snow; the E   289 cycles; E-M   ships E   ships; 1820-M   290
quivers helms & spears E   marble; 1820-M   293 ⟨no punctuation⟩ E
beasts, 1820-M   294 death 1820-M   laughed, E-M   295 destruction, 1820-M   296 vast E   297 Earth E   298 mortal E   human,
E   human; 1820-M   lie E-M   299 works, 1820-M   300 Thier ⟨sic⟩ E

302 hard E   these, 1820-M   307 thier ⟨sic⟩ E   308 crags;— E
309 alligator E   311 shores, 1820-M   312 Earth E   earth, 1820-M
315 Deluge E   cloke, 1820-M   316 gaspt E   abolished; E-M   317

Comet, past, & cried— E past, 1820-M   **318** not! And 1820-M
more E ⟨no quotes⟩ E-M   **319** madness E   **320** overflowing E
gladness E gladness, 1820-M   **321** vapourous E-1820 exultation
1820-M   **322** Animation E   **323** light E   **324** wind. 1820-M
325 wanderer E   **326** air E   **327** Spirit E-M thee E   **328**
frame E   **329** flame— E   **330** ⟨no punctuation⟩ E   **331** me!— E
332 Ha, ha,! ⟨sic⟩ E cavens ⟨sic⟩ E mountains E   **333** fountains E-
1820   **334** laughter E laughter. 1820-M   **335** Oceans E Desarts
E desarts, 1820 Abysses E abysses, 1820-M   **336** And the deep
1820-M wildernesses E   **337** after E   **338** do— E do. 1820
Curse E curse, 1820-M   **339** Universe E   **341** thunder-stones,
1820-M   **342** childrens E bones 1820   **343** blending E blending. 1820-M   **344** crag-like 1820-M tower E column E   **345** Obelisk & Temple solemn E   **346** cloud & snow E fire; 1820-M   **348**
on my bosom E   **349** mire E mire. 1820-M   **350** coverd— ⟨sic⟩ E
     352 Drain'd M (Drained M²) Desart-troop— E desart-troop, 1820
all! E   **354** Love E   **355** by thunder-ball. 1820 thunderball E
thunder-ball. M   **357** fountains E   **358** ⟨no punctuation⟩ E
Oceans E shine: 1820-M   **359** forth E   **361** bosom—oh, E   **363**
feel E know, M   **364** grow E   **365** move E move: 1820-M
366 air E   **367** there E   **368** of E   **369** Love, all Love! E   **370**
mass E   **371** pass, 1820-M   **372** delicatst ⟨sic⟩ flowers E   **373**
spread E spread, 1820-M   **374** dead E dead, 1820-M   **375** bowers E bowers. 1820-M   **376** storm 1820-M   **377** thunder, 1820-M
378 being E being: 1820-M   **379** shook ⟨sic⟩ E   **380** for ever
1820-M   **381** Hate & Fear & Pain, E fleeing E   **382** Man, E-M
manysided E many sided mirror, 1820 mirror, M   **383** error,
1820-M   **384** things, 1820-M Sea E Love; E   **385** kind 1820
Suns Heaven E   **386** oer Ocean E serene E even 1820-M   **387**
light, 1820-M move E move. 1820 move, M   **388** man, 1820
left, 1820-M   **390** poured E   **391** smile E   **393** Spirit— E then,
E-M restored. E-M   **394** oh not men; E thought E   **395** not E
396 elements E-M stress— E stress; 1820-M   **397** Sun E tyrants
E   **398** Republic E   **399** Planets, E Heavens E wilderness. E-M
400 Soul of many a soul E

401 it's ⟨sic⟩ E controul E controul, 1820   **403** thro love, E
404 ⟨no punctuation⟩ E pain, and grief, 1820-M   **405** beasts, 1820-M
be E   **406** Will, E will, 1820-M   **408** obey; E obey, 1820-M
410 rules, E-M overwhelm E   **411** Life's E sovereigns sway E
sway. 1820-M   **412** strength— E   **413** pass E pass; 1820-M
414 threads, E   **415** orphic 1820 song E   **416** Which rules 1820-M

Dædal 1820-M harmony, E   417 were E were. 1820-M   418
Lightning E Heavens E   420 numbered M²   421 Tempest E
steed,— E steed, 1820-M air! E   422 bare E   423 me, E none E
⟨no quotes⟩ E-M   424 death 1820-M hath E past 1820-M   425
Heaven E   426 sleep— E   427 bowers, 1820-M   428 paramours
E   431 Dawn E   432 half infrozen 1820 half unfrozen M dewglobe, 1820-M green & gold E   433 chrystalline, E mist E   434
Day E   435 Sun's E   436 oer the Sea; E amethyst. 1820-M
439 Heavens E divine E   441 thee, a light a life E   442 sphere—
E   444 night E   445 Heavens, E heavens 1820-M delight E
446 sleep; E-M   447 love-dreams 1820-M   448 lying E   449
keep E   450 eclipse, 1820-M

    451 lovers lips E   452 ⟨no punctuation⟩ E dull; 1820-M   453
So, M me E   454 still,— E   456 oh too full!— E   457 Sun E
sun 1820   458 World E one E one; 1820-M   459 sphere 1820-M
461 Heaven E-M   463 chrystal E paramour E-1820   465 Paradise
E Paradise, 1820-M   466 Magnet-like E-1820   467 maiden E-1820
469 love— E   470 move 1820-M   471 bride E   472 side E-1820
473 Mænad, E-M   475 wierd ⟨sic⟩ E-M (weird M²) forest— E
476 wheresoer ⟨sic⟩ E   477 hurry E   478 Thro' the Heavens E
479 Sheltered E-M   480 soul 1820-M space E space, 1820-M
481 Drinking 1820-M sight E-M   482 might E   483 or a ⟨?⟩ cameleon E a 1820 cameleon 1820-M   484 gazes on— E upon,
1820-M   485-94 ⟨lacking⟩ E   487 beholds, 1820-M   490 enfolds,
E-1820   492 snow. 1820-M   495 Oh, 1820 Gentle moon, E   497
night, 1820   498 Thro' E for ever 1820-M calm; E-M   499 Oh
Gentle E Oh, 1820 chrystal E   500 Pride's E deep Universe E
    501 tyger Joy E   502 wounds, E balm E   505 sound— E me,
sweet sister E   506 us E   507 wave, 1820-M   508 clear, 1820   509
wood nymphs E hair E   510 Peace! Peace!— E Peace, peace! a M²
A mighty 1820 Darkness E darkness M (darkness, M²)   511 Earth,
E-M   512 Night, E   514 sun-light— E Visions E   515 shone E
516 thro' E watery mist E   517 ear. 1820-M   518 An universal E-
1820 words . . . E o list E Oh, 1820-M   519 Thou, 1820-M Empire E Soul, E   520 harmonies E harmonies, 1820-M   522 Love
E skies E   523 hear,— E dies! E   524 Thou, 1820-M (Thou M²)
Moon E earth E   525 thee E thee; 1820-M   526 ⟨no punctua-
tion⟩ E   527 harmony E   528 ⟨The Moon lacking⟩ E hear— E
thee! E-M   529 Kings E stars! M   530 Dominations! M   532
Heavens E Heaven's 1820-M wilderness E   533 SD a Voice from
above E hears . . . E hears, 1820 hears; M blest M² bless E

534 Dead, E   dead! M   **535** pourtray E   pourtray, 1820   **536**
Universe E   Ye E   **537 SD** A Voice from beneath E   or E   **538**
away— E   **540** mans E   **541** lead, E   Heavens E   Heaven's 1820-
M   **542** on— E   **543 SD** a confused Voice E   hear— E   **544**
Spirits, 1820   Spirits! M   flesh— E   flesh: 1820-M   birds E   birds,
1820-M   **545** worms, 1820   fish— E   buds— E   **546** Wind— E
547 feed Airs solitudes E   solitudes. M²   **548** woods E   **549** Man
E   slave— E   **550** or a deceiver,—a Decay E

   551 Traveller E   **552** Day— E   **553** Speak— E   Speak! M
away E   **554** This the day, M   Day E   Abysm E   **555** Earth-
born's E   Despotism E   **556** Captive thro' the Deep; E   deep; M²
557 Love E   awful home E   **559** dead endurance, 1820   endurance;
E   **560** craglike Agony E   **561** wings E   **562** Wisdom & Endurance,— E   Endurance, 1820-M   **564** Destructions E   **567** length,
— E   length; 1820   **568** re-assume 1820-M   **569** o'er that E
Doom E   doom. 1820-M   **570** infinite E   **571** Death or Night, E
572 Power, E-M   Omnipotent; E   **573** love M²   **574** contemplates E   contemplates: M   **575** ⟨no punctuation⟩ E   nor flatter,
1820   faulter, M (falter, M²)   repent; E-M   **576** Titan! M   **577**
free E   **578** Empire & Victory E   Victory! M

Appendix B

The Manuscripts: A Bibliographical Listing[1]

Bodleian MS Shelley D.1. A notebook of 156 leaves, 6.2 x 8.6 in., with Shelley's translation into Italian of two passages from the poem. (See *Variorum*, pp. 677-81.)

Bodleian MS Shelley E.1. A notebook of 46 leaves, 5.6 x 8.2 in., with Shelley's fair copy of parts of Acts I and IV.

Bodleian MS Shelley E.2. A notebook of 43 leaves, 5.6 x 8.2 in., with Shelley's fair copy of parts of Acts I and II.

Bodleian MS Shelley E.3. A notebook of 38 leaves, 5.6 x 8.2 in., with Shelley's fair copy of Act III and parts of Acts II and IV.

Bodleian MS Shelley E.4. An oblong notebook of 85 leaves, 9.2 x 7.3 in., with a passage related to II.v.

Bodleian MS Shelley adds. c.4. A single folded sheet, of which the page containing a draft for II.iii measures 7 x 9.7 in.

Bodleian MS Shelley adds. e.6. A notebook of 86 leaves, 5 x 7.2 in., with a single line related to II.v.

Bodleian MS Shelley adds. e.11. A notebook of 83 leaves, 4.3 x 6.4 in., with related materials and drafts for parts of the Preface, II.i and III.iv.

Bodleian MS Shelley adds. e.12. A notebook of 117 leaves, 4.1 x 6.3 in., with related materials and drafts for parts of I, II.i, II.ii, III.ii, and IV.

Huntington MS 2176. A notebook of 56 leaves, 4 x 5.8 in., with related materials and drafts for parts of II.ii, II.iii, II.v, and IV.

Huntington MS 2177. A notebook of 94 leaves, 3.8 x 5.5 in., with related materials and drafts for parts of the Preface, II.iii, III.iv, and IV.

The Mask of Anarchy MS. Twelve leaves, 3.75 x 6.2 in., with a single page containing a draft for Act IV.

Pforzheimer Library Notebook. A notebook, containing *A Philosophical View of Reform*, from which Ingpen-Peck in the Julian Edition (7, 332) gave drafts for nine lines of Act IV. The notebook will not be available for description and collation until after its publication in *Shelley and His Circle*.

1. A literal transcription of all known draft materials is now available. See Bibliography under the present editor's name.

Appendix C

Verbal Changes from the E Manuscript
to the 1820 and Mary Shelley Editions

Following is a list of the verbal changes differentiating 1820 and M from E. These changes include substitute words, changes in tense or number, uses of the paradigm of *thou,* and additions, deletions or transpositions within phrases. Options in E (see Textual Notes at I.165, 237, 238) are not included since there are no verbal changes in the chosen words, nor are simple contractions or expansions of contractions (I.223, 745) since these involve metrical rather than verbal considerations. If M follows 1820 or E, or offers an independent reading, this is indicated under the M heading, and if M follows a reading initiated by Galignani a superior *g* is used (e.g. *A hundred*[g]). All punctuation changes will be found in the variant readings of Appendix A, with important instances discussed in the textual notes (see Index under Manuscripts, Fair copy, principal cruxes). Only those that result in an actual verbal change (e.g. *many-peopled* to *many peopled*) are given here.

	E	1820	M
Preface			
30	& the endurance	and endurance	1820
32	perfidious & successful	successful and perfidious	1820
41	perpetually interfere	interfere	1820
57	awakening of spring	awakening spring	E
71	from the study	the study	1820
89	have the form	possess the form	1820
115	or forerunners	and forerunners	1820
116	& in the opinions	or the opinions	1820
146	philosophers or painters	philosophers, painters	1820
147	or musicians	and musicians	1820
169	equally well be	be equally well	1820
181	systematical development	systematical history	1820
182	genuine sources of our human	genuine elements of human	1820
189	amuse or interest	amuse and interest	1820
D.P.			
	[omitted]	Demogorgon	1820
	[omitted]	Ocean	1820
	[omitted]	Apollo	1820
	[omitted]	E	The Spirit of the Moon

	E	1820	M

Act I

	E	1820	M
14	seem years	seemed years	1820
35	it's own ⟨sic⟩	his own	1820
48	Their wingless	The wingless	1820
54	thro wide	thro' the wide	1820
80	had ran	had run	1820
106	as hell	a hell	E
106 SD	They pass ⟨etc.⟩	[omitted]	1820
157	beam / From sunrise, leap	cloud / Of glory, arise	1820
166	lifted with	lifted by	1820
204	whirlwind-shaken	whirlwind-peopled	1820
208	throned / On burning gold	throne / Of burning gold	1820
247	Him	He	1820
253	dare not speak	cannot speak	1820
277	Its darkness	In darkness	1820
294	this universe	the universe	1820
301 SD	The Phantasm vanishes	[omitted]	1820
332	on groans	with groans	1820
338	in his eyes	into his eyes	1820
357	do more	do no more	1820
369	and savage	or savage	1820
386	trodden down	trampled down	1820
472	else are we	else we are	1820
531	was bought	is bought	1820
538 SD	A fury ⟨etc.⟩	[omitted]	1820
539 SD	The furies ⟨etc.⟩	[omitted]	1820
553	Hark	Mark	1820
577 SD	depart but one	vanish, except one	1820
589	Tho some	And some	1820
596 SD	a darkness ⟨etc.⟩	[omitted]	1820
619	ravin	ruin	E
634 SD	Exit	Vanishes	1820
637	illumed	E	illumineds
646	sawest thou more?	sawest thou?	1820
650	And nations	The nations	1820
661	and they see	they behold	1820
687	make there	make these	E
693	radiant like	radiant as	1820
733	borne	born	Eg
774	lulling footstep	silent footstep	1820
779	their shadow	the shadow	1820
779	his ⟨?⟩	he	1820
791	when snow-storms	when the snow-storms	1820

	E	1820	M
800 SD	They vanish	[omitted]	1820
825	looks wan	looks white	1820

Act II.i

		E	lonely
SD	lovely	E	lonely
25	sunrise	sunlight	1820
40	thine	thy	1820
43	yours	thine	1820
66	makes dizzy	makes giddy	1820
88	as they died	ere they died	1820
89	far melody	weak melody	1820
115	in	to	1820
122	moon	morn	1820
123	thou	thine	1820
126	oer the waste	on the waste	1820
142	mine own	my own	1820
143	among these	among the	1820
151	moving clouds	morning clouds	1820
190 SD	Echo	Echoes	1820
196 SD	Echo	Echoes	1820
207	thine hand	thy hand	1820

Act II.ii

7	when	where	1820
15	climb & wander	climbs and wanders	1820
34	stream	strain	1820
38	lake-surrounded	lake-surrounding	E
44	deep awe	sweet awe	1820
53	steams	E	E (M²: streams)
71	which the enchantment	E	which enchantmentᵍ
76	which the noontide	which noon-tide	1820
80	ride on it	ride on them	1820
87	Or in	Or on	1820
93	doom	dooms	E

Act II.iii

4	breathed	hurled	1820
12	beest	be	1820
26	illumed	illumined	1820
46	on an	on some	1820
48	which	that	1820
49	my eyes	mine eyes	1820
50	seest those shapes	I see thin shapes	I see shapes
84	that	the	1820
88	hidden, but from	treasur'd but for	1820

	E	1820	M

Act II.iv

	E	1820	M
37	have	has	1820
39	birthrights	birthright	1820
66	chase	prey	1820
100	rains	reigns	E^g
128	will	shall	1820
138	hair	locks	1820
139	Streams	Stream	1820
139	[scattered hair]	flashing hair	1820
145	What	Who	1820
150	The	That	1820
151	dust	smoke	1820
168	daughters	daughter	1820
173	ere	at	1820
174	daughters	daughter	1820

Act II.v

	E	1820	M
SD	[names omitted]	[names added]	1820
9	this cloud—	the cloud?	1820
22	thine	thy	1820
30	dwell	dwells	1820
54	limbs	lips	E
96	winds & on	winds on	1820

Act III.i

	E	1820	M
3	am I	I am	1820
4	has	had	1820
5	like unextinguished	like an unextinguished	E
13	night	might	E
20	destined	distant	E
45	though	although	1820
69	What then art	What art	E
71	shall sink in	will sink on	1820
77	The	This	1820
77	thou	thee	1820
82	the	mine	1820

Act III.ii

	E	1820	M
22	many-peopled	many peopled	1820
26	light-laden	light laden	1820
39	i'	on	E
45	streams	stream	1820

Act III.iii

	E	1820	M
8	make	made	1820
27	shall chant	shalt chaunt	shall chaunt

	E	1820	M
40	thither	hither	1820
55	rapt	wrapt	E
70	this the	this is the	E
85	their touch	thy touch	1820
102	unwithering	unwitting	E
124	whence	where	1820
126	those who	E	those thatͨ
131	among	amongst	1820
147	that	This	1820
148 SD	arises	rises	1820
163	capitals	capital	1820
164	with most	most with	1820
169	thine	thy	1820

Act III.iv

	E	1820	M
26	mine	my	1820
39	An hindrance	E	A hindrance͡g
53	The sentinel	A sentinel	1820
87	the inconstant	inconstant	1820
121	flight	light	E
133	frowned	fawned	1820
137	fawned	frowned	1820
160	make	made	1820
173	These	Those	1820
187	amid	among	1820
192	or	and	1820

Act IV

	E	1820	M
13	Of dead	Of the dead	1820
57	& earth	and of Earth	1820
61	An hundred	E	A hundred͡g
66	dream	dreams	1820
68	beam	beams	1820
79	all Spirits	the spirits	1820
80	& the sunbeams	and sunbeams	1820
82	like radiant	as in bright	1820
107	sliding	loose	1820
116	her	his	1820
138	or	and	1820
172	Oceans	ocean	1820
208	light	night	1820
210	curved	E	curbed ⟨typo⟩
212	aery	airy	1820
225	strings	string	E

	E	1820	M
230	which	that	1820
242	white & green	white, green	1820
263	Like a child overwearied	Like to a child o'erwearied	1820
274	spokes	spoke	E
276	lightenings	lightnings	1820
280	mines	mine	1820
282	poised	poured	E
336	Of	And	1820
348	on	in	1820
355	by the thunderball	by thunder-ball	E
387	life	light	1820
411	sovereigns	sovereign	1820
416	Ruling	Which rules	1820
424	hath	has	1820
432	half-unfrozen	half infrozen	E
483	or a ⟨?⟩ cameleon	or a cameleon	or cameleon
484	gazes on	looks upon	1820
516	mist	night	1820
518	An universal	E	A universal[g]
547	feed	throng	1820
550	or	and	1820
554	This is the	E	This the
557	home	throne	1820
559	dread	dead	E
569	that	the	1820
575	falter	flatter	E

Bibliography

Ackermann, Richard, *Percy B. Shelley: Prometheus Unbound, a Lyrical Drama in Four Acts: Erste kritische Textausgabe mit Einleitung und Kommentar,* Heidelberg, Carl Winter, 1908.

Blind, Mathilde, *A Selection from the Poems of Percy Bysshe Shelley,* Leipzig, Bernard Tauchnitz, 1872.

———, "Shelley," *Westminster Review,* N.S., *38* (1870), 75-97.

Forman, Harry Buxton, *The Mask of Anarchy: Facsimile of Shelley's Manuscript,* The Shelley Society's Publications, Extra Ser., No. 4, London, Reeves and Turner, 1887.

———, *Note Books of Percy Bysshe Shelley: From the Originals in the Library of W. K. Bixby* [now in the Huntington Library], 3 vols. Boston, 1911. (Printed for Members of the Bibliophile Society.)

———, *The Poetical Works of Percy Bysshe Shelley,* 4 vols. London, Reeves and Turner, 1876.

Freeman, Martin J. [with Carl Grabo], *The Reader's Shelley,* New York, American Book Company, 1942.

———, "A Text of Shelley's *Prometheus Unbound,*" Unpublished dissertation, University of Chicago, 1934. [Freeman's Introduction (pp. 1-50) was reproduced and distributed by the University of Chicago Libraries, 1937.]

[Galignani, A. and W.], *The Poetical Works of Coleridge, Shelley, and Keats,* Paris, A. and W. Galignani, 1829.

Hutchinson, Thomas, *The Complete Poetical Works of Shelley,* Oxford, Clarendon Press, 1904.

Ingpen, Roger, and Walter E. Peck, *The Complete Works of Percy Bysshe Shelley,* The Julian Edition, 10 vols. London, Ernest Benn, 1926-30.

Jones, Frederick L., *The Letters of Percy Bysshe Shelley,* 2 vols. Oxford, Clarendon Press, 1964.

Locock, Charles D., *An Examination of the Shelley Manuscripts in the Bodleian Library,* Oxford, Clarendon Press, 1903.

———, *The Poems of Percy Bysshe Shelley,* 2 vols. London, Methuen and Company, 1911.

Pottle, Frederick A., "The Case of Shelley," *PMLA 67* (1952), 589-608.

Rogers, Neville, "Music at Marlow," *The Keats-Shelley Memorial Bulletin,* No. 5 (1953), 20-25.

————, *Shelley at Work*, Oxford, Clarendon Press, 1956.

————, "Shelley's Spelling: Theory and Practice," *The Keats-Shelley Memorial Bulletin*, No. 16 (1965), 21-25.

————, "The Punctuation of Shelley's Syntax," *The Keats-Shelley Memorial Bulletin*, No. 17 (1966), 20-30.

Rossetti, William Michael, *The Poetical Works of Percy Bysshe Shelley*, 2 vols. London, E. Moxon, Son, & Company, 1870.

Schick, Joseph, See Zupitza, Julius, and Joseph Schick.

Shelley, Mary Wollstonecraft, Harvard MSS Eng. 258.2 and 258.3. [Two notebooks into which Mary copied Shelley's poems.]

————, *Letters*, ed. Frederick L. Jones, 2 vols. Norman, University of Oklahoma Press, 1944.

————, *The Poetical Works of Percy Bysshe Shelley*, 4 vols. London, Edward Moxon, 1839. [Mary Shelley's first edition.]

————, *The Poetical Works of Percy Bysshe Shelley*, London, Edward Moxon, [1839] 1840. [A corrected, one-volume edition of the preceding item.]

Shelley, Percy Bysshe, Manuscripts. See Appendix B and Lawrence J. Zillman below.

————, *Prometheus Unbound: A Lyrical Drama in Four Acts: With Other Poems*, London, C and J Ollier, 1820.

————, Prose and poetical works. See under various editors.

Taylor, Charles H., Jr., *The Early Collected Editions of Shelley's Poems*, New Haven, Yale University Press, 1958.

Trelawny, Edward John, *Recollections of the Last Days of Shelley and Byron*, London, Humphrey Milford, 1923. [A reissue, with introduction by Edward Dowden, of the same, London, Edward Moxon, 1858.]

Woodberry, George Edward, *The Complete Poetical Works of Percy Bysshe Shelley*, Centenary Edition, 4 vols. Boston, Houghton Mifflin Company, 1892.

Zillman, Lawrence John, *Shelley's Prometheus Unbound: A Variorum Edition*, Seattle, University of Washington Press, 1959.

————, *The Complete Known Drafts of Shelley's Prometheus Unbound*, Ann Arbor, University Microfilms, 1967. [A microfilm or xerographic reproduction of the literal transcription.]

Zupitza, Julius, and Joseph Schick, "Zu Shelleys Prometheus Unbound," *Archiv für das Studium der neuren Sprachen und Litteraturen, 102* (1899), 297-316; *103* (1899), 91-106, 309-34.

Index